Homilies for Weekdays

Year I

Homilies for Weekdays

Year I

Don Talafous, o.s.b.

LITURGICAL PRESS
Collegeville, Minnesota

www.litpress.org

Cover design by James Rhoades.

Excerpts from the *Lectionary for Masses for Use in the Dioceses of the United States of America, second typical edition,* Copyright © 1970, 1986, 1992, 1998, 2001, Confraternity of Christian Doctrine, Inc., Washington, D.C. All rights reserved. No part of this work may be reproduced or transmitted in any form or by any means, electronic or mechanical, including photocopying, recording, or by any information storage and retrieval system, without permission in writing from the copyright owner.

Other acknowledgments continue on p. vii.

Year I
ISBN-13: 978-0-8146-3031-0
ISBN-10: 0-8146-3031-6

Year II
ISBN-13: 978-0-8146-3032-7
ISBN-10: 0-8146-3032-4

1	2	3	4	5	6	7	8	9

Library of Congress Cataloging-in-Publication Data

Talafous, Don, 1926–
    Homilies for weekdays / Don Talafous.
        p.   cm.
    Summary: "Short, sample homilies based on the two-year weekday cycle of the Catholic Lectionary for Mass"—Provided by publisher.
        Includes bibliographical references.
        ISBN-13: 978-0-8146-3032-7 (pbk. : alk. paper)
        ISBN-10: 0-8146-3032-4 (pbk. : alk. paper)
        1. Catholic Church--Sermons.   2. Church year sermons. 3. Catholic Church. Lectionary for Mass (U.S.)   I. Title.

BX1756.T34H66 2005
252'.02–dc22

                                                                    2005019726

Contents

Acknowledgments

Continued from the copyright page:

Scripture quotations that are not from the readings of the day—or are designated as NAB—unless otherwise noted, are from the *New American Bible with Revised New Testament and Revised Psalms* © 1991, 1986, 1970, Confraternity of Christian Doctrine, Washington, D.C., and are used by permission of the copyright owner. All rights reserved. No part of the *New American Bible* may be reproduced in any form without permission in writing from the copyright owner. What is marked with brackets ([ ]) in the *New American Bible* is marked with braces ({ }) in this book.

Where noted Scripture quotations are from the New Revised Standard Version Bible (NRSV): Catholic Edition, © 1989, 1993, Division of Christian Education of the National Council of the Churches of Christ in the United States of America. Used by permission. All rights reserved.

Where noted Scripture quotations are from the New English Bible (NEB): Oxford Study Edition with the Apocrypha, © 1976, Oxford University Press.

The quotation from the Sequence of Pentecost is from the *Lectionary for Mass for Use in the Dioceses of the United States of America, second typical edition* © 1998, 1997, 1970, Confraternity of Christian Doctrine, Inc., Washington, D.C. Used with permission. All rights reserved. No portion of this text may be reproduced by any means without permission in writing from the copyright owner.

Reference to "Courage in the time of danger" is from Luke Timothy Johnson, *The Gospel of Luke*, vol. 3 in the Sacra Pagina series (Collegeville: Liturgical Press, 1991).

Reference to David Cotter is from *Genesis* in the Berit Olam Series (Collegeville: Liturgical Press, 2003).

Season of Advent

Monday of the First Week of Advent—*Call the doctor!*

Readings: Isa 4:2-6 (Year A); Isa 2:1-5 (Years B, C); Matt 8:5-11
Resp. Psalm: Ps 122:1-2, 3-4, 4cd-5, 6-7, 8-9 (L 175)—*Lectionary for Mass* number

"Lord, my servant is lying at home paralyzed, suffering dreadfully" (Matt 8:6). The opening verses of today's Gospel give us in pictorial form the basics of the Christian story. Despite the happy days and moments that we hope prevail in our lives, we have to admit, given war, starvation, disease and poverty, that in a very real sense the human race lies paralyzed and often suffering dreadfully. At some time or other each of us can be so described. We hope, of course, that the phrase "suffering dreadfully" proves to be too strong. But for some friends and members of our families it may be literally true. And "paralyzed?" That may well describe our inner life: we seem so often inert, unable to move—at least stiff and not very resilient. We feel so heavy and lacking in spiritual zest. The beginning of Advent is another one of those much-needed calls to realize that now is the time to do something or, better yet, to be responsive to the Lord's call and love. The Lord says: "I will come and cure him" (Matt 8:7). By birth as a fellow human being, the Lord comes to cure us all. In Advent we're meant to learn how to say more genuinely, "Only say the word" (8:8), Lord, and I will be healed.

Tuesday of the First Week of Advent—
There's more to see and hear

Readings: Isa 11:1-10; Luke 10:21-24
Resp. Psalm: Ps 72:1-2, 7-8, 12-13, 17 (L 176)

The words, phrases, and images which are so familiar to us from Christmas carols and pageants over the years come one after the other in the opening reading today. In the Gospel, as yesterday, we have a plea from the Lord for receptivity to the One who is to come and his message. God, Jesus tells us, reveals things hidden from the learned and clever to mere children. How do children differ from the learned and clever? The little ones are, in this contrast, individuals open to instruction, to learning something new, to being helped. From business, education, sports, and so many areas in our lives we know how absolutely essential is a stance of receptivity. The would-be golfer who will not admit that he or she needs instruction blocks his or her progress. The new person in the office who can't bother to be taught the ropes will not be able to function. The student who defies the teacher to teach goes nowhere. If we bring a child-like willingness to be taught, to be led, and to be helped to the Savior, we open ourselves to the grace and power of this season. The Son truly achieves the purpose of his entering into our world, revealing God and the divine love, if there is space in our hearts for something more than self and satisfactions. The blessing of Christmas for any one of us will be in proportion to our willingness to have our eyes and ears opened by the Lord. An attitude of smug and closed satisfaction prevents anything new from coming into our lives. The childlikeness commended by the Lord consists in a willingness to believe that there is more to see and more to hear than we see and hear so far.

Wednesday of the First Week of Advent—
A dinner fit for a believer

Readings: Isa 25:6-10a; Matt 15:29-37
Resp. Psalm: Ps 23:1-3a, 3b-4, 5, 6 (L 177)

A friend of mine who enjoys food very much says too obviously, "When it comes to eating, there's nothing like food." No matter at what level of sophistication our taste may be or our means allow, we all value food as an essential of daily life. C. S. Lewis says that God invented eating. Both readings today speak of it. Isaiah presents good and plentiful food as a sign of the time of the Messiah. In the Gospel Jesus fulfills this expectation by multiplying loaves and fish for the crowd. Satisfying our desire for good and necessary nourishment is an obvious way to indicate what God wants to do for us. Our practices of giving gifts of food to friends, invalids, and those who are grieving all echo God's care for us and continue it. If we refuse a third helping at grandma's, she's likely to take it as rejection. The image of food also reminds us to expect the necessary inspiration and strength—in other words, our nourishment—for our lives as Christians from the Lord. Just as we try to be careful about what kind of food we buy for our families, so we should be choosy about what food we give our spirit. Quality food, rich in protein and low in starch and sugar, is the food we receive from the Lord. If we live by it, in the Eucharist and the Scripture, we will, like the crowd in the Gospel, eat and be satisfied.

Thursday of the First Week of Advent—
Don't just stand there; do something

Readings: Isa 26:1-6; Matt 7:21, 24-27
Resp. Psalm: Ps 118:1 and 8-9, 19-21, 25-27a (L 178)

Aren't we afraid that the message of those first days of Advent is a bit too passive? The readings told us in one way or another to be open; receptive; ready to hear, see, and learn; and the Lord will come and do new things in us. Our part is to receive and accept, to be passive. Much of Scripture does insist on the initiative of God and that all good things begin in God's goodness to us. But, true as that may be, Scripture is never so simply one-sided nor so easily summarized. Today any such oversimplification is shot down. Jesus says very boldly: "Not everyone who says to me, 'Lord, Lord,' will enter the Kingdom of heaven, but only the one who does the will of my Father in heaven" (Matt 7:21). Essential as it is to cry out to the Lord from our need, it is not enough, he says. We have to do something, too; we have to show some evidence of good will; we have to make some effort. The practical implementation of the Lord's words, the evidence for our good will in the way we treat the neighbor, the poor, and the suffering—this is absolutely irreplaceable. Either/or language may make for memorable sayings, but reality is always more complex. In Scripture, taken as a whole, it is never simply a matter of the Lord's doing it all nor everything being up to us. God saves us, but not apart from ourselves.

Friday of the First Week of Advent—
My light and my salvation

Readings: Isa 29:17-24; Matt 9:27-31
Resp. Psalm: Ps 27:1, 4, 13-14 (L 179)

The psalm used between today's readings is one of the most uplifting of all the psalms and deserves to be well known and often used. Many of us would find it inspiring and encouraging. It is very appropriate today when we read of Jesus giving sight back to two blind men who expressed their confidence in him. "The Lord is my light," goes the responsorial psalm, "and my salvation" (Ps 27:1). The more we get to know ourselves (and that is a lifetime study), the more we recognize how blind we can be. We are blind often to our own irritating traits. We are blind to the generous and inspiring qualities of those closest to us. We are blind to the signs of God's love and care for us in the world around us. We are blind to sources of beauty and joy around us. Our

3

blindness often shows itself in our complaining and in our dissatisfaction with our lot. Prayer that the light of God may shine in our hearts and take away this blindness is necessary. Further, we learn where we are blind by taking seriously others' criticisms or comments; we learn more of it by honestly looking at ourselves in the light of Jesus' teaching. The appearance of the Messiah, Christ, is again and again spoken of in terms of light eliminating darkness and gloom as in today's first reading. As we share the Body and Blood of Christ today, a good prayer would be that this light shine in every corner of our soul and our life: "You are my light, my salvation, Lord" (Ps 27:1).

Saturday of the First Week of Advent—
No unemployment problem

Readings: Isa 30:19-21, 23-26; Matt 9:35–10:1, 5a, 6-8
Resp. Psalm: Ps 147:1-2, 3-4, 5-6 (L 180)

"The harvest is abundant but the laborers are few" (Matt 9:37). In a time like the present with a scarcity of candidates for the celibate, male priesthood, we sometimes hear this line of our Lord's quoted simply in terms of that problem. The context of today's reading, however, suggests that the poor masses of humanity, the diseased and other poor who are confused about life itself, need all the help they can get, not only from priests. Although Jesus cured "every disease and illness" (9:35), he left a lot for his followers to do. There is room for more competition to do this healing work all over the world, above all where we are. And many people do this sort of thing. One is continually impressed at how retired people are using the talents and skills they developed during their working years for others. One gives a day to the St. Vincent de Paul Society; another serves on diocesan or parish committees where his or her particular knowledge of employees' compensation is valuable; others extend the healing hand of Christ by visiting, comforting the elderly and disabled, and bringing them Communion. Most of us can find a place where our volunteering would make a difference for others, no matter what our age. We all qualify as the laborers needed for the harvest.

Monday of the Second Week of Advent—
What to accept, what to change

Readings: Isa 35:1-10; Luke 5:17-26
Resp. Psalm: Ps 85:9ab and 10, 11-12, 13-14 (L 181)

To endure the moment, the day, and even longer periods, we realistically sometimes accept the way things are—at least for now. But texts like today's first reading from Isaiah and the fact of our Lord's curing of the paralytic tell us that ultimately God does not stand for hunger, war, suffering, fear, and disease, nor even for infertile land, drought, and thirst. The desert blooms; the fearful and weak are strengthened; the blind, the deaf, and the lame are cured. All this calls us to hope and action, beyond the resignation that must be at times. People fed by the Body and Blood of the Lord and joined to him in closest union can continue the work of healing. Advent's frequent picturing of the beauty and glory of the time of the Messiah must not simply lull us into warm Christmas-card reveries, but enkindle our hope and drive our action. Today's readings offer good opportunity to reflect on this age-old question in the context of our own lives. How much of what is wrong around us (at home, at work, in the community) must we accept at least now; and what can we hope, with God's help, to change?

Tuesday of the Second Week of Advent—
The lost and forgotten

Readings: Isa 40:1-11; Matt 18:12-14
Resp. Psalm: Ps 96:1-2, 3 and 10ac, 11-12, 13 (L 182)

Too often it seems that the people who are well known and much appreciated just get more of the same, while the neglected, forgotten, unloved, homeless, and abandoned are left that way. How many of us take the initiative to seek out the people most in need? It is so much easier to spend time and attention on those with whom we feel comfortable, those who understand and appreciate us. Yet one of the distinguishing marks of the One whose coming we await is that he comes especially for the lost and forgotten. Both readings today use the image of the shepherd caring for his flock and the Gospel speaks of the shepherd leaving ninety-nine sheep in order to look for the one that is lost. This picture is another description of what God does in sending the Son to take on a human life. The lost in our society are obvious enough, especially in our cities: the homeless, the street people including children, the abused, the abandoned, and the unemployed. Then there are the victims of human greed throughout the world, the starving, and the poor. In imitation of the Lord, we Christians have been empowered to do what is in our capacity to come to the aid of these lost people. Further reflection also makes clear that all of us in some sense are among the lost whom Christ came to find and save. We may need to work at really

5

praying and at paying more attention to the suffering and lonely in our midst; we need to work at our anger and impatience and our neglect of responsibilities and commitments. Each of us knows what there is in ourselves that especially calls out for healing and restoration.

Wednesday of the Second Week of Advent—
New vigor and fervor

Readings: Isa 40:25-31; Matt 11:28-30
Resp. Psalm: Ps 103:1-2, 3-4, 8 and 10 (L 183)

Some of our heaviness, weariness, and apparent lack of energy is not simply due to the flu, being overworked, anemia, or mononucleosis. It might also stem from expecting the verve and the enthusiasm to come solely from ourselves and our natural vigor. Natural vigor and energy are not at all to be despised; in fact, having them places on us a greater responsibility—the requirement that we use them for the benefit of the more weary and weak. But even the most buoyant and bubbly among us may feel the blahs some time, a certain listlessness, indifference, ennui. "Come to me, all you who labor and are burdened, and I will give you rest" (Matt 11:28). Learning to rely more on the Lord and to expect all from God; allowing ourselves to be carried along on the energy and rhythm of God's life—this kind of surrender can fill us with a divine vitality and an ease in much that we do. His yoke is lighter and more truly adapted to us than the burdens we allow our society and its competitive spirit to place on us. No matter how important our participation in the life of our world is for ourselves, our families, and the world itself, it helps to step back and see that it is not of final importance. Surrender to the power and grace of God and allowing God more space within us and in our thoughts and desires is the way to more peace and quiet, more ease and joy. "They that hope in the LORD will renew their strength, they will soar as with eagles' wings; they will run and not grow weary, walk and not grow faint" (Isa 40:31).

Thursday of the Second Week of Advent—
Self-help and other help

Readings: Isa 41:13-20; Matt 11:11-15
Resp. Psalm: Ps 145:1 and 9, 10-11, 12-13ab (L 184)

The reading from Isaiah captures as well as anything the problem many people have with the Christian faith. In this we hear the Lord say to us, "Fear not, I will help you" (Isa 41:13). The Lord answers the needs of the afflicted and needy. "I will turn the desert into a marsh-land" (41:18), and much more. God does all this; God satisfies our needs; God delivers us from all ills. We, on the contrary, have been taught and we hear that everything we need for health and happiness lies within us, within our own powers: "You can do or be anything you want to." Any little grade-schooler can grow up to be president, etc. In many bookstores, self-help materials pretty well replace religion as we know it. Self-help instead of God-help seems to reign. The very idea that God should send the Son to save us (not simply to show us how to save ourselves) is utterly opposed to much in the spirit of our age. We are like two-year-olds, anxious to be independent, anxious to walk by ourselves even if it means falling on our face. A recognition of sin, as we saw earlier this week, and a recognition that our salvation or deliverance has to come from outside ourselves are two very hard truths for our age—very difficult facts, possibly, for human nature any time. To surrender to God by trustingly turning over the controls to God is one attitude Advent can teach us.

Friday of the Second Week of Advent—
There's no pleasing some people

Readings: Isa 48:17-19; Matt 11:16-19
Resp. Psalm: Ps 1:1-2, 3, 4 and 6 (L 185)

"There's no pleasing some people." We've all heard or used some simi-lar phrase at times. If, for whatever reason, some people oppose us or oppose a public figure, there is almost nothing that we or they can do which is not criticized. The words of Jesus in today's Gospel, of course, refer to his life among his contemporaries who, out of envy or fear, jumped at every opportunity to fault him. If he fasts, they say he is mad; if he eats and drinks with the wrong people, he's a drunk and glutton. There are at least two applications to our own lives. First, we can expect that if we put ourselves out to undertake anything worth-while in public, there will be carping from several contradictory direc-tions. Service doesn't infallibly bring appreciation. Second, we learn to temper our own criticism of others who are trying to do some-thing worthwhile. Genuine incompetence and crookedness should be exposed, but so often our faultfinding is merely petty and negative and does nothing to help the situation. "There's no pleasing some people."

Saturday of the Second Week of Advent—
The crib and the Cross

Readings: Sir 48:1-4, 9-11; Matt 17:9a, 10-13
Resp. Psalm: Ps 80:2ac and 3b, 15-16, 18-19 (L 186)

No more than we can forget the poor and suffering and the victims of so much of the world's cruelty and indifference, can we in Advent forget the suffering of the Savior. Speaking of John the Baptist today, Jesus says that in him Elijah has come and they "did to him whatever they pleased." "So also will the Son of Man suffer at their hands" (Matt 17:12). This seems to be a reference to the way John was beheaded by the king for his straightforward speaking out and a reference to how Jesus will suffer at the hands of the authorities. Jesus, the prophets, and John the Baptist all shared in the hostility of fellow human beings to the message of God and to the Good News. On a most general level and in a way applicable to all of us, the point is that coming close to God and allowing God entry into our lives inevitably entails some suffering. On an even broader level, we may say that no good thing is accomplished by any of us without the acceptance of some suffering, pain, and at least minimal difficulty involved in the undertaking. Advent—which celebrates the initial steps in our relation to God and our opening ourselves to God—adds this note about suffering in order to be realistic about what discipleship entails. Human life, as the celebration of the Nativity of the Lord shows eloquently, is shot through with a mixture of sadness and joy, pain and pleasure, life and death. As we enter into the warmth, cheer, and good will of the Christmas season, we can be more aware of and practically concerned about those in our midst who do not share our joy but share so much of the Cross.

Monday of the Third Week of Advent—*Commitment*

Readings: Num 24:2-7, 15-17a; Matt 21:23-27
Resp. Psalm: Ps 25:4-5ab, 6 and 7bc, 8-9 (L 187)

Avoiding commitment might be a good way to describe the chief priests and elders who question Jesus in today's Gospel. Whether it's John the Baptist or Jesus, it's the same thing; they are met by people who look for ways to avoid a decision and avoid any commitment. Commitment certainly carries with it risks and we should think, reflect, and weigh these risks before we make serious commitments. Friends, parents, priests, and counselors all urge this on those thinking of marriage. In one sense, our society is all too aware of the seriousness of commitment; in fact, there seems to be a great fear of any commitment beyond the next ten minutes or so. The chief priests and elders of today's Gospel had other personal reasons for fearing commitment; they feared for their own authority and position. They gave too much weight to their relation to the political powers and to their position in that society. Part of our annual preparation for the celebration of the birth of the Lord is the renewal of our own commitment to Christ. We may dither around about too many secondary things, and thus put off making a fuller commitment of our lives to Christ. We may paralyze any likelihood of commitment by endless discussion and worry. We may fear what the consequences and demands of a commitment may be. But all this only highlights our need to explore the nature and depth of our commitment to Christ during this Advent.

Tuesday of the Third Week of Advent—
Yes or No or "I dunno"

Readings: Zeph 3:1-2, 9-13; Matt 21:28-32
Resp. Psalm: Ps 34:2-3, 6-7, 17-18, 19 and 23 (L 188)

At some time in our lives we have said to the Lord with the elder son in the Gospel, Yes, I am on my way. Like him, we may still be sitting at the breakfast table dawdling over the comics, not much nearer to the vineyard and the work we promised. An essential part of Advent for all of us is repentance—a recognition that we have failed coupled with a will to change. We may have in effect said "no" by our inertia or putting things off. Continuing yesterday's theme, today's Gospel holds up commitment for us to look at it and think about. What does our yes to new life in Christ which we repeat every Easter mean? The son in today's Gospel who said "yes" and then did nothing suggests that we look at the content of our commitment. At this or any Eucharist, we offer our lives and work to God through Christ. Through him also we have the energy and strength to carry out our promises and decisions, our yes. Most of us may need to emphasize more in our prayer a trusting petition for God's grace to make us more generous and active in carrying out that original yes.

Wednesday of the Third Week of Advent—*Which guru?*

Readings: Isa 45:6c-8, 18, 21c-25; Luke 7:18b-23
Resp. Psalm: Ps 85:9ab and 10, 11-12, 13-14 (L 189)

Are we awaiting he who is to come or "should we look for another?" (Luke 7:19). The One whose coming we await in this Advent season is called in John's Gospel the "Word of God," the sum total of what God has to say to the world and to us. Do we expect enough from Christ, from his word, and from the sacraments? So often it seems we give them a back seat, while some current guru or popular teacher on TV with a book or a seminar gets most of our attention and effort and even at times quite a bit of our money. Don't we often look for someone else when we have not given sufficient time and thought to the word of God? The opportunities to study the Scriptures in groups or alone abound today, but so often we Christians have never given God's word persevering and generous attention. We could gauge the reality of our devotion to God's word by asking how much time and reflection we are willing to give it. The word speaks to us of he who is to come, but only if we allow it some space in our lives. The words of Isaiah today are absolute, and a good reminder to us of what position God's word should have in our thought and heart: "Turn to me and be safe, all you ends of the earth, for I am God; there is no other!" (Isa 45:22).

Thursday of the Third Week of Advent—
Endless thanksgiving

Readings: Isa 54:1-10; Luke 7:24-30
Resp. Psalm: Ps 30:2 and 4, 5-6, 11-12a and 13b (L 190)

We don't often focus the homily on the responsorial psalm, but today's psalm is one of those gems that would enrich anyone's inner life and relation to God. It is full of thanksgiving for God's deliverance, a theme which is probably applicable to the life of any one of us. Looking back, we can all find instances of how we were saved from difficult or trying situations or given a new outlook on a desperate situation. The God of Judaism and Christianity is not, of course, a short order cook at a fast food place. Our faith, trust, and thanksgiving are not based on some magical certainty that God will free us from the hardships, pains, and difficulties of ordinary life, if we only ask. God's care and love for us show themselves often—usually, in less obvious ways. We may remain with our physical ailment, but hopefully we have learned through prayer a better way of facing it. We may see how our freedom from a damaging and fearful episode in our life took a form we could not have predicted or asked for. Our responsorial phrase is: "I will praise you, Lord, for you have rescued me" (Ps 30:2). "You changed my mourning into dancing; O LORD, my God, forever will I give you thanks" (30:12-13). To come to a position of continual thanksgiving is a central goal of Christian life, and enough reflection on our life in the light of our faith can show us all how appropriate this is. The central act of our faith is the Eucharist, thanksgiving in and with the Lord.

Friday of the Third Week of Advent—*Who needs testimony?*

Readings: Isa 56:1-3a, 6-8; John 5:33-36
Resp. Psalm: Isa 56:1-3a, 6-8 (L 191)

"Better to light one candle than to curse the darkness." By now we've all heard this saying. John, Jesus says, was a "burning and shining lamp," and elsewhere in John's Gospel Jesus says of himself, "I am the light of the world" (John 8:12; 9:5). Jesus says that his works testify to him and certainly, as we know from elsewhere in Scripture, our works and our lives testify to what we believe and to the Lord in whom we hope and trust. But then Jesus says rather disconcertingly in today's Gospel that he does not need our testimony; in fact, he does not even accept it. But perhaps it's we who need our testimony to the Lord? Don't we need each other's testimony in our weakness and fear? Our often faltering and frail faith benefits when we see or hear others testify to their trust and hope, often when they are in much more difficult straits than ours. Testimony of the kind we need doesn't have to be in stirring words. In fact, we are probably more impressed by another's life and example than by mere words. We need the help of others. The strong, silent loner is more fiction than reality. Real people are aware of how much they depend on others and how much they influence others, for good or ill, by their lives and actions.

December 17—*An all-inclusive genealogy*

Readings: Gen 49:2, 8-10; Matt 1:1-17
Resp. Psalm: Ps 72:1-2, 3-4ab, 7-8, 17 (L 193)

"Obed became the father of Jesse, Jesse the father of David the king" (Matt 1:5-6). The list of ancestors of Jesus with their strange names may seem dull and irrelevant to us, but it was important to the Jews of Christ's time. It showed that the person in question was truly a Jew and truly a member of the people of the covenant. Implicitly, of course, in doing this it also makes plain that this person is truly a human being. There are some peculiarities in this particular list tracing Jesus' lineage back to Abraham; it shows a family tree which is by no means completely Jewish. Among Jesus' ancestors are non-Jewish women and women of ill repute. The very inclusion of women in the genealogy runs counter to the usual practice of tracing lineage only through the male line. Jesus is truly human. He comes as the Savior of not only the Chosen People but of all peoples and not only of men but also of women; he likewise comes very clearly for sinners and not just for those of unquestioned probity. The genealogy may seem boring to us, yet this information about the various people in Jesus' background is really not what we would expect, for it includes sinners and non-Jews. All this was quite revolutionary for those who heard; it was the unexpected and "good" news. In our day when exclusion of others for race, ethnic background, sexual orientation, or unusual customs is, unfortunately, still all too prevalent, we may need to take the lessons of this family tree more to heart, more seriously. The Messiah comes for everyone.

December 18—*What does the Messiah mean to me?*

Readings: Jer 23:5-8; Matt 1:18-25
Resp. Psalm: Ps 72:1-2, 12-13, 18-19 (L 194)

Today Jeremiah says the coming Messiah, the king to come, will be the "righteous shoot" (Jer 23:5). The text tells of how the Israelites have always referred to the Lord as the one who brought them out of slavery in Egypt; now, in different circumstances, they speak of the Lord who brought them back from exile, "up from the land of the north" (23:8). In the Gospel the angel says, "You are to name him Jesus, because he will save his people from their sins" (Matt 1:21). Between the two texts we have three ways of looking at or speaking of what the Lord does: he saves his people from harsh servitude; he brings them back from exile; and he saves them from sin. One of the three should fit each of us specifically. Either, one, we have been under the domination of some habit or tendency which has amounted to a kind of slavery. Or, two, we have simply been distant from God (in exile); our prayer life has been perfunctory and superficial; we have not developed a genuine relation with God. Or, three, we have sinned in some way which has cast a dark shadow over our life. While being in exile, slavery, and sin have different tonalities, each can also be used interchangeably for our situation. To lack a close relation to God is a kind of exile; to be under the domination of the world's standards and values is a kind of slavery. *Jesus, come, save us from our sins; be Emmanuel for us, be God with us in all the moments of this day.*

December 19—*The future is open*

Readings: Judg 13:2-7, 24-25a; Luke 1:5-25
Resp. Psalm: Ps 71:3-4a, 5-6ab, 16-17 (L 195)

Two unlikely pregnancies urge an always necessary lesson, one we need to hear during this Advent and any time: there can be new beginnings and the unexpected can happen; things can change. Better yet, God can bring about the unexpected. Around us there are people who believe and teach that we have no choice about what happens in our lives; it is all settled in advance by our chemistry, genes, heredity, etc. There are others who come to the same conclusion in a less scientific way. They are the people we hear so often say after the death of a young person in an accident, "His time was up; it was meant to be." In the shock of grief, of course, many of us do not think clearly. But this certainly sounds like what we call "fatalism." Couldn't the young man have had fewer drinks? Couldn't there have been better lighting on that stretch of the highway by the cliff? Couldn't he have accepted that friend's offer to drive him home? There are many instances in human life where a different exercise of our freedom or better use of technology or science could have changed things. And, as these stories illustrate, there is also the fact of God's initiative. We too easily buy the fatalism and resignation which are around us. Advent and Christmas tell us that God and our freedom can make things different. We need more confidence in both—in God and our freedom, in that order.

December 20—*How to hear and respond*

Readings: Isa 7:10-14; Luke 1:26-38
Resp. Psalm: Ps 24:1-2, 3-4ab, 5-6 (L 196)

Too often we tend to forget or ignore the fact that some popular practices of Catholic piety are rooted in the Bible. Today's Gospel suggests, for one, devotion to angels—recently pretty close to a fad in our otherwise secular world. And then there is that prayer which seems so exclusively Catholic to many, the Hail Mary. That, too, has its origins in the opening chapters of Luke's Gospel. We hear the first part of it today in the angel's greeting to Mary: "Hail, full of grace! The Lord is with you" (Luke 1:28). The next part of the Hail Mary prayer comes in Elizabeth's words to Mary, a little later in the same chapter of Luke. Honoring Mary with these words is doing nothing less than what the angel of the annunciation did. The last part of today's Gospel gives us probably the most basic reason why we give Mary such an exalted position. She is the model for how we Christians best receive the word of God: "I am the handmaid of the Lord. May it be done to me according to your word" (1:38). If it means anything for us to regard Scripture as the standard for our belief and Christian life, then this is a good example.

13

We find in Scripture models for our response to God. Like Mary, our willingness to be receptive to God's word can bring forth in our lives and for the world much good. The effectiveness of our Communion at Mass relies on such receptivity in us to God's grace.

December 21—*Where to put our confidence*
Readings: Cant 2:8-14 or Zeph 3:14-18a; Luke 1:39-45
Resp. Psalm: Ps 33:2-3, 11-12, 20-21 (L 197)

Much of the motivational talk of our culture is built around telling us that we can do anything with the right sort of self-confidence. Elizabeth today commends Mary because the great things happening to her are the result of her trust in God: "Blessed are you who believed that what was spoken to you by the Lord would be fulfilled" (Luke 1:45). In the face of so much apparently successful stress on self-confidence in our society, Christians need to take what is of value in that and join it to the confidence in God which fills the pages of Scripture. Confidence in God does not replace the appropriate confidence in ourselves or our God-given powers that functioning in ordinary life requires. Figuring out the relationship of the two kinds of confidence is not simple and, in many ways, is the work of a lifetime. It seems that coming to appreciate how much we need to trust God is the result of experience and living. We can't force that insight on young people, for example, who must learn some decent confidence in themselves and in their powers. To constantly repress that or downplay it seems likely to produce fearful, hesitant people. All of us must be allowed to learn by trial and error and through experience the limits and capabilities of our own powers. Ultimately it seems that any thoughtful and prayerful person reaches the point of appreciating more profoundly how much we depend on the power and help of God. Blessed is she or he who trusts that God's promises will be fulfilled in his or her regard.

December 22—*Turning things upside down*
Readings: 1 Sam 1:24-28; Luke 1:46-56
Resp. Psalm: 1 Sam 2:1, 4-5, 6-7, 8abcd (L 198)

Yesterday we heard where the center of our joy at Christmas should be: in the Savior. Mary's song, the *Magnificat* (the text for today's Gospel) spells out what the Savior does. It is almost comforting to realize that the singing of this canticle by Christians has at times been considered subversive by repressive regimes. It confirms that Christ's coming and teaching can have a powerful impact even in the present. One of the persisting criticisms of Christians has always been that we are only interested in the future, the world to come, and, consequently, preach acceptance of injustice now in view of eternal hope. The coming of Christ, in practice, should herald the introduction of concern for the lowly and the hungry in our world. Whether it does that or not, of course, depends on our willing cooperation with God's desire for justice and compassion. Preachers of class hatred, racial prejudice, and selfishness (whether religious or political) should not expect or find support among Christians. Our God comes to confuse the proud, depose the mighty, and raise up the lowly.

December 23—*The great reconciler*

Readings: Mal 3:1-4, 23-24; Luke 1:57-66
Resp. Psalm: Ps 25:4-5ab, 8-9, 10 and 14 (L 199)

"To turn the hearts of the fathers to their children, and the hearts of the children to their fathers" (Mal 3:24). The task of John the Baptist described in the reading from the prophet Malachi is one of reconciliation; that is the way he prepares people for the Lord who is to come. That is certainly part of our preparation for the hoped-for entry of the Lord into our lives. Our willingness to be reconciled, to forgive, and to ask forgiveness is not a luxury, but an essential part of our preparation. Christmas, like Easter, is genuinely celebrated if we are willing to be reconciled and to begin anew relationships soured by past events. As the words of Malachi suggest, that reconciliation is often most needed with those we are closest to: family members and friends. The Christ who comes does not change our vindictive and spiteful hearts and thoughts independently of our willingness. But he welcomes and perfects our turning to love and our willingness to be reconciled.

December 24—*Evidence of hope and life*

Readings: 2 Sam 7:1-5, 8b-12, 14a, 16; Luke 1:67-79
Resp. Psalm: Ps 89:2-3, 4-5, 27 and 29 (L 200)

On a day when everyone else is engaged in last minute preparation for Christmas (gift buying, giving, food preparation, more Christmas cards) those at Mass this day before Christmas are undoubtedly a dedicated group. In contrast to the frenzy around us, we gather to prepare in another way for the coming of the Lord. The words we hear are those of one who can't wait; they speak of salvation already accomplished, already here although there is still one more day until we celebrate the birth of the Savior. The words of Zechariah about his son, John (to be called the Baptizer) sound like a hymn to the complete salvation brought by the Messiah. God has ransomed his people; has given us salvation from our enemies; and has shone on us in our darkness with light to "guide our feet into the way of peace" (Luke 1:79). To appreciate what Jesus brings, we need some sense of the darkness of a world without him and a sense of how the threat of death hangs over our existence. On this day before Christmas, think of what our world and life would be like without the hope, strength, and encouragement we get from believing in Jesus, hearing his word, and sharing his life in this Eucharist. Many of our contemporaries do live in darkness—unsure of what it's all about, where it's going, why we're here. Some do live oppressed by fear of death and the void and emptiness they see beyond this life. But, with Zechariah, we believe that in Jesus God has shone "on those who dwell in darkness and the shadow of death." Christians feel it is their mission to evidence the joy and light which come with Christ. They know a joy much more profound than whatever comes from abundance of food and drink, from gifts and giving, and even from friends and family.

Season of Christmas

December 26, Saint Stephen, First Martyr—
Celebration and Suffering

Readings: Acts 6:8-10; 7:54-59; Matt 10:17-22
Resp. Psalm: Ps 31:3cd-4, 6 and 8ab, 16bc and 17 (L 696)

None of us, filled with the spirit, good food, and music of Christmas, would ever have thought to place the feast of St. Stephen on the day after Christmas. To celebrate a man who was stoned to death for his belief in Christ on this day is about as unsentimental as one can get. Even that carol, "Good King Wenceslaus," which does mention this feast, doesn't touch on Stephen's martyrdom but on a story in the usual spirit of Christmas about a good king who helps a homeless man. The brutal realism of celebrating St. Stephen today is a real plus for the church's liturgy. It reminds us in the midst of the good fellowship, song, fun, and family reunions that all this can be a bit unreal. There is certainly nothing wrong with enjoying the delights which accompany our celebration of Christmas. God has made us for ultimate delight and joy, not for suffering and sadness. But even in our Christmas celebration, as in the picture given us of St. Stephen, there can be suffering: someone is missing from our family celebration or some who are there don't get along; someone else may not have come because so-and-so was going to be there. It could even come to, Matthew tells us, "Brother will hand over brother to death . . . children will rise up against parents" (Matt 10:21). Our joy and celebration as Christians and as human beings is always bittersweet. Aunt Jenny is not here because she's getting chemo; Larry and Jill split up a month ago; Marilyn's husband is not here because he's overseas with the military; Bill was afraid to come to the big dinner because of his alcoholism. The feast of Stephen tells us that following Christ brings with it the Cross, as does simply living human life. The Eucharist tells us this same reality every day, and points ahead to resurrection.

December 27, Saint John, Apostle and Evangelist—
Little less than gods

Readings: 1 John 1:1-4; John 20:1 and 2-8
Resp. Psalm: Ps 97:1-2, 5-6, 11-12 (*L* 697)

Much in popular culture—its music, films, language, stories, famous people, crime—presents a low evaluation of human life. Despite our touchiness about how we are treated, we tolerate an awful lot of low talk and ways of acting about human beings. Terms which have been ordinarily used as insults become trendy. The spirit of the writings which go under the name of John (the Gospel and three letters) is quite the opposite. Here we have language that again and again links us very closely to God. The author seems breathlessly excited by what he is telling us. This is what he proclaims to us: "what we have heard, what we have seen with our eyes, what we have looked upon and touched with our hands" (1 John 1:1)—the Word of life. The eternal life of the Father, he says, has become visible in the Son and we are able to share in that life: "We are writing this so that our joy may be complete" (1 John 1:4). To be able to tell us about it and share this life with us is the writer's joy. The various sciences may tell us correctly about all that we share with the earth and its living creatures and with the stars of the universe, but John is on another plane. He stresses our dignity as sharers of the divine life and how in Christ the life of God has become visible, become flesh. No other New Testament writer seems to dwell so continually on the mystery of Christmas. We may be subject to suffering and disease and even to violence; but (we learn in John, through the gift that is Jesus) we share the life of God, an eternal life which has already begun in us. God has made us little less than gods, crowned us with glory and honor (Psalm 8 tells us), and given us power over the work of God's hands.

December 28, The Holy Innocents, Martyrs—
A mother's slant

Readings: 1 John 1:5–2:2; Matt 2:13-18
Resp. Psalm: Ps 124:2-3, 4-5, 7cd-8 (*L* 698)

History seems to go from one battle or war to another and from one political leader to another, at least as it's ordinarily recorded. It would sound quite different if it were written from the point of view of mothers, the mothers whose offspring (infants or twenty-year-olds) were the casualties of those wars. This history would give us one long line of mothers weeping for their children, children like the infants massacred in today's Gospel story. The Rachel to whom today's Gospel refers wept for children carried off into captivity. The innocents of this history would not simply be those under the age of the use of reason, but the sons and daughters of all ages who are caught in the crossfire of crime and war. Sorrowful, sorrowing mothers fill the pages of human history. As so often, some particular moment in the life of Jesus or some specific person like his mother Mary, for example, or the mothers of the Holy Innocents—such persons or moments are typical of ordinary human life. The sorrowing mother of our day has seen her child die in an accident, of crib-death, of a drug-overdose, as a soldier in some nation's war, of famine in the sub-Sahara, of suicide and mental illness, or as a bystander in a gang war. There is no easy consolation for them. As we all have a fellow sufferer in the Lord, they have a soul mate in the mother of the Lord, as well as with many mothers worldwide, throughout time.

December 29, The Fifth Day in the Octave of Christmas—
High expectations

Readings: 1 John 2:3-11; Luke 2:22-35
Resp. Psalm: Ps 96:1-2a, 2b-3, 5b-6 (L 202)

It's probably small consolation, but the violence about which we complain in our world is not something new. Good people, the bearers of light, have frequently met with violent hatred. The sword or the gun is never far from those servants of light close to God. Although many of us may lead relatively tranquil and unperturbed lives, violence is never lacking for those who would bring the light of Christ to it. Think of the martyrs and persecuted in our time in the Iron Curtain countries or in Central America. At times violence seems to diminish; conditions now seem better for Christians in the countries of Eastern Europe. Violence diminishes, the first reading suggests, insofar as neighborly love gains the upper hand: "Whoever loves his brother remains in the light" (1 John 2:10). Christians support their hope for a better world based on mutual love by not giving up on bringing that love and that light into human life. The "true light is already shining" (2:8) when we curb our tongue, our badmouthing; when we encourage the good; when we forgive and expect the best even of those who seem to have failed; when we expect everything good from the Savior whose birth we are celebrating.

December 30, The Sixth Day in the Octave of Christmas—
Persevering in service

Readings: 1 John 2:12–17; Luke 2:36-40
Resp. Psalm: Ps 96:7-8a, 8b-9, 10 (L 203)

The widow Anna in her faithfulness to Temple worship and prayer reminds us of the many women who form the core of the faithful at
daily worship, who probably do more than anyone to foster and pass
on faith. The real guarantee of any virtue is perseverance in it through
thick and thin, in fervor or dullness. Anna "never left the temple, but
worshiped night and day with fasting and prayer" (Luke 2:37). It's so
much easier to do things by fits and starts and to pray by whim and
feeling. The wisdom and insight which Anna has—that those who have
stayed with prayer over the years gain—is to a large degree the result of
staying with prayer in dry periods and times of fervor, when our heart
sings, and also when it is heavy as a rock. Some insights come from
constant attentiveness to God and prayer which cannot be gained from
books or study. Anna's recognition of the Child and his significance is an
example of such insight. The poor, hungry, abandoned, abused, and dis-
carded children of our world, of our big cities, and elsewhere need more
people who see the Christ Child in them and feel obliged to care and help.
The world of which John speaks so negatively today is not God's creation as such, but a world which is under the domination of selfishness
and self. Those who do see the identity of these children with the Child
Jesus can pressure the powers of our world and work themselves to see
that they are given respect and love. The children of the world require
more than an occasional smile or gasp of admiration at how cute they
are; each one of them requires someone to show God's love to them.

December 31, The Seventh Day in the Octave of Christmas—
Leaving self-pity behind

Readings: 1 John 2:18-21; John 1:1-18
Resp. Psalm: Ps 96:1-2, 11-12, 13 (L 204)

The last day of the year—"it is the last hour" (1 John 2:18)—of which
John speaks is here. If we allow ourselves some time for reflection, we
may have many thoughts about what has happened and not happened
as well as what we hope will continue or be different in the new year
starting tomorrow. Today we hear John's account of the nativity. There
are no shepherds, Magi nor angels, and no manger in this one. John,
instead, speaks of the theology of the birth of Christ and the meaning

of this event for those who embrace it by faith. The acceptance of the one who came as a human child to reveal most concretely God's love for his creatures opens the way to the transformation of our lives. No matter how poorly this past year may have gone in terms of our personal lives or our hopes, today's gospel tells us once more how much has been given us in Christ and how much, therefore, can still come to pass in us. Those who have accepted him, John writes, are empowered to become sons and daughters of God; those who believe in him have a share in his fullness and in the waves of love flowing from God toward us. A man who had the terrible experience as a ten-year-old of finding his mother murdered writes that over the years he has learned that the abandonment of self-pity is the beginning of wisdom. Rather than moan about what should or might have been last year, about failures and losses, we are able, through the love of God available to us, to face the new year with hope and strength. The real light has come into the world; the Word of God has made his dwelling among us; God's enduring love for us has come in and through Jesus Christ.

January 2—*The abiding presence*

Readings: 1 John 2:22-28; John 1:19-28
Resp. Psalm: Ps 98:1, 2-3ab, 3cd-4 (L 205)

Secular and social calendars mark the end of Christmas on December 26th. Christmas trees already removed from living rooms and abandoned on the boulevards of city streets are a sign that Christmas is over for some. But the church keeps a Christmas season which lasts at least eight days, the octave just completed. Even twelve days of Christmas aren't too long to extend this joyful season. Like Mary, we need time to ponder in our hearts the message of God incarnate in Jesus Christ. These days give us the time to do that. The frenetic pace of planning and parties and presents is over. Now we take time to abide in the Word made flesh who dwells among us. The First Letter of John calls us to abide in Christ and to remain in him. This kind of abiding is not merely suffering the misfortune of waiting in line at the bank or at the drive-up window of a fast-food restaurant, impatient to get on to the next thing. The scriptural sense of abiding is to stay in one place long enough to watch and listen and look for the presence of God among us. There is no "next thing" to get on to. God has made a home among us. That's the message of John the Baptist in the Gospel. The Mighty One stands among us now. God's anointed Son dwells with us so that in our day we may dwell with God.

January 3—*Living as daughters and sons of God*

Readings: 1 John 2:29–3:6; John 1:29-34
Resp. Psalm: Ps 98:1, 3cd-4, 5-6 (L 206)

Both readings today speak of Jesus as the one who takes away sin. A good number of people in the last couple of decades have worried out loud that sin has been taken away too much from our world and not by Jesus, but because we have lost consciousness of sin. Undoubtedly, some have let sin be erased too easily by substituting genes, environment, and society for individual responsibility. Public figures have erased it by a new vocabulary of "misspoke" for lying and similar stratagems. But isn't some of the apparent lessening of sin-consciousness among Christians really a rediscovery of other biblical ways in which to speak of our failure in relation to God? Other language has been rediscovered in Scripture: unfaithfulness, coldness, lack of responsiveness, and the disobedience of children to their Father. In John's first Letter there is much talk of our relation to God by faith and baptism as that of children to the Father. Other terms are there too, of course; "sin is lawlessness," John says (1 John 3:4). But believers today find it more inspiring to look at their moral and religious life as an effort to live up to their baptismal dignity as sons and daughters of God than simply as a matter of obeying laws or of avoiding sins. John says that the one who remains in God does not sin. Stressing our life in God or God's life in us may result in less talk of sin, but it certainly need not result in less responsibility. Rather, it encourages us to live as God's children and to live up to that dignity.

January 4—*In person*

Readings: 1 John 3:7-10; John 1:35-42
Resp. Psalm: Ps 98:1, 7-8, 9 (L 207)

"Behold, the Lamb of God" (John 1:36)—the Lamb of God who is the sacrifice for our sins. And "We have found the Messiah" (1:41), the One who ushers in a new world. Whether we easily identify with the terms or not, Scripture is speaking of Jesus as the fulfillment of all human hopes and desires and the answer to our question about how to live and what is truly important. Not the answer to questions about life on Mars or the age of the universe, but in Jesus we have the answer to our questions about what or whom to trust. Earlier Jesus says to them, "What are you looking for?" (John 1:38). Christmas is a celebration of the arrival in our world of "the meaning of life," Jesus.

Faith is finding that meaning and embracing it. Isn't it most interesting that the answer to the question about the meaning of life comes in the form of a human being? Other questions are answered in formulas or propositions or with numbers. But the big question has its answer in a Person. The most precious, dear, and loved part of creation for most human beings is another human being. Relationships, marriage, love, and friendship all mean more to us than ideas and facts. Martyrs don't die for an idea, but for a person; and none of us lives generously except for a person—for *the* person, Jesus Christ.

January 5—*The surprise in the human*

Readings: 1 John 3:11-21; John 1:43-51
Resp. Psalm: Ps 100:1b-2, 3, 4, 5 (L 208)

"Can anything good come from Nazareth?" (John 1:46). The question of Nathanael reminds us of the prejudicial remarks we may make or hear others make about the neighboring state or the little town down the highway. Jesus doesn't take it amiss; he attributes it to Nathanael's simplicity. In the bigger picture, of course, it almost sounds as if Jesus were enjoying the irony: this local boy is surprised that the Messiah should come from Nazareth. Wouldn't it have been just as unlikely that he would come from Jerusalem? On one level the story reminds us to avoid judging others in terms of from where they come or in terms of their background. But in John's Gospel we're usually safe looking for several layers of meaning. Nathanael's remark in a broader sense can refer to the basic improbability of the Messiah coming from *any mere human town*—from Boise or Kuala Lumpur, Nairobi or Caracas. Nothing about his human origins ever explains sufficiently the real meaning of the Messiah. That is just what is so astounding: that the Christ should have come into the world as the Son of a young virgin from any human town. God's appreciation for all that is simply human shines out in the birth of Christ. God loves and acts through all that is simply human, through any part of the creation, through bread and wine. For the same reason God uses any energy, personality, smiles, or generosity we have to show love to others.

January 6—*What believing does*

Readings: 1 John 5:5-13; Mark 1:7-11 or Luke 3:23-38 or Luke 3:23, 31-34, 36, 38
Resp. Psalm: Ps 147:12-13, 14-15, 19-20 (*L* 209)

Someone once defined belief as that which gets us out of bed in the morning. What we hear in today's first reading goes further: "the one who believes that Jesus is the Son of God" (1 John 5:5) is *victorious* over the shaky convictions and superficial values of our world. Believing makes us victorious over the attitude which would say: "Why get up? Nothing will change. What am I doing that will make any difference?" Once we're up, we are able to live with the confidence and assurance that our belief gives us; we are no longer on shaky ground, but possess a basic conviction from which to live. Believing, in other words, is an assurance we get from God that we are justified in living with hope and spirit because we put our trust in the life, teaching, death, and resurrection of Jesus. We know it's worthwhile to get up and face the daily battles and often seemingly the very same ones. With Jesus as the center of our belief, we can have confidence that the forces causing suffering, sin, and death can only be temporarily victorious. The kind of belief we are talking about here does not claim to have or give the answer to all sorts of scientific questions or questions about the nature of the universe, for example, the number of islands in Indonesia or how genetics work in each of us. It would be nice to know the answers to all these issues, but that's the purpose of the human quest for knowledge and understanding. What belief in God tells us is, rather, that we are not wrong in practicing self-giving love and in seeing even life's crushing moments as something that will be overcome by the power of the resurrection in our lives.

January 7—*The joy and abundance of the Messiah's feast*

Readings: 1 John 5:14-21; John 2:1-11
Resp. Psalm: Ps 149:1-2, 3-4, 5 and 6a and 9b (*L* 210)

We're used to hearing the exuberant trumpet sounds of composers Henry Purcell and Jeremiah Clarke at weddings. Such music would go well with the wedding celebration at Cana. This first of seven signs worked by Jesus in John's Gospel is a high-spirited and lavish declaration that the Messiah has come. The traditional prophetic utterances about the age of the Messiah frequently pictured it in terms of a joyous banquet and a wedding. In related fashion, the same prophets spoke of how copious will be the fruit of the vine in the days of the Messiah. That is unmistakable in today's Gospel when Jesus transforms the water prescribed for Jewish ceremonial washings into wine, in fact, into a better wine than the guests were drinking earlier. The abundance of good food and drink with which Christians like to celebrate Christmas echoes this conviction. While the more sober and mundane accounts of the appearance of the Messiah in Matthew, Mark, and Luke emphasize the difficulties and slowness of recognition of the Messiah, here the kingdom of the Messiah is pictured in bold colors and celebration untouched by negatives. In the eucharistic banquet we share in at this altar we have made present for us a foretaste of the ultimate Messianic Banquet. We can go forth from our participation at this altar full of confidence that the Messiah, Jesus the Christ, has come and begun his reign in us. Indeed, before the coming of Christ, "they [had] no wine" (John 2:3). Jesus has revealed his glory and we have begun to believe in him.

Monday after Epiphany or January 7—
Healing and comfort and peace

Readings: 1 John 3:22–4:6; Matt 4:12-17, 23-25
Resp. Psalm: Ps 2:7bc-8, 10-12a (L 212)

John's Gospel presents the coming of the Messiah (in the story of the wedding at Cana) in terms of the joyous and lavish wedding feast of the kingdom. The coming of the Messiah signals an end to want and sorrow. Today, in Matthew, we hear a more subdued but equally meaningful picture of the time of the Messiah—here given in terms of the healing of human disease and pain. Quoting Isaiah, Matthew writes: "The people who sit in darkness have seen a great light, on those dwelling in a land overshadowed by death light has arisen" (Matt 4:16). In emphasizing that Jesus went around Galilee "curing every disease and illness among the people" (4:23), the evangelist stresses the signs of love and care for the sick and the poor that characterize the arrival of Messianic times. The church and we, members of Christ's Body are responsible for continuing in the sacraments and in our deeds the healing presence of Christ, of the Messiah, among our fellow human beings and above all, among our neighbors and the poor and abandoned in our midst. Healing, reconciliation, peace, food for the hungry, and consolation for the sorrowing are the ministry of the Body of Christ, which we are.

Tuesday after Epiphany or January 8—
Something (someone) has got to give

Readings: 1 John 4:7-10; Mark 6:34-44
Resp. Psalm: Ps 72:1-2, 3-4, 7-8 (*L* 213)

To relinquish what is in our own interest and good for the sake of others is what love means in today's first reading. We know this is what love means for two reasons: first, God has sent the Son, given him to us; and, second, the Son has come to be an offering for our sins. Both actions tell us of God's character and, specifically, that God forgoes self-interest for us. In an age of self-assertion and concern (if not obsession) with rights, this may sound too submissive to some. Our world is more likely to see love as a good feeling encouraging the fulfillment of each party. That this fulfillment might require some yielding of self-interest by at least one party is not usually part of the package. But even among those who consider fulfillment and self-expression the highest values, there is often the experience of someone giving up his or her self-interest. The proponents of self-fulfillment often owe a debt to someone's yielding. They must be grateful that someone else is yielding enough of his or her self-interest to listen to their ideas. At a minimum we all must recognize that our life in the world depends to some degree on us and/or others yielding self-interest. But the Christian ideal and the life of Jesus go further; they tell us that this self-forgetting and self-emptying is the way to a higher life. Every day at this altar this is put before us under the signs of bread and wine.

Wednesday after Epiphany or January 9—*Fear nothing*

Readings: 1 John 4:11-19; Mark 6:45-52
Resp. Psalm: Ps 72:1-2, 10, 12-13 (*L* 214)

Young people like to sport messages on T-shirts and decals like, "Have no fear"; "Fear nothing." Surely much of this is meant as youthful derring-do, a sort of flaunting of the "I will never die" implicit in youthful spunk. But every so often even such flamboyant excesses contain a kernel of truth. Ultimately, we all should come through our faith to a freedom from fear and a trust which carries us beyond the fear of death. As it is, however, fear stalks almost all of us in some form or other. Fear keeps some indoors at night. Living in a large apartment complex makes us fearful of what these unknown people might do or be. The doctor's prognosis, no matter how gently delivered, sets us shivering and fearful of the future. A weakening of the economy or a word from the Federal Reserve Board chairman gives us fears for our job and tomorrow. Jesus tells the disciples in the wind-tossed boat, "Take courage, it is I, do not be afraid!" (Matt 6:50). And John tells us that genuine love has no place for fear: "There is no fear in love, but perfect love drives out fear because fear has to do with punishment, and so one who fears is not yet perfect in love" (1 John 4:18). Thus the way to true and warranted fearlessness is by learning to love perfectly. Such a great ideal understandably is not achieved overnight; a life of prayer and the accompanying intimacy with God are what bring us to this perfect love. Freedom from fear, John tells us, results from love and the confidence and trust that love breeds. Our sharing in the offering of Christ helps foster that love and fearlessness in us.

Thursday after Epiphany or January 10—
Love of God begins next door

Readings: 1 John 4:19–5:4; Luke 4:14-22
Resp. Psalm: Ps 72:1-2, 14 and 15bc, 17 (L 215)

These continuous readings from the First Letter of John can sound, after a while, pretty heady and lofty. And they are. But they are also downright practical and leave us few outs with respect to actively loving others. Today's first reading tries to cover all the bases. We hear at least three reasons why love of neighbor is so central. First, John says we're liars if we claim to love God and yet hate our neighbor. That neighbor is our here-and-now opportunity to show God's genuine love. Second, how can we claim to love God whom we have not seen and not love our neighbor who is right here, visible and close at hand? If we claim to love the invisible God, we can easily show it by how we treat the neighbor. Third, because we believe in Christ, we have been begotten of God and so we are God's sons and daughters; if we claim to love the Father, we must love the children also. It would indeed be an odd father or mother who did not expect that friends would show at least minimal respect for their children. Like John's style, these incentives may be a bit repetitive, saying the same thing in different ways; but the point is clear. The more we become familiar with the New Testament, the clearer it is that John's themes (belief in Christ as God's Son and love of neighbor) are its pivots. How close what we hear today is to the words of Jesus in Matthew 25 where he tells us that whatever we do for the least of his own we do for him. *Lord, we celebrate your love for us in the sacrifice recalled on this altar; fill us with the same love for the people you love.*

27

Friday after Epiphany or January 11—*Learning to overcome*

Readings: 1 John 5:5-13; Luke 5:12-16
Resp. Psalm: Ps 147:12-13, 14-15, 19-20 (L 216)

Earlier the First Letter of John told us that through faith we conquer the world; we are able to go beyond appearances to see the love and power of God behind it. After hearing First John for almost two weeks now, we've all noticed the author's odd style—odd in that it is not organized by the kind of logic with which we're familiar and it seems repetitive. But as it moves on, the writer does bring in new elements just as we do in a conversation when we say a few times, "And besides . . ." or "Another thing . . ." Today a new point is made: "God gave us eternal life, and this life is in his Son. Whoever possesses the Son has life . . . I write these things to you so that you may know that you have eternal life, you who believe in the name of the Son of God" (1 John 5:11-13). Not only does faith overcome the world we see by telling us of so much more; faith also assures that even now we have eternal life. Our life in and with God has begun. The faith and eternal life we already have are what enable many a Christian to survive devastating experiences, losses, or illnesses with the assurance that there is more to life than this car accident, this illness, or this disappointment. Thinking this way does not come easily. It isn't a matter of a very strong and vivid imagination, but of a gift from God. This faith is nourished by practice and through our union with Christ here at the altar.

Saturday after Epiphany or January 12—
The gifts around us

Readings: 1 John 5:14-21; John 3:22-30
Resp. Psalm: Ps 149:1-2, 3-4, 5-6a and 9b (L 217)

"He must increase; I must decrease" (John 3:30). John the Baptist is aware that he is not the Messiah, that One more important than he is present. It's unfortunate that for many in our society today, any kind of self-effacement is seen as weakness or even slavery. Behind this attitude may be the denial that anything or anyone is more important or significant than any other thing or anyone else. But isn't it true that some people are better athletes than we, more attractive or sociable than we, or more talented in writing or art or fixing things than we? The crowds who fork over so much money to attend concerts of rock stars seem to suggest some recognition that this rock star is better than another. The fact that many of us sit enthralled watching Olympic stars do their stuff points to the same idea—we do appreciate superior talent. To appreciate what others can do and who they are without looking for chinks in their armor or finding fault with them is simply a decent approach to other people. Life would be pretty flat and dull if we never felt that there was anyone with some gift that we wanted to see or hear. It's part of our dignity as human beings to be able and willing to appreciate the accomplishments and gifts of others. When we are willing to recognize that a slowing down due to age or a certain inflexibility have become ours, it's wonderful and so helpful to others if we recognize that some younger person may do the job better. A willingness to see the good and talent in others makes life better for everyone.

Season of Lent

Ash Wednesday—*Spring, at least in the heart*

Readings: Joel 2:12-18; 2 Cor 5:20–6:2; Matt 6:1-6, 16-18
Resp. Psalm: Ps 51:3-4, 5-6ab, 12-13, 14 and 17 (L 219)

The word "Lent" probably comes from an Old English word for spring. Today, no matter how much the temperature dips outside, how bitterly the wind howls, or how deep the snow, we begin the springtime of the church. True, some of us in other parts of the world may be entering autumn. But in the church and, it is to be hoped, within each of us, spring is coming. This springtime is a renewal of life: a new beginning, the revival of freshness and hope in our life with each other in Christ, the radiance of our baptismal white. To get to spring we have to go through the sometimes gray and barren look of winter or late winter. The ashes we receive today are a good reminder that spring grows from gray to green. The yearly return of Lent tells us, as does what we see in the mirror, that change is urgent and not to be put off. Reminders about urgency are often what get us going and make us "get serious" about what is at hand. "Even now," says the Lord, "return to me with your whole heart" (Joel 2:12). St. Paul says it his way: "Behold, now is a very acceptable time; behold, now is the day of salvation" (2 Cor 6:2). We hasten the spring in our hearts by watering and cultivating them with more regular and heartfelt prayer, with practical care for the poor and unfortunate around us, and with more discipline in our lives. To paraphrase St. Paul: do not receive the grace of God offered in this season in vain. "Now is a very acceptable time!"

Thursday after Ash Wednesday—*Giving up, adding to—or?*

Readings: Deut 30:15-20; Luke 9:22-25
Resp. Psalm: Ps 1:1-2, 3, 4 and 6 (L 220)

Our first reading is from a book (Deuteronomy) containing some of the harshest teaching of the Old Testament. Yet we can find in today's selection some positive words for this early part of Lent. "I have set before you life and death . . . Choose life" (Deut 30:19). Although the text seems to be referring only to this earthly existence, we can be encouraged by these words to choose the life-giving vigor of Lent. In the Gospel our Lord tells us that true life, genuine life, is found when we are willing to surrender the comforts of this life or, put another way, to accept the inherent hardships in living a good life. Many of us are tempted to reduce Lent to "giving up" something or, somewhat better, adding something. These expressions can be misleading, especially for people who are already excessively busy or burdened with responsibilities. For these, adding something is just another way of feeling more put upon. Many a faithful Christian needs more time to reflect and to get away from a crowd of responsibilities. Possibly for such (and there are many) Lent must consist in choosing the life we already have along with its built-in crosses and demands—choosing it and trying to live it with a new spirit, a spirit of more gentleness and patience and more love and compassion. In other words, we pray to God to help us do what must be done (about which we have no choice) and to do so more fully in the spirit of Jesus and with his help. *Continue your earthly life, Lord, in us; may all we do and say point to you from whom comes our strength and joy.*

Friday after Ash Wednesday—*Priorities of Lent*
Readings: Isa 58:1-9a; Luke 5:27-32
Resp. Psalm: Ps 51:3-4, 5-6ab, 18-19 (L 221)

If Catholics are ever accused of putting too much emphasis on externals (on laws, regulations, practices like fasting or abstinence from meat), it certainly can't be blamed on the Scripture we hear these days. Today, for a second time since Lent began, we are warned against trusting externals and neglecting their purpose. The eloquent words from Isaiah give us God's idea of what fasting and external acts in general are all about. Anything we may do by way of a religious practice to revive our spirit during this season is aimed at the heart. The last half of the first reading puts in very concrete language what God expects: freeing the unjustly imprisoned and the oppressed; feeding the hungry, clothing the naked, sheltering the homeless. All of this, written centuries before Christ, retains its appropriateness for those of us living almost two thousand years after Christ. The voices—and the votes—of each one of us can help even our nation and world keep the right priorities, putting human need before everything else. A bishop in Brazil expressed this well when he said he was more concerned about all the naked street children and poor people in his diocese than about the naked vacationers at the beach. If we Christians are to be anywhere near innocent of charges of externalism and pettiness, it is because we are more often in the forefront of efforts for justice in our world, in our neighborhood, and our city. The daily reminders at Mass during Lent help sharpen our consciences about these matters.

Saturday after Ash Wednesday—*Saved but sinners*

Readings: Isa 58:9b-14; Luke 5:27-32
Resp. Psalm: Ps 86:1-2, 3-4, 5-6 (*L* 222)

On our better days, we may feel that the daily invitations to be sorry for our sins and to repent are a bit excessive. We're not that bad! The Church seems hung up on sin. Let's grant that the criticism may fit some periods and places in our history; insofar as it does, we are reminded that Christ came to bring us freedom and salvation, not to grind us into the dust. On days other than our better days, we may feel grateful that the liturgy does recognize that we are always sinners to some degree. Think of how impatient we've been, how sharp-tongued, how complaining, how hard and cold to some, or how simply selfish in any number of ways. Yes, we are sinners, the ones Christ came to call to repentance and to a change of heart, as he says today. Scripture urges us to be open to this internal change, this change of heart, which is what Lent is all about. To recognize our need for change and for repentance is part of being realistic about ourselves. We may be generally moving ahead, but almost every day some little thing reminds us that we are still capable of going backwards. The old and bad habits die hard and slowly. Lent serves us well with daily opportunities to say we're sorry and to begin again.

Monday of the First Week of Lent—
More than feelings and forms

Readings: Lev 19:1-2, 11-18; Matt 25:31-46
Resp. Psalm: Ps 19:8, 9, 10, 15 (*L* 224)

Words like today's from the first reading from the Book of Leviticus and our Lord's Gospel story about the sheep and the goats echo the concern we've heard several times already this Lent: that we do not fool ourselves into thinking that faithfulness to some form of prayer, fasting, and almsgiving (charity) is by itself genuine religion. These traditional ways to do penance have to be accompanied by a change of heart (an interior turning from what is wrong) and a concern for justice and compassion. It has always been a temptation for spiritual people to imagine that a set of religious practices carried out carefully is some kind of magic. Along with this is the temptation to take one's feelings for reality and for action as enough. Feelings of spiritual enthusiasm and being deeply moved by prayer or Mass don't mean much unless these produce practical, moral results in our lives. The Scripture writers are concerned that we don't let practices or feelings fool us into thinking we are holy. It's pleasant to have good feelings from our religion, but by themselves they prove nothing. Genuine religion consists in what we hear in Leviticus and the Gospel today: speaking the truth, not defrauding others, paying just wages, being honest in all our dealings, not speaking ill of others, not judging, avoiding revenge and, most positively, showing compassion to the suffering of our world. Leviticus says: "You shall love your neighbor as yourself" (Lev 19:18). And Jesus reaffirms these words with strong approval. Active love is the real test and proof of religion.

Tuesday of the First Week of Lent—
How God can get a word in
Readings: Isa 55:10-11; Matt 6:7-15
Resp. Psalm: Ps 34:4-5, 6-7, 16-17, 18-19 (L 225)

Perhaps we can let today's words from Jesus, helped by Isaiah, remind us that our prayer includes listening and not simply saying words. At times we act in prayer to God in the same way as a person sitting nervously with a new acquaintance. We feel we have to be saying something every minute; we find little pauses in the conversation embarrassing. How different it is with someone we know very well; we can sit together, gazing at a fire or listening to music, without feeling that one of us has to be saying something every moment. Jesus says that in prayer we shouldn't just rattle on or multiply words. Isn't it true that what our prayer lacks so often is just some space and silence which allow God actually to influence our minds and hearts? The author of Isaiah says that the word of God is like rain or snow that softens the earth and makes it fertile, eventually bringing forth its crops. True prayer is a dialogue and not merely a one-sided conversation dominated completely by us. God's work in us requires that we leave God some opening, a chance to be heard. In our world of so much noise and so little tolerance for silence, it may be hard for us to learn to be quiet before God. But it's definitely worth the effort. In silence we may experience our minds wandering all over the place. To minimize these distractions, it may help to take a phrase from the Gospel or one of the readings and keep coming back to those inspired words gently, while trying to focus our attention. Silence and attentiveness can be learned. This may be a helpful way to stay with what is going on at Mass, too: coming back to some favorite phrase.

Wednesday of the First Week of Lent—*Blessed by technology*

Readings: Jonah 3:1-10; Luke 11:29-32
Resp. Psalm: Ps 51:3-4, 12-13, 18-19 (*L* 226)

Jonah preached to non-believers and they repented after hearing him. A famous queen in Old Testament times came to see and hear for herself the wisdom of the renowned King Solomon. Yet these phenomenal people were nothing compared to the Son of God who came and preached to the people of first century Palestine. And this same Son of God still speaks to us through the word of Scripture and in the life of our fellow Christians. He is present among us by the sacrament of his Body and Blood. We, like his contemporaries, are blessed by his closeness. We could push this further and think of all the great advances of civilization that benefit us in so many ways and which at least theoretically make Christian life so much more accessible for us. We have such easy access to the word of God: in easily available printed form, in inexpensive commentaries, in courses, and in churches where we hear it more easily through electronic advances. Getting to Mass every Sunday (even daily for some) is made so much easier by modern transportation. All in all, it is so much easier for us to hear the word of God, to be exposed to it, and to understand it. Our lives are so much easier in terms of time spent in obtaining food and shelter, which allows us some leisure time to study and meditate. Does all this result in more holiness? Obviously, these same advances allow us to spend more time and energy on material satisfaction and on our own comfort and recreation. How do we use the wonderful opportunities, unknown to our ancestors, that we have available to us and that help us to be close to the word of God? Do we take it all too much for granted?

Thursday of the Week of Lent—*Prayer without qualifications*

Readings: Esth C: 12, 14-16, 23-25; Matt 7:7-12
Resp. Psalm: Ps 138:1-2ab, 2cde-3, 7c-8 (*L* 227)

The first reading tells of the prayer of Esther as she and her fellow Jews faced extermination at the hands of a king. She prays, "Now help me, who am alone and have no one but you, O LORD, my God" (Esth C:14). Esther's prayer implies her total trust in God, who knows and sees more than she can; this God can be trusted to answer her prayer in ways she may not be able to imagine. In the Gospel Jesus tells us in a number of ways that God always answers prayer. The tone of Jesus' words is not one encouraging us to lay out in specific detail for what we are pray-ing (for example, the model, unit number, size, and color of something we want), but the tone is simply that we trust God. We need Esther's trust. We need confidence in God and confidence that God will do what is best for us whether it's what we pray for or not. Possibly more prayer should be about asking to be in tune with God rather than asking for specific items which we think we absolutely need. Prayer doesn't really change things around us like altering the laws of meteorology or phys-ics; it more likely changes us. Too bad we are so conventional about prayer! "I'll pray for you" ends up being as significant as "We'll have to do lunch sometime." Only persistence in prayer and regular practice of prayer can teach us how life-changing prayer really is.

Friday of the First Week of Lent—
Worship of God and respect for persons

Readings: Ezek 18:21-28; Matt 5:20-26
Resp. Psalm: 130:1-2, 3-4, 5-7a, 7bc-8 (*L* 228)

As we heard loudly and clearly recently, Scripture supposes some free-dom on our part to change. Today's readings continue this theme: "If the wicked man turns away from all the sins he committed, . . . he shall surely live, he shall not die" (Ezek 18:21). Ezekiel goes on to speak of how the virtuous person could similarly make a turn for the bad. A most practical example is given or, better, asked of us by the Lord. He says: "If you bring your gift to the altar, and there recall that your brother has anything against you, leave your gift there at the altar, go first and be reconciled with your brother, and then come and offer your gift" (Matt 5:23-24). We do not sincerely worship God while harboring ill will toward another or while being conscious that some-one has something against us. Obviously, in some situations we un-avoidably make others unhappy or disappoint them. Teachers find that there are always some students who take a well-deserved low grade as a personal attack. In many areas of life standards of workmanship, courtesy, and safety have to be upheld. Those in charge must face the fact that the offender may take correction personally. But the Gospel text is concerned with situations where something unkind or harsh

Season of Lent

has caused another's enmity. Of such behavior the Lord speaks. The same idea—the inseparability of the worship of God and the respect due to others—is behind the custom of greeting others before Communion. As with so many things we do habitually, there is danger that it may cease being a real indication of our good will toward all. We preserve its real purpose when we greet not simply our family and friends but those we do not know.

Saturday of the First Week of Lent—
Forgiving love for deficient love

Readings: Deut 26:16-19; Matt 5:43-48
Resp. Psalm: Ps 119:1-2, 4-5, 7-8 (L 229)

Yesterday Jesus said that "unless your righteousness surpasses that of the scribes and Pharisees, you will not enter into the kingdom of heaven" (Matt 5:20). We hear the final demand of this holiness in today's Gospel reading. Our love is to be like God's; it is to be like the rain which falls on the just and the unjust. Somehow we are to go way beyond just responding to our attractions or simply loving those whom we know are in a position to do good for us. All of us, Jesus says, even without any directive from God, love or at least value those who love us and do us good. To love only those who love us is something like demanding an eye for an eye. To love others indiscriminately with God's own breadth of love is a demand we fulfill, if at all, only fitfully and occasionally. To pray for our enemies, speak kindly and sincerely to those who have injured us, resist getting even, come to the aid of another who may have hurt us at another time, forget past insults and congratulate and rejoice with the accomplishments of an enemy—all this we probably do only fitfully. For the other times, when we are so much less generous, we know how much we depend on the forgiveness and mercy of God. Every time we come to Mass we at least implicitly admit our dependence on God's forgiving love.

Monday of the Second Week of Lent—
Growing more generous and all-embracing

Readings: Dan 9:4b-10; Luke 6:36-38
Resp. Psalm: Ps 79:8, 9, 11 and 13 (L 230)

Hearing various parts of the Bible over a long time, we unavoidably come to the conclusion that there have been some pretty serious changes. In

36

some parts of the Bible written five or six hundred years before Christ, we come across a pretty stern, even revengeful picture of God. Although today's readings have in common a statement that God is compassionate, there is what we could call an improvement or a broadening of God's compassion in the Gospel. The opening verse of the reading from Deuteronomy says that God is merciful toward those who love God. Thus, there seems to be a limit to God's mercy; it's extended toward those who love him. In the Gospel Jesus asks us to be compassionate like the Father, and has earlier told us that the Father shows the same forgiving and loving face to both the good and the bad and not to just those who love God. The changing picture of God in the Bible is probably more in the minds and hearts of believers over the centuries than in God. It takes us human beings a long time to realize or understand some things. Being compassionate like God, Jesus tells us today, means not judging and not condemning. If it took the human race a long time to comprehend the breadth and depth of God's love, it also takes us individually a long time to begin to imitate that all-embracing love. How constant is our tendency to judge and even condemn others! We sometimes find ourselves making judgments (usually pretty rash ones) about others almost automatically. If we could only turn our critical eye on ourselves, how much we and others would benefit!

Tuesday of the Second Week of Lent—*Preaching and practice*

Readings: Isa 1:10, 16-20; Matt 23:1-12
Resp. Psalm: Ps 50:8-9, 16bc-17, 21 and 23 (L 231)

Jesus' quarrel with the scribes and Pharisees is not with their teaching, but with their practice. ". . . do and observe all things whatsoever they tell you, but do not follow their example" (Matt 23:3). The Lord wants us to put our money where our mouth is. If we are going to proclaim great ideals and strict requirements, then we should exemplify them. This suggests a warning, first, to those of us who preach and teach professionally, and, second, to those of us (whether clerical or not) who may too easily moralize and condemn. Preachers have to proclaim the Gospel of Jesus while recognizing that they cannot perfectly exemplify it. One solution is to recognize explicitly that we are preaching ideals toward which we too strain; secondly, we do good to include ourselves in all our exhortations. The same advice holds for all who feel called to condemn others' actions. Such condemnations are honest if everyone, including ourselves, is included and this might temper any absolute and harsh judgment we are tempted to make. We have seen fairly often among well-publicized religious leaders situations where they castigate vice and moral laxity only to be exposed themselves as guilty of the same sins (sexual most often) they have singled out for attention. Jesus' strictures on religious leaders of his day remind us that the ideal is high and we are weak. The last sentence of the Gospel fits here: "Whoever exalts himself will be humbled; but whoever humbles himself will be exalted" (23:12).

Wednesday of the Second Week of Lent—
Competition versus humility

Readings: Jer 18:18-20; Matt 20:17-28
Resp. Psalm: Ps 31:5-6, 14, 15-16 (L 232)

Competition in our world almost always means aggressively vying with others for power, wealth, or prestige. We talk about cutthroat competition in business, commerce, education, and government—in fact, in any human enterprise. Jesus' words and history tell us that this competitive spirit is as old as Cain and Abel. No matter how old, Jesus was not about to accept it. After Zebedee's sons and their mother petition Jesus for choice spots in his kingdom and the other disciples hear about it, Jesus shows his opposition to this approach. He says the peoples of the world regularly act this way: "the great ones make their authority over them felt" (Matt 20:25). They lord it over the masses. However, he says to the disciples and to us: "But it shall not be so among you" (20:26). What we all have a part in, as true disciples, is in his suffering, in the Cross. He says the way to compete for greatness in his kingdom is to seek to be the one who serves everyone. There may not be that much room at the top, but there is plenty of room for all of us who generously serve each other. There should be so many of us serving others that there would be a significant diminution of poverty, suffering, abandoned and abused children, ignorance, and strife; and even in the home there might be more willingness to do the dishes and clean the bathrooms than there is to get the cushiest chairs before the TV! While we wait for our big opportunity to serve the world, we might begin right at home or on the job by being willing to serve those with whom we live and work. Jesus, the model servant, shows us how.

Thursday of the Second Week of Lent—*This mysterious heart*

Readings: Jer 17:5-10; Luke 16:19-31
Resp. Psalm: Ps 1:1-2, 3, 4 and 6 (L 233)

"More tortuous than all else is the human heart, beyond remedy; who can understand it?" (Jer 17:9). This is one of those sayings which almost requires us to throw up our hands as we say it. Who can understand it? Another translation says that "the heart is the most deceitful of all things, desperately sick" (NEB). The word tortuous means "marked by repeated turns or bends; winding, twisting" *(American Heritage Dictionary)*. There may be times in our life, long periods even, when we don't feel this way but somewhere, sometime we are going to experience our own complicated and shifty heart. St. Paul speaks in the Letter to the Romans of how he (and he speaks for all of us) at times does what he doesn't really want to do (see Rom 7:15-16). Self-knowledge and the experience of living eventually show all of us how "tortuous," how mysterious, and how incomprehensible are our thoughts and desires. We so often know what we should or shouldn't do, but having this knowledge equally often seems to have no effect. This tension involves everything from eating a lot of cholesterol-filled foods although we know they're bad for us to the way we walk into a temptation with full knowledge. In today's Gospel the rich man thinks that some dramatic event like the return of one from the dead will shake up his brothers so that they avoid his fate. But, Abraham says, they have Moses and the prophets and, therefore, all the necessary knowledge to behave according to God's will; if people can't act on this knowledge, they won't be changed by seeing someone risen from the dead. We have the Scriptures, the sacraments, and the presence and power of the Lord here at Mass; these can help straighten out our own complex hearts.

Friday of the Second Week of Lent—*Christ will be the victor*

Readings: Gen 37:3-4, 12-13a, 17b-28a; Matt 21:33-43, 45-46
Resp. Psalm: Ps 105:16-17, 18-19, 20-21 (L 234)

The great stories of any religion aim to help us penetrate more deeply into the mysteries of daily life such as the suffering of the innocent, the prosperity of the wicked, and the seeming indifference of God to tragedies. Today's readings involve two great and parallel stories of the Jewish and Christian faiths. The Gospel, in fact, refers to the central story of the Christian faith: that of the suffering, death, and triumph of Jesus. Here it is, of course, alluded to in the story of the tenant farmers and the owner's son. Joseph's story (not complete here) is so well known that we easily find ourselves thinking ahead to when, as a result of his brothers' treachery, he becomes a powerful man in Egypt, able to help his family in a famine. Simply put, both stories tell us more vividly and memorably than any theology or philosophy could that God can bring good, even superlative good, out of human tragedy. A great part of the faith which distinguishes believers from non-believers and which sustains us in our sorrows, disappointments, worries, and fears is this trust that these negative things in our lives do not have the last word. The hard part of faith is hanging on and continuing to trust when the cancer persists, the tragedies follow one another, too many relationships sour, and hardship follows upon hardship. Our eucharistic acclamation, "Christ has died, Christ is risen, Christ will come again," is not a comment on history but the expression of Christian hope which is strengthened whenever we share in this meal.

Saturday of the Second Week of Lent—
Leaving and finding home

Readings: Mic 7:14-15, 18-20; Luke 15:1-3, 11-32
Resp. Psalm: Ps 103:1-2, 3-4, 9-10, 11-12 (L 235)

Although many thoughts come to mind upon hearing the famous parable of the Prodigal Son (or, one might say, of the all-loving Father), time only permits looking at one point. An aspect of ourselves that we see in the prodigal son is the conviction, so often reached in adolescence, that things would be so much better if we could get away from this oppressive family and religion and live our own life. We are driven to strike out and find our own way and satisfaction, even if it looks like a huge mistake to our family. Undoubtedly, some experiment and some breaking of the bonds is necessary, and those of us who are on the parent end need patience and great understanding as this occurs. The wandering away may be physical or spiritual or both. Part of this wandering rests in our need as we mature to find ourselves and assert our independence. As we know from experience or observation, leaving home can be anything from civil and orderly to brutal and disruptive. How hard it is to see those we love seemingly turn their backs on us and on all we value! The revolt of our children or our revolt against our parents is often a messy and unpleasant business. Hard feelings and hurt sensitivities abound. Parents need to keep the doors open and make sure communication is possible. The son or daughter may not see any need for that at the moment. But a welcoming, forgiving parent is most accepted when the prodigal one discovers that there are, after all, some genuine values at home. Most of us have the rich opportunity at some time or other in our lives of playing from the heart the forgiving and welcoming mother or father. We have been forgiven much; forgiveness always rests on the condition that we forgive, too.

Monday of the Third Week of Lent—*Open to something new*

Readings: 2 Kgs 5:1-15ab; Luke 4:24-30
Resp. Psalm: Ps 42:2, 3; 43:3, 4 (L 237)

While today's Gospel concerns the lack of reception of Jesus by his townspeople, it is read here for our sake. In the opening verses of John's Gospel we hear that Jesus came to his own and they did not receive him. Isn't that always the basic question about Jesus: do we truly, adequately receive him and accept him? More basic than what we ever do (the active side of things) is the receptive side of our relation—how open we are. Jesus' reference to Naaman the Syrian (the center of the first reading) is an indication to his fellow Nazareans that because of their rejection he will go to others (Gentiles) who are more receptive. The implicit warning is here for all of us. To remain open to something, to Someone, from outside ourselves, to be ready to accept something new, to change or revise long-held attitudes and ideas is not at all easy. With age, education, and experience, we often tend to become more certain of our positions and approaches and, therefore, less willing to change. We all know (if the person is not, in fact, our own self) the usually elderly type we call "set in his or her ways" who has settled views on nearly everything. It is difficult to know when we have firm convictions or when we are just hardened. We ask the Holy Spirit, whose domain this is, to keep us open to new influence from God, receptive to the Spirit's own new promptings, and ready to hear what new things Jesus still has to say to us.

Tuesday of the Third Week of Lent—*Those trespasses*

Readings: Dan 3:25, 34-43; Matt 18:21-35
Resp. Psalm: Ps 25:4-5ab, 6 and 7bc, 8-9 (L 238)

The parable in today's Gospel illustrates the meaning of our daily prayer: forgive us our trespasses as we forgive those who trespass against us. That little word "as" seems almost negligible, but upon this word turns the whole point. The forgiveness we expect from God requires that we demonstrate the same forgiveness to others and indefinitely: seventy-seven times. If this number stands for forgiving without limit, the other numbers in this story further underline the point. The figure used for the official's debt is meant to suggest a huge

41

sum equivalent to the national debt or, another commentary suggests, $10 million. By contrast, the debt of a fellow servant to the official is something like a mere $20. Obviously, the numbers are included here to make a point and not to record some historical situation. The story describes God's forgiveness of us and suggests that God forgives us on the same order as someone canceling an incredibly large debt. The forgiveness we are asked to extend in daily life to others is, on the other hand, more on the lines of forgetting the postage stamp we gave someone. We who have been on the receiving end of such generous forgiveness have ample daily opportunities to deal mercifully with those who may have offended us.

Wednesday of the Third Week of Lent—*Love and patience*
Readings: Deut 4:1, 5-9; Matt 5:17-19
Resp. Psalm: Ps 147:12-13, 15-16, 19-20 (L 239)

Many a parent must respond with anguish to the admonitions in today's first reading about passing on what they believe and have experienced. That's the whole problem—they've tried to do it, one hears so often, and are so disappointed that sons and daughters seem to place so little value on what their parents treasure. First we hear Moses stressing in his instruction to the people that they should pass on to their children the convictions and faith they have acquired from experience and from those before them, those, for example, who experienced the Exodus: "Take care and be earnestly on your guard not to forget the things which your own eyes have seen, nor let them slip from your memory as long as you live, but teach them to your children and to your children's children" (Deut 4:9). Jesus' remarks in today's Gospel from the Sermon on the Mount are in continuity with those of Moses. He himself has not come to abolish the Law, and "whoever obeys and teaches these commandments will be called greatest in the kingdom of heaven" (Matt 5:19). Has it always been that parents feel their efforts to pass on their faith are flouted? We hear so often, "We brought them up as good Catholics, gave them good example and I don't think we nagged them, but today none of them attends Mass." Or we hear, "They are living together but they haven't been married in the church." There are no easy answers to these situations and certainly none to be given in a short homily. One suspects that it's safe to say that good example and persevering and trusting prayer, without nagging and tiresome moralizing, are about the best anyone can do.

Thursday of the Third Week of Lent—*Those painful prophets*

Readings: Jer 7:23-28; Luke 11:14-23
Resp. Psalm: Ps 95:1-2, 6-7, 8-9 (L 240)

In Luke Jesus is often presented as a great prophet, one who speaks on behalf of God—and today's Gospel is no exception. The first reading from Jeremiah summarizes the usually hostile reception the prophet gets. The tendency has not disappeared from among us. Think about how difficult it is for most of us to receive genuine criticism of our way of acting or thinking. In a broad sense the friend (or even the less well disposed) who points out our impatience, our abruptness, our self-absorption, our indifference, or our carelessness is like a prophet for us. But how resistant we are to such criticism! We'd so often prefer our relations with others to stay on a superficial but not disruptive level than face real issues in our character. We are so ready to point critical remarks in Scripture at someone else or some other group, doing anything to deflect them from hitting us. The poet Robert Burns spoke of the gift of seeing ourselves as others see us. It's one of those gifts we'd just as soon not be given. Is there some easy solution to this? No. As we renew our relation to God in Jesus Christ at Mass, this would be a good prayer: *May I be open, receptive to what is for my good, have a heart not hardened against every helpful suggestion.* On a more mundane level, a good principle (again, not easy to execute) is to take anything critical or even unkind said about ourselves or to us as containing some nugget of truth. If someone sees us as ungenerous or hot-tempered, there must be some smidgeon of truth in the remark. God and conscience often speak to us through uncongenial messengers.

Friday of the Third Week of Lent—*Love beyond the Mass*

Readings: Hos 14:2-10; Mark 12:28-34
Resp. Psalm: Ps 81:6c-8a, 8bc-9, 10-11ab, 14 and 17 (L 241)

". . . Jesus saw that he answered with understanding" (Mark 12:34). The scribe had just confirmed what Jesus had said and added a note to the effect that this love of God and of neighbor was superior to any kind of sacrificial offering. It is clear that we are being told that love is more important than even anything we do in church although, of course, ideally they should all hang together. When we share the Bread and Cup in church, the understanding is that it commits us to love those with whom we share our daily lives and to love all our fellow humans. But to love both God and neighbor can be pretty easy statements until we think in concrete terms. That neighbor, for example, includes the people whose mannerisms really annoy us, those who may have injured us in the past, the person who has said false things about us, the person who called us a fool or an idiot at a meeting, the person who pulled a fast one on us financially, the person who thinks our work performance is incredibly poor, the little kid who taunts our child at school. When we look at the neighbor up close, he or she (ourselves included) has a way of making that love seem very unrealistic and very difficult at times. Before we mouth the command to love our neighbor too easily, it's good to think about how we'd carry it out with all these people and the others we might add to the list of those who annoy us. The answer, of course, is we can love our neighbor when we remain in our Lord and celebrate well the Eucharist, as long as we realize neither dispenses us from effort and imagination. *Be with us, Lord, to show your love as we leave this church building.*

Saturday of the Third Week of Lent—
God's acting in our world

Readings: Hos 6:1-6; Luke 18:9-14
Resp. Psalm: Ps 51:3-4, 18-19, 20-21ab (L 242)

Love of neighbor in the Gospels, we've heard often in Lent, never stays at the level of lofty sentiments but proves its reality by concern for individuals. Today's famous parable of the Pharisee and the tax collector can be understood as telling us that faith in God, similarly, is genuine to the degree that it shows itself in practice and in heartfelt prayer. Both the Pharisee and the tax collector are instructive with respect to prayer. The former shows us someone who really does not feel that he needs to pray; he considers himself already perfect. Rather than feeling any need to put any trust in God, he informs the Creator about how he fasts and gives tithes beyond the call of duty. The rest of his "prayer" time is spent in putting down others as "greedy, dishonest, adulterous" (Luke 18:11). Faith minimally means recognition that there is a God on whom we depend for everything. To use God as a sounding board for our boasts and criticism of others is missing the boat and ignoring the living and real God. To ask forgiveness and to know our need of God is faith in action. Pascal said that to believe in a God who is remote and uninvolved in our world or lives is practically the same as atheism. True faith supposes a God concerned about this world, a God who is able to respond to those calling for help. Such thoughts prompt us to ask that same God to assure that we do have genuine faith: "Lord, I believe, help my unbelief" (Mark 9:24).

Monday of the Fourth Week of Lent—*Helping to heal*

Readings: Isa 65:17-21; John 4:43-54
Resp. Psalm: Ps 30:2 and 4, 5-6, 11-12a and 13b (*L* 244)

To say as the old hymn to Mary does that human life is a "vale of tears" often seems only too true. At any given moment most of us, even apart from the world news, know of friends and relatives who have been crushed by the death of an infant or of a high school age daughter. We know of a mother or father battling a serious illness likely to take them away from their young children. All this is undoubtedly background for the unfettered joy of the age to come, of which the prophet speaks today. In the Gospel Jesus intervenes in just such a case and cures the son of the royal official. It hardly seems likely that the prophet's vision is going to be realized in this world, but we should expect that the power of Jesus' working in and through those who believe in him does change the lives of those around us for the better. To hope only for some dramatic, final intervention by God in our world seems not to expect enough from the power of God working now in us. God wipes away all our tears, destroys suffering and death, and restores all those who have been lost to us—all this in the world to come. But in the meantime, we are to continue to live with the help of God's presence and power, and with the help of all those around us who have been energized by that same power. It helps our world immensely and turns our thoughts away from self when we sense a mission to assist in the healing and consoling of our world. In Communion with the Lord at this Mass, we are empowered to do just that.

Tuesday of the Fourth Week of Lent—*Signs and words*

Readings: Ezek 47:1-9, 12; John 5:1-16
Resp. Psalm: Ps 46:2-3, 5-6, 8-9 (*L* 245)

Today's readings point to basic elements in the sacraments: signs and words. In the very odd story in Ezekiel of the water flowing out of the Temple and of the fruitfulness of all that borders on the river, we have a picture of the water of baptism. By rebirth in the waters of baptism, we become fruitful and life-filled. Interestingly, there is a pool of water in the Gospel story, a pool where the sick man had been hoping to be cured and thus restored to more vigorous life. Apparently being cured depends on entering the water immediately once it had been disturbed. The man is always too late. Jesus doesn't help him get into the pool immediately after its stirring, but instead by his word cures him: "Rise, take up your mat, and walk" (John 5:8). Water, of itself, does serve to nourish life on this planet. Soldiers back from the Middle East tell of the arid desert country, but then they tell of the lush, green area immediately adjacent to the two famous rivers of biblical times, the Tigris and the Euphrates. The new life of the human being, reborn in God, comes not simply from water but from the word of Jesus enabling this element to give us new life. To be plunged, dunked, washed in the water in the name of the Father and of the Son and of the Holy Spirit is what makes the water of baptism so special. Christianity is not a superstitious religion of natural elements, important as they are, but of certain elements given more profound meaning by the word of God. Attention to signs is necessarily accompanied by similar attentiveness to the word of God.

Wednesday of the Fourth Week of Lent—
Revitalized by God's word

Readings: Isa 49:8-15; John 5:17-30
Resp. Psalm: Ps 145:8-9, 13cd-14, 17-18 (L 246)

"For this reason they tried all the more to kill him, because he not only broke the sabbath but he also called God his own Father" (John 5:18). The Gospel today points to the passion and death of Jesus, to be recalled shortly during Holy Week. The Gospel and Isaiah together give us a plate full of themes. One theme suggests Easter, but is relevant for us now during Lent: ". . . the hour is coming and is now here when the dead will hear the voice of the Son of God, and those who hear will live" (5:25). Not only will the dead in the tombs hear the voice of the Son of God and come forth to resurrection, but even now the dead in homes, offices, businesses, schools, churches, and even we here today—all who hear Jesus' word—can be brought back to life. We all must experience at times feelings of complete inertia toward our faith, a lack of enthusiasm, or a feeling of *déjà vu* about every element of our Christian life. Those of us who have gone through the church year many times over may be especially prone to sometimes being lukewarm. We pray appropriately that our faith and hope be brought back to life. Jesus says, ". . . whoever hears my word and believes in the one who sent me has eternal life." For creatures like ourselves for whom feelings are so important, it can be very difficult to believe when we seem to "have lost that lovin' feeling." There is no way to guarantee exuberant feelings toward our faith, but we can, perhaps, remember more fervent moments when God truly rescued us from despair or sin. With the help of this interior testimony, we can hear God's word with a more open heart and ready generosity.

Thursday of the Fourth Week of Lent—*More witnesses*

Readings: Exod 32:7-14; John 5:31-47
Resp. Psalm: Ps 106:19-20, 21-22, 23 (L 247)

All the talk about the various witnesses to Jesus today should encourage us to be open to so much around us that testifies to God's goodness and power. While Jesus is crucified again and again the world over in the starving, the persecuted, the oppressed, the exploited, refugees, the homeless and abused, abandoned children and neglected old people, there are still signs all around us of God's love working. We need to balance our temptations to despair and discouragement with seeing these hopeful signs and evidence of great generosity. Aren't there people around us who make a point of watching out for some poor family, who spread cheer and hope instead of gloom, who give an example of generous use of their means, and who have something for everyone in need? Even beyond individuals, we can look for signs of corporate responsibility, of civic pride and care; we see foundations and movements and church groups that make a difference for farm workers, illegal immigrants, overburdened mothers, and the disabled. Jesus is hunted down and crucified in the members of his Body, but he is also comforted and cared for in those same members. Strengthened by prayer and our sharing at the altar, we can be witnesses for others to God's love either as individuals or by our participation in some larger movement. We can do our part to assure that the number of witnesses to God's love exceeds the number of those denying it.

Friday of the Fourth Week of Lent—
Preparing now for tougher times

Readings: Wis 2:1a, 12-22; John 7:1-2, 10, 25-30
Resp. Psalm: Ps 34:17-18, 19-20, 21 and 23 (L 248)

So much of what we claim to believe can have an air of unreality about it as long as we live in comfort and peace. Our trust that God will care for us is, in a sense, too easy when we lack nothing essential, when our relations are happy, or when we are not involved in any great struggle. By saying this, we're not implying that we should reject peace and comfort and make every effort to destroy them. Peace, comfort, order, and sufficiency all are helpful; they enable us to build some solid foundations for helping others and working for our world and society. They require hard work and persistence in unexciting but necessary activity. But the point here is that the bitter struggle of Jesus and many of our fellow human beings calls on other powers not tested in peace and quiet. Peace and quiet provide the opportunity for us to develop the qualities we need in more difficult times. By perseverance in prayer and deepening our relation to God, we prepare ourselves for times when we may feel totally alone. Should we really expect God to rescue us in such dark hours or that we will know the power of God's presence, if we have otherwise had only a formal and superficial relation with God? There may or may not be individuals who plot against us (as in the first reading and the life of Jesus), but we deal with cancer, divorce, old age, and disease. There are always forces in human life that put us through suffering and desolation. Like the enemies of Jesus, they test us to see if, as we claim, God does take care of us. *We believe that, Lord; help us to grow in awareness of your constant care and presence, to be more ready for the tests.*

Saturday of the Fourth Week of Lent—*God in our pocket*

Readings: Jer 11:18-20; John 7:40-53
Resp. Psalm: Ps 7:2-3, 9bc-10, 11-12 (L 249)

Looked at carefully, the quibbles and evasions of the chief priests and Pharisees come too close to our own tendencies—the tendency to use legalism for our own benefit *and* the tendency to want everything settled, secure, and predictable. We may like surprises, but we get pretty uncomfortable when *too many* items are up for grabs. We expect not only physical reality to act in certain ways, but we also like God to be pretty consistent, rational, and to fit into our boxes. The leaders of the Jews had certain expectations about the Messiah; that Jesus didn't fit every one of them perfectly helped them justify their rejection of him. While we call Scripture "revelation" because it tells us of God and God's ways, it doesn't pull the veil aside completely. We need to allow God, and Christ too, at least the same freedom we allow other human beings, that is, the freedom to *be more* and to *do otherwise* than we think they must. God is always going to be beyond our grasp and thought. A God we could completely comprehend would be, by that very fact, too small to be God. Let us be happy that we will never know all there is to know about God or Christ! Not having this knowledge allows for greater surprises to come as God's love for us plays itself out in our lives.

Monday of the Fifth Week of Lent—*More gentleness*

Readings: Dan 13:1-9, 15-17, 19-30, 33-62 or Dan 13:41c-62; John 8:1-11
Resp. Psalm: Ps 23:1-3a, 3b-4, 5, 6 (L 251)

One reads laments occasionally that really good people in our country—persons of integrity and character—don't run for public office. One reason advanced for this is that once someone puts him- or herself forward in this way he or she becomes a constant target for attack and for probing; one's private life is over. Even the slightest lapses in one's past become fodder for the press and other politicians. Think of what an unforgiving enemy or press could do with the histories of two people like those we hear about in today's first reading! The two women there stand for all of us. Like the woman taken in adultery, most of us have sins and failures in our past if not in our present. Like Susanna, any one of us is open to accusations—whether false or with some truth, or based on misunderstanding or misinterpretation. Our only security is God and our conscience. If, despite failures in the past, we are trying to live a good life today, we need to trust in what we know to be true of ourselves; we need to trust in our intentions and God's acceptance. Further, we all contribute to the climate of our society by the severity or gentleness with which we judge each other. Do we possibly impose outrageously unrealistic standards on others, while excusing ourselves? We need to know ourselves honestly and allow for the fact that we cannot know others as well. Through our communion with Christ in this Mass, we can learn some of his gentleness, forgiveness, and understanding.

Tuesday of the Fifth Week of Lent—*Beyond the Cross*

Readings: Num 21:4-9; John 8:21-30
Resp. Psalm: Ps 102:2-3, 16-18, 19-21 (L 252)

Like the bronze serpent which was salvation for those who looked on it in that first reading, Jesus lifted up becomes salvation for all who look on him in faith. As used here, to be lifted up has two meanings: first, it means to be raised up on the cross; and, second, it means to be taken from earthly existence into glory with the Father. In the process of being raised from death to resurrection Jesus, the Son of Man, is shown to be also the Son of God: "Then you will realize that I AM" (John 8:28). The suffering, death, and resurrection of Jesus are the means by which God has overcome death and sin. All the famous traditional expressions about being saved by Jesus on the cross, by his blood, and by his

49

sacrifice refer to death and sin being overcome. This is, therefore, the source of our hope. The lifting up of Jesus is also the pattern for our own lives, a pattern we need to recall in order not to see human life as simply one meaningless thing after another. The inevitable Cross in our life (suffering, death, hardships) is our way, too, to be lifted up and to enter new life even here and now. By seeing the elements in our life that cross us (those that seem to be so contrary to our desires and good) as instruments of growth in unselfishness, we are allowing these events to transform us. We are being lifted up. *Help us, Lord, to look for the good which comes through the harsh aspects of our life, to see beyond the present difficult moment to your desire for our good.*

Wednesday of the Fifth Week of Lent—
Faith that God is with us

Readings: Dan 3:14-20, 91-92, 95; John 8:31-42
Resp. Psalm: Dan 3:52, 53, 54, 55, 56 (L 253)

The opening verse of today's Gospel speaks of some Jews who believed in Jesus. It's really hard to credit them with having faith in Jesus when, within a couple of verses, this belief seems to have evaporated, to say the least. In fact, as pictured in John, some of the Jews and Jesus are in a hostile relationship. But shifting, changing, and undependable faith is a theme in John's Gospel. By exhibiting this, John warns us that faith is not simply a matter of saying the right words; instead, faith is something much deeper that often costs us something. It is probably always premature to label an attitude toward God as faith when it has just been declared. A word, a feeling, or a momentary rush of assurance needs to be tested in the drudgery and difficulties of daily life. While faith probably doesn't mean much when we've never felt the need to be saved from anything (illness, betrayal, disappointment, the loss of someone dear to us), these painful events are what do test our faith. We might link the two readings today by saying that genuine faith is only such when it has been tried by fire. The three young men in the first reading were cast into the fiery furnace for refusing to worship a false god. They told the king they would stay with their faith even if they were not delivered from that fire. To the king's utter amazement, they were soon joined, "unfettered and unhurt," in the furnace by a fourth figure who looks like "a son of God" (Dan 3:92). Genuine faith believes that God is with us in whatever trials overtake us. We are never alone is what true faith tells us. One is with us who is the Son of God.

Thursday of the Fifth Week of Lent—
On not blaming "them"

Readings: Gen 17:3-9; John 8:51-59
Resp. Psalm: Ps 105:4-5, 6-7, 8-9 (L 254)

The disputes we hear daily between Jesus and the Jews in the Gospel lead up to next week, Holy Week. In them we hear about Abraham, the father of the Jews. Judaism, Christianity, and Islam are often called the "Abrahamic faiths," that is, religions rooted in the faith of Abraham. All three share the history of God's concern for human beings which stems from God's calling of Abraham. Spiritually, we are all related. For that reason, it is all the more necessary that we not be misled by expressions in the Gospels that blame the Jews for Christ's death. In today's Gospel we do hear three references to Jesus' enemies as "the Jews." A close look at all the Gospels and specific details about the death of Jesus shows us that this is a shorthand expression for the *leaders* of the Jews: the scribes, chief priests, Pharisees, etc. The Second Vatican Council and various popes have stressed that there is no justification for anti-Semitism on the part of Christians and no excuse for anti-Jewish behavior and talk. Jesus himself, of course, was a Jew. The references in Gospel readings should remind us not to buy into anti-Semitism or, even worse, contribute to it by our language or actions. The sins of humankind led to the crucifixion of Jesus. If he had been born in Ireland, his opponents would have been the establishment and leaders of that country, the Irish. We can profitably apply this further as part of our following of Christ by opposing any prejudicial behavior or talk about any group: African Americans, Native Americans, Hispanics, etc. If we look for applications of the love we celebrate at this Eucharist, this is a most important and obvious place to begin.

Friday of the Fifth Week of Lent—*Genuine dedication*

Readings: Jer 20:10-13; John 10:31-42
Resp. Psalm: Ps 18:2-3a, 3bc-4, 5-6, 7 (L 255)

In the first chapter of his Gospel, John wrote that the Word of God, Jesus, had come to his own people and they had not received him. Our recent Scripture readings amply show this rejection of Jesus by his own people. Despite Jesus' signs and the integrity of his life, his own people cannot see in him anything but a challenge to their way of life and traditions and, in some cases, their authority. So, "He went back across the Jordan . . . And many there began to believe in him" (John 10:40, 42).

We think of ourselves as "his own people" often. Does Jesus, perhaps, get a more generous hearing at times "across the Jordan"? Isn't it appropriate to see Lent as a time of challenge to our way of living and the reality of our faith? Isn't it a time for some self-examination about how we receive Christ? We may not dispute with him about his relation to the Father, but couldn't our belief be stronger and deeper? What about those other Christians whom we see as deviating from our Catholic faith tradition? We must admit that at times they embarrass us not so much by not believing in certain doctrines as by their very dedication to the One they call so constantly the Lord Jesus. Don't these other believers often shame us by their willingness to speak about the Lord and their practical exercise of love? As we near the annual commemoration of the Lord's loving sacrifice for us, we ask ourselves these questions: Are we forthright enough in telling others of the Lord and our faith? Do we look for practical instances where we can exercise the love with which he has loved us and which is put before us daily in the Mass?

Saturday of the Fifth Week of Lent—*Let peace begin with me*

Readings: Ezek 37:21-28; John 11:45-56
Resp. Psalm: Jer 31:10, 11-12abcd, 13 (*L* 256)

In the words of the high priest Caiaphas, we have the paradoxical blending of bad intentions regarding Jesus with God's will for our salvation. Caiaphas, from the viewpoint of John and the Christian reader, probably said a lot more than he understood ("He did not say this on his own . . ."). "He prophesied that Jesus was going to die for the nation, and not only for the nation, but also to gather into one the dispersed children of God" (John 11:51-52). When we read daily of new ethnic strife, new wars in this or that part of the world, and warfare in our city streets, it's hard to trust that all of us are going to ever live in peace as God's children. But just this is what our faith in Jesus as the redeemer of humankind means: that God will ultimately transform this cruel and war-stricken world into something better, with our help, effort, cooperation. Critics have complained, maybe justly at times, that Christians sit on their hands and wait for God to right wrongs and bring peace instead of doing anything themselves. Elusive and far off as it may seem, the task of peace-making is one for all of us. We can look here and now for opportunities to make peace more real for more people, beginning in our own neighborhood.

Monday of Holy Week—*Worship and work*

Readings: Isa 42:1-7; John 12:1-11
Resp. Psalm: Ps 27:1, 2, 3, 13-14 (L 257)

On this Monday of the week during which many Christians spend a large amount of time in prayer and worship, it helps to remember that the Lord himself felt it necessary at times to get away from his active ministry to pray. Some people around us see all the time spent in church during this week as a monumental waste of time. They would say something along the lines of what Judas said: all this time and energy could be better spent on the poor and otherwise deprived. True, the touchstone of our love for God is the love we show for the least of Jesus' sisters and brothers. No one can deny that. But two other points must be kept in mind. First, concern for the poor does not have to be in competition with our worship of and love for God. Why can't people who are regular in worship of God also be devoted to the cause of the poor? In fact, what motivates many of us really to do something practical about the poor is our prayer and worship. Second, love for and worship of God cannot be reduced simply to the good we do for the poor and suffering. While we show our love for God by what we do for our fellow human beings, they do not, even all added together, equal God. God is still beyond and above all those we serve. The two commandments call for love of God and love of neighbor. May the time we spend in prayer and worship only further invigorate the time and energy we give to the works of love of neighbor.

Tuesday of Holy Week—*Sorrow and joy*

Readings: Isa 49:1-6; John 13:21-33, 36-38
Resp. Psalm: Ps 71:1-2, 3-4a, 5ab-6ab, 15 and 17 (L 258)

Even while John's Gospel sets the scene for the final events of the life of Jesus, the first reading from Isaiah is full of assurance that wonderful good (salvation) comes out of these tragic happenings. God says to his servant Israel (Jesus for us) that through him "I show my glory" (Isa 49:3). And the servant's reward is with God; God makes him a light to the nations so that salvation reaches all. Here in Holy Week, as in all of human life, joyous elation and suffering walk side by side. While we recall the suffering and death of Jesus this week, we cannot do so apart from our knowledge that Jesus is risen. Similarly, during Eastertide, we celebrate Jesus' resurrection while also remembering his passion and death. Once we're past the carefree days of our youth (if we were so blessed), usually our laughter is mingled with tears and our tears mingled at least with a smile. Most of human life is a mixture of joy and sorrow and pain and pleasure. Especially in pain and tragedy, we may not be able to see the other aspects; but usually some good things remain. Even the worry and sorrow brought on by serious illness in a family member is often balanced by the closeness of the members in those moments or by the love and care shown by the neighbors. Conversely, our joy at the success of a daughter or son may be tempered by the fact that other members of the family have not survived to share the success. As life tells us in so many ways, the experience of Jesus is ours also, and we have every reason to confidently come to him in prayer in any part of our life, be it filled with sorrow or joy. He has been there.

Wednesday of Holy Week—*A word for the weary*

Readings: Isa 50:4-9a; Matt 26:14-25
Resp. Psalm: Ps 69:8-10, 21-22, 31 and 33-34 (L 259)

The words of the prophet Isaiah, words of encouragement and confidence for the suffering one, almost sound as if we were trying to encourage Jesus as he enters his darkest hour. Possibly the words can prompt us to take more seriously our role in supporting the sick and suffering around us, those going through weeks of chemotherapy, or those caught into a seemingly unending family problem. Perhaps we can strengthen their faith with the comfort that "he is near who upholds my right" and "the Lord God is my help" (Isa 50:8, 9). Overwhelming tragedies or crushing illnesses leave us feeling as abandoned as the Lord felt on the cross. We appreciate all that Holy Week is the more we ourselves have had to walk in the valley of the shadow of death. The Gospels do not dwell on how Jesus felt about betrayal by a disciple, but that must have been for the human Jesus a most devastating sorrow. Similar experiences of our own help us sense not only what Jesus must have felt, but also feel a deeper kinship with the daily offering of his sacrifice before us at the altar. We need the strength which took him through his passion and death; and he gives it to us in this sacrament. And, please God, may our sharing here and the harsher experiences of life make us so much more sensitive to what many around us are going through. Reflection on the passion and death of the Lord and on the more difficult moments of our own lives help us know how to help others who share Jesus' passion so profoundly. God help us to "know how to speak to the weary a word that will rouse them."

Season of Easter

Monday of the Octave of Easter—
Joy in the presence of the Risen Christ

Readings: Acts 2:14, 22-33; Matt 28:8-15
Resp. Psalm: Ps 16:1-2a and 5, 7-8, 9-10, 11 (*L* 261)

To triumph over death summarizes perhaps most completely the deepest hopes of the human heart. So much of life is spent in overcoming illness, disappointments, heartbreaks, and bereavements. But to overcome death—that is the final and most wonderful victory beside which all these short-term successes fade. In his Pentecost address, Peter voices our profound desire to overcome death by quoting the words of the psalmist and finding their fulfillment in the risen Christ: "[M]y body, too, abides in confidence; because you will not abandon my soul to the nether world, nor will you suffer your faithful one to undergo corruption . . . you will show me the path to life, fullness of joys in your presence" (Ps 16, 9-10, 11). In the freshness and joy of Easter, we celebrate the realization of these great hopes in Christ and, through him, for all those who put their trust in him. During these days of Easter we can let our being breathe deeply of the expansive joy and hope that are ours in the risen Christ. The narrow confines of this life have been surpassed. As we celebrate this risen life year after year, we can expect that our sense of overcoming of sin, suffering, and death grows and becomes more deeply rooted in us. We can't simply wish this peace and joy into existence within ourselves. It is God's gift and comes to us to the extent that we put our trust in God's power over all life's hardships and pains. Making our own the words of the psalmist can help strengthen this hope and joy: "With him [the Lord] at my right hand I shall not be disturbed. . . . my body, too, abides in confidence; . . . You will show me the path to life, fullness of joys in your presence . . ." (Ps 16:8, 9, 11).

Tuesday of the Octave of Easter—*Coming to faith*

Readings: Acts 2:36-41; John 20:11-18
Resp. Psalm: Ps 33:4-5, 18-19, 20 and 22 (L 262)

Hearing how John himself and others such as Mary Magdalene and Thomas came to faith in the risen Christ is more helpful to us than mere speculation. The fact that Mary Magdalene did not at first recognize the risen Lord and that this happens with others suggests a number of things. Despite any number of hints about it, the followers of Jesus still were not prepared fully for the resurrection. Many a modern day non-believer tells us that such things just cannot happen. Often the fact that we do not expect to see something prevents us from seeing it. We only see what we expect to see. Too, the inability of Mary Magdalene and others immediately to recognize the risen Lord tells us that faith in the risen Christ is a gift of God and not a natural accomplishment. We can suspect that many of us only come to believe that the Lord is truly risen with prayer, time, and God's grace. Our belief in the resurrection of Jesus is probably at times too glib, too easy, and too superficial. Except for those few of us who may have experienced some awesome flash of insight on the matter, most of us must pray and hope for a more profound realization of what it is we celebrate at Easter. With trust and prayer, a time comes when, like Mary, we hear his voice and his words, and truly know that he is risen, is with us, and is even now overcoming sin and death in us. Or we are some day more profoundly struck by his presence at this altar, in this bread and wine, in these people. *Lord, open us to truly know your resurrection.*

Wednesday of the Octave of Easter—*Stay with us, Lord*

Readings: Acts 3:1-10; Luke 24:13-35
Resp. Psalm: Ps 105:1-2, 3-4, 6-7, 8-9 (L 263)

Many rightly find today's Gospel the most moving and impressive in the whole New Testament. It seems boundlessly rich and suggestive. It speaks in such concrete terms of the central matters of our faith and of our following of Christ. It tells us that, like and with Christ, our suffering and death are only part of the story. Suffering and death are part of the pattern of human life, now crowned with hope and joy because the Lord is risen. After he has explained all this to them, the disciples ask the Lord to stay with them: "Stay with us, for it is nearly evening" (Luke 24:29). Stay with us and be with us always, maybe especially as we see our days running out: "the day is almost over" (24:29). Our faith tells us and the Eucharist shows us that Christ is always with us and always close. Should not our hearts burn with more excitement and joy, as we are able, even daily, to be in his presence here at this table? We hear his words and we share the bread he gives us, his Body and Blood. "The Lord has truly been raised . . . !" (24:34). We can help the joy and hope of this season to stay and grow within us by taking such a piece as today's Gospel and often reading it over slowly and reflectively.

Thursday of the Octave of Easter—
Beautiful, godlike, and eternal

Readings: Acts 3:11-26; Luke 24:35-48
Resp. Psalm: Ps 8:2ab and 5, 6-7, 8-9 (L 264)

Lines from the English thinker Thomas Hobbes on human life have become famous. Human life, he wrote, is "nasty, brutish and short." Those who observe only its economic and social aspects may feel the same way. And the lot of millions in our world certainly is "nasty, brutish and short." Not all the world's population enjoys the benefits of electricity, clean water, and freedom from devastating diseases. Progress and evolution seem spotty. Irrespective of whether all share in these material blessings, our Easter faith adds an important dimension to human life: what God does for the baptized in Christ dignifies human life more than any of these material benefits. Our responsorial psalm today, Psalm 8, celebrates a life no longer "nasty, brutish and short": "O LORD, our Lord, how glorious is your name over all the earth! What is man that you should be mindful of him . . . You have made him little less than the angels, and crowned him with glory and honor" (Ps 8:2, 5-6). In other words, we are not simply highly developed beings able to think, feel, plan, build, and invent. The resurrection has taken the course of evolution beyond time and space to life in God. In our head, Christ, who has gone before us, we have been made little less than the angels, given a place of honor at the eternal banquet. Human life has become beautiful, Godlike, and eternal, not "nasty, brutish and short." This is the new creation we celebrate at Easter.

Friday of the Octave of Easter—*Anything to eat?*

Readings: Acts 4:1-12; John 21:1-14
Resp. Psalm: Ps 118:1-2 and 4, 22-24, 25-27a (L 265)

Another meal with the Lord! This one is an early morning brunch on the beach. The point of attention to so many meals throughout the

Gospels is not that the disciples were gourmets. Meals underscore the reality of the resurrection: we are not talking simply about the spirit of Jesus risen again after a period of despair in the disciples. Further, what is more natural than that the risen Lord and his disciples be re-united around a meal? We regularly arrange to spend time with newly returned friends at a meal or at least over a coffee or coke. But even more, the emphasis on meals stresses that we can find the risen Lord in the company of other human beings, in community, in relationships, and in love and friendship. The Eucharist itself discloses its meaning in our understanding of what meals do. Because we eat the one bread, St. Paul says, we are one Body (see 1 Cor 10:17). The Eucharist exists to make us one with God and each other. Remembering that Eucharist is a supper, a meal (despite the token amount of food and drink), keeps us aware that it is never simply a matter of God and us being joined together, but God and us and everyone else. Eating in the Gospels is never a matter of taking food and going off by oneself before one's own TV to eat. Eating in the Gospels is apparently what it has been in most cultures: a social event, a time to get together with others. Our sharing in the Eucharist tells us forcefully that God is encountered in others and in the elements of ordinary life.

Saturday of the Octave of Easter—*Living and proclaiming*

Readings: Acts 4:13-21; Mark 16:9-15
Resp. Psalm: Ps 118:1 and 14-15ab, 16-18, 19-21 (L 266)

When Mary Magdalene announces the Good News to the followers of Jesus, "they did not believe" (Mark 16:11). Similarly, when the two who had walked with Jesus on the way to Emmaus tell of the Good News, "they did not believe them either" (16:13). Finally, Jesus in an appearance to the Eleven rebukes them for their disbelief "because they had not believed those who saw him after he had been raised" (16:14). The Good News and the disciples' lack of faith are two poles of this Gospel. In this conclusion to Mark's Gospel, faith and belief seem to mean, first, the acceptance of the truth of Jesus' rising from the dead (the Good News) and, second, trust, hope, and confidence in the way the Good News changes our lives. The strong emphasis on faith is re-inforced by all the evidence in this Gospel telling us that our forebears in the faith, the disciples, did not lightly nor easily take it up. They accepted the Good News only with difficulty—it was too good—and then learned to live by it, even to the point of a further share in the suffering and death of the Lord. We see this in the difficulties the disciples had with the Jewish leaders as recorded in Acts. Jesus commanded, "Go into the whole world and proclaim the Gospel to every creature" (16:15). Proclaim it and suffer for doing so while trusting in the Lord. As today's responsorial psalm says, "I shall not die, but live, and declare the works of the LORD" (Ps 118:17).

Monday of the Second Week of Easter—*Let the Spirit work*

Readings: Acts 4:23-31; John 3:1-8
Resp. Psalm: Ps 2:1-3, 4-7a, 7b-9 (L 267)

So often in John's Gospel, words and phrases play on ambiguity or on two different but possible meanings. "Unless one is born from above, he cannot see the Kingdom of God" (John 3:3) can also mean that no one can see the rule of God unless that person is born *again*. Either meaning is way beyond the simple physical meaning of being born all over again, to which Nicodemus refers. The point is that we can only fully share in the kingdom of God and have life in the risen Christ if we receive that possibility as a gift from the Spirit in baptism. After saying we must be born this way (from the Spirit), Jesus seems to push very heavily the idea that the Spirit's actions in us are entirely out of our control. Our baptism, in other words, must be fully implemented or realized by the work of the Spirit in us. If we were baptized as infants, we had the necessary receptivity for the Spirit to work in us. It's only with age that we learn to set up obstacles to the Spirit. Our work now is to demonstrate receptivity to the Spirit, remove the obstacles, and realize how much we need the Spirit's power in us to transform us more perfectly into the likeness of the risen Christ.

Tuesday of the Second Week of Easter—
It takes a village . . .

Readings: Acts 4:32-37; John 3:7b-15
Resp. Psalm: Ps 93:1ab, 1cd-2, 5 (L 268)

We will be hearing much from the Gospel of John for the next several weeks and we have already dealt somewhat with Nicodemus, so today we look at that idyllic passage from the Acts of the Apostles. To call it "idyllic" is not to take away from it; we need to see and imagine such spotless pictures of what the Christian community should be. Here we see the early Christians praying together, living in mutual love, and sharing wealth. We know that, given our tendencies to self-seeking, such an ideal life is never totally realized. But, to the degree that some of these ideals are realized, such communities testify to the presence and power of the risen Lord and his Spirit within them. Such a community would elicit the famous remark made about the early Christians: "See how they love one another" (Tertullian). It takes a community of such people to show the world around it what belief in the risen Lord can do. Such Christians show by their lives that there is One who conquers sin, death, poverty, hatred, and suffering. And, it must be emphasized, an individual cannot do it alone; it really requires a community. Christian love, concern, and patience are only clear in our interaction with others. We can probably demonstrate our innate self-love in isolation. The vision we hear about today inspires us to make real in our own lives the love and unity we celebrate in this Eucharist by the way we live with others.

Wednesday of the Second Week of Easter—*Acting in truth*

Readings: Acts 5:17-26; John 3:16-21
Resp. Psalm: Ps 34:2-3, 4-5, 6-7, 8-9 (L 269)

Although there is, perhaps, the temptation to leave Easter at the lofty level of words of joy and hope and of new life and resurrection, Scripture (even a book like John) does not let us avoid the concrete demands of Christian life. Jesus tells Nicodemus that God did not send him into the world to condemn it, but so that the world might be saved through him. But if there is no such external judgment, there is an interior judgment going on all the time: "Whoever believes in him [the Son] will not be condemned, but whoever does not believe has already been condemned" (John 3:18). We are being judged here and now by our actions and by our response to the Son of God. We judge ourselves by our acceptance or rejection of the revelation of God in Jesus Christ and the actions—good or bad—which follow. While Easter, like every other great moment in Christian life, is primarily about God's gift to us (God's constant giving love), that gift must be received. God's action is part of the story, the major part; but the response of the believer is the other part. Jesus puts it another way: the light came into the world and we either welcome it or hide from it in darkness. Really, Jesus is talking here about what we call "conscience." If we respond generously to the Light which is the Son, we have no reason to fear that Light: "But whoever lives the truth comes to the light, so that his works may be clearly seen as done in God" (3:21).

Thursday of the Second Week of Easter—*No rationing here*

Readings: Acts 5:27-33; John 3:31-36
Resp. Psalm: Ps 34:2 and 9, 17-18, 19-20 (L 270)

"He does not ration his gift of the Spirit" (John 3:35). If one looks at enough commentaries on this passage, one could spend a very long time discussing whether it is God the Father who gives the gift or Jesus. Further, some commentators make the point that "of the Spirit" is missing in some very ancient texts. Time spent on who gives the Spirit could be a way, too, of avoiding the more personal point for each one of us: how *we receive* God's gifts—"He does not ration his gift of the Spirit." In any case, we are left with an essential bit of revelation: God's giving to us is boundless. The practical question must rise: if that is so, how come we are so lacking in some areas like love and patience, so inadequate in our discipleship, and so undeveloped as the Body of Christ? It's pretty clear that if God does not ration the Divine Gift to us, the Spirit's limited effectiveness is due to a lack in us. We limit the Gift by implicitly saying, "Sure, I'd like a gift but . . ." (like the polite Midwestern guest at dinner: "not too much, please"). The intrinsic difficulty is our fear of allowing God control, of trusting God that much, and of letting go of our own plans. The detailed planning of our self-fulfillment that is such a part of our culture is in direct contradiction to how Scripture says it is done. Scripture says it is achieved by self-surrender. But we hesitate to trust God to do it. By the Gift of God, however, we can pray appropriately and maybe more fervently in this Easter season for more receptivity to all of God's gifts.

Friday of the Second Week of Easter—*Thanksgiving*

Readings: Acts 5:34-42; John 6:1-15
Resp. Psalm: Ps 27:1, 4, 13-14 (L 271)

This miracle of the multiplication of the loaves is the only one we find in all four Gospels. In John it becomes the springboard for a long discourse read at Mass over a period of eight days. It suggests to us how central was the celebration of the Lord's Supper for the early Christians, although they hadn't developed all the terms we use for it today. The other accounts of this miracle speak of Jesus in words we hear at Mass: he took the bread, blessed it, broke it, and gave it to those present. John adds that he gave thanks, something we also hear every day at Mass. From the Greek for "thanksgiving" we get our word "Eucharist." In some of our more negative moods we may ask, thanks for what? Very likely most of us have gotten beyond that stage, but our growth as Christians may be measured by thanksgiving. Recalling the reasons we have for being thankful is always in season and can have immediate effects on how we live. There are some basic reasons for being thankful. We're thankful for life. For many, God's love and care is another reason for thanksgiving. Why we should be thankful varies a great deal from person to person. We probably shouldn't expect an African refugee to be thankful in the same way as a comfortable American suburbanite. People caught in the crossfire of warring nations are hardly thankful for God's care in the same way as a middle-class mother just home from the hospital with a healthy baby and a loving husband. Thinking of our reasons for being thankful against the backdrop of the misery of so many of our fellow human beings may make having grateful hearts easier. Being thankful counters our tendency to self-pity and self-absorption.

Saturday of the Second Week of Easter—*Do not be afraid*

Readings: Acts 6:1-7; John 6:16-21
Resp. Psalm: Ps 33:1-2, 4-5, 18-19 (L 272)

"It is I. Do not be afraid" (John 6:20). These words of Jesus recur in the Gospels and may be, for many of us, the most helpful words for our everyday living. Especially if we're the worrying type, we know there is a whole index of fears we can easily bring to mind, given a little quiet or a sleepless night. At these moments the fears jostle each other for our attention, for the chance to disturb us and destroy our peace. We can worry about everything from immediate financial problems to our eternal lot and everything in between: that new job, an upcoming marriage, the health of our spouse, the faith of our children, the state of the Middle East, and the problems of the church—even what to pack for that trip to see the parents. Trust in the Lord is not some panacea which does away with every worry or solves every problem; but with enough prayer and practice, trust can give us a deep assurance that no matter how strong the wind or how turbulent the sea, the Lord is still with us and for us. The light, radiance, and joy we associate with Easter are justified by this great victory of Christ over suffering and death. Daily and often during the day, it helps to state our trust in God and pray for more. *We know you are here, Lord, risen and living in your Body, the church; help us to not be afraid and worried.*

Monday of the Third Week of Easter—*The work asked of us*

Readings: Acts 6:8-15; John 6:22-29
Resp. Psalm: Ps 119:23-24, 26-27, 29-30 (L 273)

The crowd that followed Jesus to the other side of the lake begins a dialogue with Jesus. After a while it becomes mostly a monologue, filling a chapter in John's Gospel with what is called the Bread of Life discourse. We will hear the entire discourse in the course of this week's readings. In the dialogue, as is true so often in John's Gospel, Jesus speaks on one level about faith and his gift to us but the crowd hears on another level, seemingly about the possibility that Jesus might provide fresh baked goods daily. Jesus tries to make clear very quickly that he is not a baker and that they must show some faith in him in order to benefit from what follows. The signs worked by Jesus are never entertainment or sideshows. They help us see more clearly some aspect of our life in God. They are not worked to force us to faith. In that sense these signs demonstrate God's respect for our conscience and human dignity. Some elemental trust in the Lord has to be there first before any miracles can be perceived. Faith makes the meaning or insight of miracles evident to us, from the Eucharist to the resurrection. Without faith we do not see beyond the bread or recognize the risen Lord: "This is the work of God, that you believe in the one he sent" (John 6:29). Trust is our work.

Tuesday of the Third Week of Easter—
Taste and see how good the Lord is

Readings: Acts 7:51–8:1a; John 6:30-35
Resp. Psalm: Ps 31:3cd-4, 6 and 7b and 8a, 17 and 21ab (L 274)

As he is being stoned Stephen exclaims: "Behold, I see the heavens opened and the Son of Man standing at the right hand of God" (Acts 7:56). This statement so offends his persecutors that they hold their hands over their ears so as not to hear. This is a very clear way of stating that Jesus is central to Christian belief and much more than any mere mortal teacher. Jesus confirms this in the Gospel: "I am the bread of life; whoever comes to me will never hunger, and whoever believes in me will never thirst" (John 6:35). Jesus is as close to the Father as is imaginable and he claims that all human desire for life and happiness is fulfilled in him. He is the bread of life. Other claimants who offer us fulfillment or happiness by comparison are light pastry—cream puffs or donuts. Jesus—his life and teaching—is solid food and essential nourishment. The closing words of the Gospel are another invitation to us to take this seriously, to look to him rather than to some week-end seminar or psychological technique for a substantial satisfaction of our deepest hopes. Jesus' promise is that a life lived in faith, prayer, and closeness to God produces results deep within us: "Whoever comes to me will never hunger, and whoever believes in me will never thirst." Only by regular sharing in the heavenly Food Jesus offers can we learn the truth of these words.

Wednesday of the Third Week of Easter—
The food of Christians

Readings: Acts 8:1b-8; John 6:35-40
Resp. Psalm: Ps 66:1-3a, 4-5, 6-7a (L 275)

Today's Gospel repeats the last verse of yesterday's and further develops the theme of believing. All who believe in the Son find, as we heard yesterday, full satisfaction; further, everyone who believes in him will have eternal life, we hear today. The condition which allows us to be nourished by this Bread which is Jesus is believing. In its most basic sense, to believe means to be open to the wisdom, strength, and love that come from God. Not to rely on our own thought, schemes, and human wisdom but to trust the God we cannot see is faith. From the point of view of our reason, that means a risk; faith even seems foolish. But we have to surrender some control and surrender ourselves to God in order to receive what God gives. One can spend much of one's life trying to find reasons to believe. And some of that we should expect of people who think about politics, living wills, and mortgages. Faith and religion deserve our best thought. But somewhere along the line we have to get on with living and have to make a decision about believing just as someone in love, for example, eventually decides in the interest of getting on with life that this is the person to marry. Once we commit ourselves to believing in Jesus as the true Bread of life, we have opportunities to verify our believing by our experience of living this teaching. Taste and see, Psalm 34 says (v. 8, NRSV). The real proof of faith is in the living. The power and value of believing become apparent over the years in the peace, trust, and insight that come from daily practice. The risen Lord eventually shows us, no matter how quietly and simply, that he is true nourishment and true life for us.

Thursday of the Third Week of Easter—
The risen life is here and now

Readings: Acts 8:26-40; John 6:44-51
Resp. Psalm: Ps 66:8-9, 16-17, 20 (L 276)

We are likely to see the eternal life promised by Jesus as something in the future, as something which occurs after death. In the first verses of today's Gospel Jesus says of those who come to him, "I will raise him on the last day" (John 6:44). And toward the end we hear, "whoever eats this bread will live forever" (6:51). We're less accustomed to the idea that what Jesus promises is already ours. But we do hear that promise in today's Gospel: "Amen, amen, I say to you, whoever believes has eternal life" (6:47). Possibly we make too much of a distinction between this present life and the one to come. But by faith and our relation to the Lord, we have already begun the life which has no end. The life in us by virtue of our baptism is the same life which will come to its full realization only in the world to come. Although it can be accompanied now by pain, tears, anguish, and even terror, this life is already in us. We live in Christ or Christ lives in us; we have become sons and daughters of God; the Holy Spirit quickens us. Even in ordinary life there are many things which we know are true, but of which we don't always have some emotional awareness. Even our love for those closest to us is not always accompanied by bells and singing; the same is true with respect to eternal life. More attention to this as we share in the Body and Blood of Christ and in our personal reflection and prayer could help us through some of the more terrifying aspects of our present life. In the Mass for the dead we often hear: "For your faithful people life is changed, not ended." Our eternal life of loving fellowship with God and God's Beloved has begun; it remains for it to blossom and be freed from its limitations.

Friday of the Third Week of Easter—*The change in us*

Readings: Acts 9:1-20; John 6:52-59
Resp. Psalm: Ps 117:1bc, 2 (L 277)

The story of the conversion of Saul (later renamed Paul) is fascinating and also exceptional. It seems safe to say that most of us do not acquire a new vision of reality, of God, and the world in so dramatic a manner as this. To be knocked to the ground and blinded, to hear the voice of Jesus, to have a stranger enter our life as Ananias did—all this and Saul's transformation is undoubtedly out of the ordinary. But a change in our hearts and outlook and the acceptance of the Lord by an unbeliever—this is ordinary and essential to the Christian faith. Believing in Jesus entails change, a turning around of attitude, and a reversal of priorities. The great picture of this in Saul's case is his receiving his sight again. From what follows (the reception of the Holy Spirit, baptism, and Paul's subsequent preaching) we know his vision was never the same. It now included the Lord Jesus as the key to life and death. Often we think of the Eucharist primarily in terms of the change of the elements of bread and wine into the Body and Blood of Christ. More fruitful for our own life as Christians would be to concentrate on the transformation the Eucharist can bring about in us. We receive the Body and Blood of Jesus in this sacrament in order to live by the life which he has from the Father and to share God's view of the world and life. The Eucharist changes us.

Saturday of the Third Week of Easter—*To come to believe*

Readings: Acts 9:31-42; John 6:60-69
Resp. Psalm: Ps 116:12-13, 14-15, 16-17 (L 278)

We know of or at least have heard of members of our family, parish, or church who have for some reason or other "left the faith," as we say. Today in John's Gospel selection, after Jesus has concluded his discourse on the Bread of Life by insisting that one must eat his flesh and drink his blood to have life, some of the disciples murmured in protest and said this was really too much: "Many of his disciples returned to their former way of life and no longer walked with him" (John 6:66). We might say they lost their faith in him. Leaving the faith of one's youth or, as we say, "losing the faith," is not a new phenomenon. It's as old as the Christian religion, as old as religion itself. But that expression "losing one's faith" bears a bit of scrutiny. The phrase makes losing one's faith sound like losing a pair of glasses, a pen, or some loose change. We don't develop or have faith without our cooperation, receptivity, and struggle; and we don't "lose" it except, similarly, with some willingness on our part. We hear in Acts that "many came to believe" (9:42), and also we hear it from Martha: "I have come to believe that you are the Messiah" (John 11:27). The phrase indicates the necessity of work and of the endurance of difficulty and doubt as we work our way toward the commitment of faith. Not only young people getting married must wrestle with commitment, but all of us must. We only come to believe and stay believing after struggle, the consistent practice of prayer, and the endurance of doubt. We don't lose our faith; we either keep it by conscious effort or throw it away by neglect and non-practice.

Monday of the Fourth Week of Easter—*Celebrating life*

Readings: Acts 11:1-18; John 10:1-10 or John 10:11-18
Resp. Psalm: Ps 42:2-3; 43:3, 4 (L 279)

Most of us have heard the phrase "a celebration of life." It is certainly an apt description of what being a follower of Jesus is about. Both readings today end on this note. In the first reading, once the Jewish Christians are convinced that the Gentiles have received the Holy Spirit, they say: "God has then granted life-giving repentance to the Gentiles too" (Acts 11:18). Jesus concludes his discourse about the true shepherd and the sheep gate with the words: "I came so that they might have life and have it more abundantly" (John 10:10, first option for the Gospel). Much as we equate life with youthful vigor, mobility, and all the accompanying effervescence, life (as in "celebration of life") must be something more profound, often even hidden. For Christians, the Spirit is the life-giver and that life, happily, can persist and thrive even when vigor and elastic limbs have disappeared. The life that Jesus gives through the Spirit is within, a pulse of the life of Father, Son, and Spirit transmitted to us to bear us up now and bear us ultimately to the heart of God. Faith can remind us that even when we feel "dead" (as we say), physically drained and in pain, we are alive in the Spirit with the life Jesus has given us. We pray that it may show itself in our patience, love, courage, trust, and hope—maybe even, if it isn't too presumptuous, in good cheer.

Tuesday of the Third Week of Easter—
Change, always change

Readings: Acts 11:19-26; John 10:22-30
Resp. Psalm: Ps 87:1b-3, 4-5, 6-7 (L 280)

We hear often that so-and-so does not accept change or does not take it easily. Even allowing for temperamental differences in this regard, we have to admit that change is right in front of us, almost daily. Change abounds, from those little two-year-olds growing into college students to improvements in that new hybrid car we just bought. The early Jewish disciples of Christ had to accept some startling changes. Just to accept that the Messiah had come for the Gentiles as well as the Jews, and that one didn't have to be a Jew first before becoming a Christian was very tough for many of them. And, in following this Jesus, they eventually had to believe that he was more than a mere human being, that he was somehow God like Yahweh, which was another bitter pill for them to swallow. After it became clear that their fellow Jews were not going to accept this Jesus, they had to split from the synagogue, another traumatic decision. Following Jesus meant a split with their families for many of them. Talk about change! One after another! We could go on listing the changes they had to make. Perhaps all this is a good reminder to us fairly comfortable Christians that to be a faithful follower of Jesus today asks changes in our mentality and in our values, probably more than we first realize. As new immigrants, for example, enter our parish and community, changes are required of all of us. Much of our development in Christian life consists in a willingness to change (a word for repent), to look at the world in a different way, and to adjust our customs to new circumstances.

Wednesday of the Fourth Week of Easter—
Bridges not walls

Readings: Acts 12:24–13:5a; John 12:44–50
Resp. Psalm: Ps 67:2-3, 5, 6 and 8 (L 281)

Paul says that Jesus is the icon, the image of the unseen God, the Father (see Col 1:15). In today's Gospel Jesus proclaims: "Whoever believes in me believes not only in me but also in the one who sent me, and whoever sees me sees the one who sent me" (John 13:44-45). This is a strong statement of what we might call the idea of Jesus as the sacrament of God—the visible, palpable sign of the Father we do not see. Elsewhere in John's Gospel Jesus calls himself the way, the sheep gate, the door, etc. (see, for example, John 14:6; 10:7) which suggest the same kind of use of a sign. Everything about our faith points to the Father, to God. The church with all of its ritual, customs, and activities is sometimes referred to also as one great sacrament, a sign which exists to point to and bring us to God. The pope, bishops, priests, sacraments, laws, practices, etc., of Christianity are all meant to be these pointers, aids to our union with God. One of the titles given the pope is *pontifex* or pontiff which means "bridge builder." Everything in our religious practice is meant to be a bridge to God—not a wall, not a dead end, not, above all, an obstacle or barrier. Insofar as members of the church, ourselves included, do not point beyond to the Father, we can be obstacles or barriers for others. Possibly an examination of conscience is in order on how we use the church and its rites and how we ourselves function as signs of God's presence in our world.

Thursday of the Fourth Week of Easter—*Like the master*

Readings: Acts 13:13-25; John 13:16-20
Resp. Psalm: Ps 89:2-3, 21-22, 25 and 27 (L 282)

Ministers of the Gospel are part of a very noble chain beginning with Jesus. Those who accept him are accepting the Father who sent him; those who accept the ministers of Jesus are, in turn, accepting Jesus. By virtue of our baptism we are all called in some way to represent Christ and through him we represent God to those around us. All this points to the heavy responsibility we all have of doing this fittingly and without reflecting poorly on the One whom we represent. Our time, like every period in the history of the church, has seen its share of scandals and misery caused by those who should be serving and representing God. Jesus stresses that the initiative in choosing representatives is his, but he also implicitly recognizes that those chosen must also agree to the task. They do not become robots. The brief reference to Judas makes this clear. In saying that "no slave is greater than his master" (John 13:16), Jesus is also telling us that those who in any way are his spokespersons and his representatives in the world must expect some of the same treatment he received. We are called to be conscious of the high duty we have and of the danger it brings. Our union with the whole Christ at this table assures us of strength and help for the task of bringing Christ to the world.

Friday of the Fourth Week of Easter—
A place and a love for us

Readings: Acts 13:26-33; John 14:1-6
Resp. Psalm: Ps 2:6-7, 8-9, 10-11ab (L 283)

"There's a place for us," the stars of "West Side Story" sing. And Jesus tells his disciples and us in today's Gospel that he goes to prepare a place for us. Besides that all-satisfying union with that ideal Person, there is probably no other comparable ideal or desire of the human heart than for a place or a condition where one feels totally comfortable and at rest. Songs and poetry about home, sweet home are almost as frequent as those expressing our longing for love. We can say, it seems, that Jesus is the answer to both of these profound longings of the human heart. We pray for eternal rest for the deceased, suggesting this same point about a place for us. Like all of our language about God and life in Christ, our desire for a comfortable place of rest is inadequate and expresses only one aspect. This Easter season reminds us that eternal life is a much richer reality than simply rest; it is life and vitality at their fullest. If we assume that our profound human longings are not accidental but part of the way God created us, then they really do help us understand what God has prepared for us. This place that Jesus goes to prepare for us, we might say, is in the heart of the Trinity, sharing the life and love of Father, Son, and Holy Spirit. There's a place for us; there's a love for us.

Saturday of the Fourth Week of Easter—*Praying in unison*

Readings: Acts 13:44-52; John 14:7-14
Resp. Psalm: Ps 98:1, 2-3ab, 3cd-4 (L 284)

"If you ask anything of me in my name, I will do it" (John 14:14). That promise, the last line in today's Gospel, must sound to some like a kind of magic. We just mention Jesus' name when we pray and we will have whatever we ask: that Lexus, that vacation in Tahiti, cure of illness, restoration of sight, peace in the family and in the Middle East, and food for all the starving. But, of course, that's not it. The teaching of the Lord is not about magic and shortcuts, but about growth in discipleship and in union with God. Jesus has pointed out in these discourses in John's Gospel that the Father lives in him and that all who believe in him live in him and, therefore, in the Father as well. Genuine union with Jesus means a growing assimilation of our own thoughts and desires to his. We become one with him not simply in some mystical sense, but one with him in his will to praise and thank God and to live for the fulfillment of God's plan for our world. Living in the Lord and praying in his name means oneness of thought, sentiment, and will with him in order that what we pray for will be in line with the will of the Father. It is not a matter of trying to bend God to our narrow and shortsighted perspective. Just as we pray repeatedly in the Our Father, we always qualify our petitions with "thy will be done." Genuine prayer to the Father by one who lives in Christ is always in the context of the Father's will for us and all of creation.

Monday of the Fifth Week of Easter—*Bridges, not walls*

Readings: Acts 14:5-18; John 14:21-26
Resp. Psalm: Ps 115:1-2, 3-4, 15-16 (L 285)

In our society, it's not very likely that anyone will go so far as to worship a missionary or preacher. The time of the Acts of the Apostles was quite different. After the cure of the crippled man, the local people thought that Paul and Barnabas were gods "come down to us in human form" (Acts 14:11). But Paul and Barnabas told them they were simply bringing them the Good News. We are more likely to treat as gods, to "idolize" sports heroes, charismatic politicians, movie stars, and doctors who work wonders for the sick. In religion we may approach this kind of "worship" when we forget that all the ministers of the church (lay ecclesial ministers, priests, bishops, popes) and all the apparatus of our faith (sacraments, rituals, religious practices) are means to our union with God. They exist to continue the work of the apostles: that of bringing the Good News to people and bringing people to God. While we turn to the ministers of the church for advice, counsel, or instruction, they can never replace our consciences or the decisions and choices which make us followers of the Lord. All the external practices of our religion similarly exist to help us to God. If we don't go beyond them and see through them to God, we are taking them for more than they are. Rituals, practices, and ministers are to be bridges to God for us; if given too much importance in themselves, they become walls instead. We can cherish and honor sincerely the priests and teachers who feed our faith; we can treat reverently and with love the practices of our faith. We can do all this without forgetting they are to help us to God.

Tuesday of the Fifth Week of Easter—*Instruments of peace*

Readings: Acts 14:19-28; John 14:27-31a
Resp. Psalm: Ps 145:10-11, 12-13ab, 21 (L 286)

Although the apostles were preaching the Good News and its accompanying peace all over present-day Turkey, Greece, and Syria, they often met not peace but hatred and persecution. Yet Jesus' farewell gift to them and to us is peace. "My peace I give to you. Not as the world gives do I give it to you" (John 14:27). The peace Jesus promises his followers flows from their trust in Jesus. It's the kind of peace the apostles could experience within themselves even while suffering the belligerent attention of persecutors. The peace which comes from Christ is to a great degree independent of outward circumstances; it is a deep assurance within us of God's love and presence with us. In the world around us, it usually takes at least two to make peace. And Christians should be in the forefront of all efforts to achieve international peace as well as peace within countries and within families. We cannot simply hug to ourselves our inner peace and ignore the strife and disharmony all around us and even in our own families. Extending a sign of peace to those around us in church is meant to be a sign of our pledge to work for peace. There is no more appropriate moment to promise to work for peace than before we are united to Christ and to each other in sharing the one Bread and the one Cup. "Lord, make us instruments of your peace. Where there is hatred, let us sow love; where there is injury, pardon; where there is doubt, faith; where there is despair, hope" (prayer attributed to St. Francis of Assisi).

Wednesday of the Fifth Week of Easter—*Productivity*

Readings: Acts 15:1-6; John 15:1-8
Resp. Psalm: Ps 122:1-2, 3-4ab, 4cd-5 (L 287)

Productivity is a big and important word in our world; its only other rival in the commercial world may be the "bottom line." Pursuit of productivity results in too much stress for many people. Further, the world's productivity is the kind that can be measured, weighed, and evaluated monetarily. The comforting and beautiful words of today's Gospel are about a more profound kind of productivity. We hear Jesus say that he is the vine and we the branches and that the Father is the vinedresser who prunes the vines to make them more fruitful. More-over, he reminds us that we can only be productive if we remain united with him and if the branches continue to receive the nourishment com-ing from the vine itself and its roots: "Whoever remains in me and I in him will bear much fruit, because without me you can do nothing" (John 15:5). Putting commercial activity alongside that fruit spoken of by Jesus makes us question ourselves: in what way, how are we productive in the Lord? What are the signs of our union with him? From the teaching of Jesus elsewhere in the Gospels, we pretty well know what the signs of our union with the life of the risen Christ are: genuine, practical love; effective care and concern for others; patience and perseverance; and witness and dedication. But, again, all this is not automatic. Paradoxically, those of us who celebrate Mass daily may be in more need of warning about this than those who come weekly or only occasionally. Our productivity appears in what we do once we leave the church building.

Thursday of the Fifth Week of Easter—*Variety and diversity*

Readings: Acts 15:7-21; John 15:9-11
Resp. Psalm: Ps 96:1-2a, 2b-3, 10 (L 288)

Our reading from the Acts of the Apostles deals with how or if the Law of Moses is to be applied to Gentile converts; the reading also deals with the increasing diversity of the early Christian community as the word spread outside the Jewish community. What the early church as described in Acts was about to become, a gathering of people from various backgrounds, is what many of our parishes actually are becoming after years of being simply German or Italian or middle class. Variety is something in which we should rejoice, but before that can happen we need within ourselves the love which the Lord transmits to us in our union with him. "As the Father loves me, so I also love you," Jesus tells us, and then continues with the admonition, "Remain in my love" (John 15:9). The Gospel speaks of our union with God in Christ, keeping the commandments, and abiding in love and of its result: "I have told you this so that my joy might be in you and your joy might be complete" (15:11). Joy comes to us from a variety of sources as well as from opening ourselves to what's new and to diversity. Joy can come from a call or visit from a friend, good food, a fine performance of some kind, music, the beauty of little children, the smiles and graciousness of others, a beautiful day, a happy surprise, etc. Joy can come from appreciating the diverse ways people of different cultures have of celebrating their faith. The diversity of our world and environment can be a source of joy and stimulation. But this requires a love of great breadth and generosity. Love for all that is and joy in it stem from our life in Christ.

Friday of the Fifth Week of Easter—*Five basics*

Readings: Acts 15:22-31; John 15:12-17
Resp. Psalm: Ps 57:8-9, 10 and 12 (L 289)

The more practical among us, as we like to call ourselves, like to have things laid out one, two, and three. Today's Gospel verses from the last discourse of Jesus to his disciples at the Last Supper do that without using the numbers. And the whole passage is a strikingly simple but profound look at the essential elements of the Christian life. The circular movement of the discourse in John does not give us an outline, but we can reconstruct it. Looking at it in terms of how it begins, what happens, and where it ends, we find these elements. First, our life in Christ begins with his choice: "It was not you who chose me, but I who chose you" (John 15:16). It was God's initiative, not ours. Second, Jesus chose us in order to open to us God's revelation: "everything I have heard from my Father" (15:15). The followers of Jesus gain an insight into life in our world not accessible by simple observation and experiment. Third, because of our relationship with Jesus, we cannot be thought of as slaves: ". . . because a slave does not know what his master is doing" (15:15). Instead, God's willingness to open the divine heart to us indicates that we are God's friends. One doesn't open one's interior to just anyone. Fourth, from our side, God expects that we do something with this gift of relationship, that we "bear fruit" (15:16) and that means primarily to love one another. This is not merely an ideal, but a direction that has been modeled in the highest degree by Jesus' death for us, his friends. Fifth and finally, living this life in response to God's loving revelation and as God asks assures us of what we call fulfillment: ". . . so that whatever you ask the Father in my name he may give you" (15:16).

Saturday of the Fifth Week of Easter—*How to witness*

Readings: Acts 16:1-10; John 15:18-21
Resp. Psalm: Ps 100:1b-2, 3, 5 (L 290)

"If the world hates you, realize that it hated me first" (John 15:18). At any one time in some part of the world, there are Christians who really experience a hatred for themselves and their belief, often government-sponsored hate. In other parts of the world where this is not evident, there is a temptation to define ourselves by people we consider our enemies, rightly or wrongly. This is a cheap way to define ourselves; we define ourselves better in terms of what our faith positively means and requires of us. In the more affluent parts of the world where people are lost in the abundance of material things, we are more likely to face a stony indifference. This may be more difficult than hostility because it doesn't take Christian belief seriously enough to have any problem with it. Whether we confront hostility—general or individual—or simply indifference, we are all left with personal decisions about how to react. Each must respond as conscience dictates. What and how much do we say to the hostile or indifferent? Do we say anything? When is an appropriate time to speak? How much do we say? Do we take the initiative or simply react? Whatever may be our answers, the one constant: is our best witnessing to those around us through the quality of our life as Christians, our genuine love and concern for the world around us, and the witness of faith in what cannot be seen.

Monday of the Sixth Week of Easter—
To witness by consoling

Readings: Acts 16:11-15; John 15:26–16:4a
Resp. Psalm: Ps 149:1b-2, 3-4, 5-6a and 9b (L 291)

"When the Advocate comes whom I will send you from the Father, the Spirit of truth who proceeds from the Father, he will testify to me. And you also testify" (John 15:26-27). The Spirit will be sent to enable the disciples to give testimony to what they have seen and heard. In other words, we are also called to witness. Everyone is familiar with the aggressive door-to-door type of witness. Scripture tells us that the disciples of the Lord were no slouches when it came to announcing the Good News. But there are also quieter ways of announcing the Good News, and we may have heard of this in today's first reading. In Acts, Paul and those with him (included in the "we") go to a place of prayer and "witness" their faith to the women there: "We sat and spoke with the women who had gathered there" (Acts 16:13). It all sounds pretty quiet and non-confrontational, as we would say today. And this little impromptu meeting has some good results. Witnessing to the word of God is not only for the naturally brassy; it's a call to all of us to realize the various ways in which we can witness without a lot of fuss. When friends or neighbors are sorrowing, or discouraged, for example, we believers are able to offer hope, encouragement, or suggest prayer or some Scripture. Perhaps we offer our best witness in times of grief and sadness by our presence or by the dinner we provide for the bereaved family, for example. Thoughtfulness and concern and treating others as genuine persons with feelings like our own are other forms of witness. At this table we are joined to the Great Consoler and strengthened to be consolers in our daily life.

Tuesday of the Sixth Week of Easter—*Phases in believing*

Readings: Acts 16:22-34; John 16:5-11
Resp. Psalm: Ps 138:1-2ab, 2cde-3, 7c-8 (L 292)

Faith comes across at times in the Scriptures as very swift and clean; at other times its difficulty is more apparent. In the first reading today we have the impression that the jailer, struck by the miraculous freeing of Paul and Silas, asked a basic question, heard the answer, and was baptized with his whole family. The reading ends: ". . . and with his household rejoiced at having come to faith in God" (Acts 16:34). In the Gospel reading today, however, the closest disciples of Jesus are so disturbed and at a loss over the things Jesus has been saying that grief fills their hearts. Possibly the two readings taken together reflect the different moments of our faith. Sometimes our faith does seem clear and strong. We say, "Where would I be without it?" At other times our faith is cause for torment and sorrow. We ask, "Why did this happen?" We should not be surprised that our faith goes through various phases and that it may be alternately strong and weak, joy-giving and frightening. Most likely faith involves some struggle, such as the two aspects of faith appearing in today's readings. The words heard elsewhere in Mark's Gospel are also fitting for any one of us at some time or another, or all the time: Lord, "I do believe; help my unbelief" (Mark 9:24).

Wednesday of the Sixth Week of Easter—
Nothing good and human is lost

Readings: Acts 17:15, 22–18:1; John 16:12-15
Resp. Psalm: Ps 148:1-2, 11-12, 13, 14 (*L* 293)

Paul's address to the Athenians in today's first reading is very concil-iatory, aiming to move from what these people believe to specifically Christian beliefs. Taking people where they are, he tries to bring them to what has been revealed in Jesus Christ. After recounting some areas of closeness, Paul tells how Jesus was raised from the dead. There are three reactions to this: some sneer; others more politely say they'll have to hear more some other time; and a few become believers. The resurrection is, as we hear elsewhere in the New Testament, "too good to be true." The rationalistic human tendency is to dismiss the resur-rection as something too much like our dreams to be true. Earlier, his hearers seem to think, Paul has been speaking rationally enough about how God is everywhere, not contained in a statue, and able to be found by those who seek him. But now he goes off the deep end in talking about resurrection! Like other peoples, many of the Greeks followed systems which taught that the soul did live on forever. But that the whole person should be restored to new life, that was too much and probably too "materialistic." All this pushes us to face the true depth of our belief in resurrection. All this reminds us that this belief does affirm that the body is good, an essential part of us, and that all the best in human life will be saved. It's only "too good to be true" if we attempt to limit God's goodness by our limited reason.

Thursday of the Sixth Week of Easter—
He is always coming, always near

Readings: Acts 18:1-8; John 16:16-20
Resp. Psalm: Ps 98:1, 2-3ab, 3cd-4 (*L* 294)

Jesus talks today about a "little while" and he has the disciples thor-oughly confused. What Jesus probably means is that in a "little while" he would leave them (the Ascension) and that in a short time after that he would come again (his Second Coming). For the community for which the Fourth Gospel was written, the return of Jesus took place with the coming of the Spirit at Pentecost. With the descent of the Spirit Jesus returns and remains truly present and active in the midst of believers. Jesus could well say that in a "little while" he would be seen again, for Pentecost is always coming, always coming soon. Jesus is always coming into our lives and always coming soon when the presence of Jesus is newly recognized, newly accepted, and newly served. This "soon" becomes the watchword for all believers. It puts the spirit of anticipation and discovery in our lives. It can fill us with courage and trust. It instills within us the constant eagerness to serve. All the qualities which the Gospel seeks to inculcate become the more pressing, the more exciting, and the more urgent because soon the Lord will come. The Lord is always coming soon—not to relieve us of the struggle, but to confirm us in it. This is the source of courage and abiding joy.

Friday of the Sixth Week of Easter—
Tears at night, joy in the morning

Readings: Acts 18:9-18; John 16:20-23
Resp. Psalm: Ps 47:2-3, 4-5, 6-7 (L 295)

John's circular and repetitive style makes us wonder at times how relevant this Good News is to us. With its lack of logic according to our Western sense of the word, the Easter message seems very far off and foggy at times. But the words of Jesus today bring things down to earth with his use of the childbirth image. He tells the disciples that they will grieve when he is taken away from them in his suffering and death, but that their grief will be turned to joy in his resurrection: "When a woman is in labor, she is in anguish because her hour has arrived; but when she has given birth to a child, she no longer remembers the pain because of her joy that a child has been born into the world" (John 16:20). The experience of the woman in childbirth and of the disciples is parallel to events in the lives of all of us. How many times have we experienced the passage from pain and sorrow to joy and delight! This passage from sorrow to joy can be as simple as the relief we experience after our persistent and debilitating two-week-long cold finally goes away or as serious as the remission of a husband's cancer. Or, we've had the experience of being tightly wound by worries and fears only to see everything in a brighter and more hopeful perspective the next morning. This is a pattern in any human life, but the suffering, death, and resurrection of the Lord make the joyous outcome the norm, the last word, even when sorrow and misery seem to prevail: "You also are now in anguish. But I will see you again, and your hearts will rejoice, and no one will take that joy away from you" (16:22). The psalmist says, "At night there are tears, but joy comes with dawn" (Ps 30:6).

Saturday of the Sixth Week of Easter—
Trusting God to answer

Readings: Acts 18:23-28; John 16:23b-28
Resp. Psalm: Ps 47:2-3, 8-9, 10 (L 296)

Is prayer perhaps the most practical application of faith and trust in God? A good case can be made for this. Where else or how else other than in prayer do we show so thoroughly that our final trust is in God and not in ourselves or anything of the visible world? The kind of prayer about which the Gospels speak is more concerned with this trust in God than with guaranteeing us some particular good. Jesus says that the reason we can trust to receive what we need from God is not that he, Jesus, assists our petition, but that the Father loves us. Why wouldn't God give us the good we need? Implicit in the teaching of Jesus on prayer is this: God loves us and, therefore, desires what is for our good; the Father knows better than we do what is for our good. Trusting prayer without too much insistence on a specific outcome is what we gradually learn. Strong, absolute statements about how we need only ask the Father and God will give us that for which we ask are rooted in trusting confidence in God, a confidence eventually leading us to quit trying to tell God *what* we need. God loves us, cares for us, and has done so much for us—why not make known our needs and then simply trust God? If that is not our practice now, it seems at least to be the ideal for which we strive, as our prayer life deepens.

Monday of the Seventh Week of Easter—
Ups and downs of faith

Readings: Acts 19:1-8; John 16:29-33
Resp. Psalm: Ps 68:2-3ab, 4-5acd, 6-7ab (L 297)

"Whoa!" This might be the right word to say to the disciples at this juncture. Their response to Jesus is definitely premature: "Now we realize that you know everything . . . Because of this we believe that you came from God" (John 16:30). He tells them in return, "Do you believe now? Behold, the hour is coming and has arrived when each of you will be scattered to his own home and you will leave me alone" (16:31-32). These first disciples had to learn what each new generation of believers and each individual believer must learn: that belief in Jesus is not that easily attained. Sure, there are and have always been some who, like the disciples here, feel that they have achieved in one fell swoop a pure and total belief. Let us grant that one or two people (possibly St. Paul) have had this experience. For most of us, as for the disciples, the required total saving trust in the Lord is only fitfully and gradually gained. The belief in the Lord that saves us and even cushions us against despair comes about only by being tested in life's every circumstance. It is tested by prosperity and poverty, by success and sorrow, each in different ways. Like the old Israel, we must pass through the waters and the desert of disappointment, betrayal, grief, loss, fear, numbing dryness—one or some of these—to come to the promised land of genuine belief. Our awareness that in so many ways our faith is provisional and not fully developed gives us good reason to pray to the Holy Spirit for this gift of faith as probably the most basic gift of all.

Tuesday of the Seventh Week of Easter—
Strength from the Holy Spirit

Readings: Acts 20:17-27; John 17:1-11a
Resp. Psalm: Ps 68:10-11, 20-21 (L 298)

The Paul we hear in his address to the elders of the church is the Paul we recognize so well from his letters. He is firm, convinced, courageous, and powerful in word, confident in his mission and in his manner of carrying it out; in a word, Paul demonstrates his integrity and faithfulness to the Gospel. For example, Paul says in today's first reading, "I did not at all shrink from telling you what was for your benefit" (Acts 20:20). Paul's decisiveness after his dramatic conversion and his forthrightness in preaching the Gospel bring before us mere mortals the image of an extraordinary man. He almost seems free from the hesitancy which grips all of us at one time or other. Our image of him makes all the more surprising the episode recounted last Friday in the Acts of the Apostles in which Paul hears the Lord saying to him in a vision, "Do not be afraid. Go on speaking, and do not be silent, for I am with you. No one will attack and harm you" (Acts 18:9-10). We do not know for sure everything about Paul's interior state, but the Lord's consoling words suggest that Paul must have had his fainthearted moments, his temptations to withdraw and avoid confronting nonbelievers. This is helpful for us who usually can only stand in awe of Paul's courage.

God can and will encourage and strengthen us if we faithfully express our weakness and fear in prayer. "Come, Holy Spirit, come. . . . Heal our wounds, our strength renew. On our dryness pour your dew . . ." (Pentecost sequence).

Wednesday of the Seventh Week of Easter—
Giving is at the heart

Readings: Acts 20:28-38; John 17:11b-19
Resp. Psalm: Ps 68:29-30, 33-35a, 35bc-36ab (*L* 299)

Both readings today come from farewell messages, the first from Paul as he leaves Ephesus and his sorrowing Christians. In the Gospel we hear part of the Priestly Prayer of Jesus in the midst of his farewell at the Last Supper. Elsewhere in Scripture we've read farewells which included the hope that those left behind would revenge the dying man on his enemies. The message in the two farewells we hear today is quite different; both are free of that spite and full of the self-giving spirit of Jesus. We may take for granted that the Christian should be free of desires for revenge or from holding a grudge, but we must also admit that the temptation to get even is strong. Much of the spirit of the world around us is centered on self, on its protection, rights, and getting its due. Each time we assist at the altar of the Lord, we have put before us the self-giving sacrifice of Jesus and his gift of self to God and us. To hear the same message in our readings only reinforces its centrality. Paul quotes an otherwise unreported line from Jesus—"It is more blessed to give than to receive" (Acts 20:35)—to support his exhortation to the elders to put service as good shepherds and the needs of others first in all they do, rather than self-seeking interests. The language of Jesus about "consecrating" is of the same tenor. This is not about consecration in the narrower sense of the change in the bread and wine at Mass, but in the sense of giving oneself, dedicating oneself, to God and for the good of others: "I consecrate myself for them, so that they also may be consecrated in truth" (John 17:19).

Thursday of the Seventh Week of Easter—
Honoring the dignity of others

Readings: Acts 22:30; 23:6-11; John 17:20-26
Resp. Psalm: Ps 16:1-2a and 5, 7-8, 9-10, 11 (*L* 300)

The discourses given us in John are almost hypnotic in their repetition of words and phrases; in today's Gospel we hear an example: "So that they may be one, as we are one, I in them and you in me" (John 17:22-23). If the words are not to lull us into vague dreaming, we need to draw some down-to-earth implications. God's love for us in the Son shows itself in respect for our own dignity and that of fellow believers and for the potential in everyone. There is so much in our society that we Christians could counter with reverence and respect. Language about human beings and their activities degrades and reduces all that we do to something cheap and valueless. Some behaviors treat individuals as interchangeable units of no distinction. An acceptance of violence and an indifference to the sufferings of people is counter to any human dignity. How easy it is for all of us to forget this! We begin to see every client or customer as just another number; we see our students or neighbors as just so many nuisances; we see the homeless and poor simply as so many losers. Reflection on the words of Jesus helps us to show some honor and consideration for all those we meet and a determination to look for their uniqueness. Unlike God, we are limited, of course, in our ability to see every human this way. Time and immediate family responsibilities make unavoidable demands on us. But there is room for greater imitation of the Mother Teresas, with those who spend their lives for the neglected.

Friday of the Seventh Week of Easter—*Moving on with Peter*

Readings: Acts 25:13b-21; John 21:15-19
Resp. Psalm: Ps 103:1-2, 11-12, 19-20ab (L 301)

We have moved from the Last Discourse of Jesus at the Last Supper to the very end of John's Gospel, where Christ appears to his disciples after his resurrection. By his threefold protestation of love for Christ, Peter makes up for his threefold denial before the Passion. Christ not only rehabilitates Peter, but gives him a special mission. Again, we see how far is the spirit of Christ from not only any desire for retribution but even for justice as we understand it. Forgiveness is total; Peter can begin again and be entrusted with a new mission. Faced with such a Savior and Friend, none of us has any cause or excuse for remaining at a distance or for indulging despair and hopelessness. Even our protestation of unworthiness before Communion, for example, is situated in the context of the ever-forgiving love of God revealed in Christ. We are certainly unworthy of this union with God, but God is ever ready to forgive and to have us begin again. As the situation with Peter suggests, God is not only ready to forgive but is also ready to erase the past and start with new hope for us and even new responsibilities. On

81

our part it requires a willingness to begin anew and not let the past hang around our neck like a millstone. Ignoring this generosity of God's can lead us to a kind of paralysis which does no one any good and helps no one. God expects this generosity to be met on our part with thankful and willing receptivity.

Saturday of the Seventh Week of Easter—*Respectful concern*

Readings: Acts 28:16-20, 30-31; John 21:20-25
Resp. Psalm: Ps 11:4, 5 and 7 (L 302)

Difficult as it may be to state, there must be a line drawn between being a busybody and being concerned for others. The latter is an obvious consequence of discipleship; New Testament teaching is full of emphasis on helping the poor, consoling the sorrowful, and coming to the aid of all who suffer or are in want. But putting our noses into everyone else's business is something else. Even Peter seems to get a rebuke related to this in today's Gospel. His queries about what will happen to John are answered by Christ with a clipped reminder that Peter should follow him and not be worried about John's destiny. Certainly we have no right to abandon legitimate concern for others. But today's Gospel reminds us of the need for sensitivity even in helping others. We can't just barge in. People who lack physical necessities or are in pain still have a basic dignity they want to maintain. That calls for respect. To give help without humiliating the one being helped is sometimes a difficult achievement. Our Lord tells us in the Sermon on the Mount not to blow a trumpet before ourselves when we do some good. Like Peter, we're told to follow Jesus and to be respectful of others in our efforts to help them. "Following" the Lord is first; an unselfconscious assistance of others is the obvious consequence about which we needn't make a lot of noise.

Ordinary Time

Monday of the First Week in Ordinary Time—
God has spoken through a life

Readings: Heb 1:1-6; Mark 1:14-20
Resp. Psalm: Ps 97:1 and 2b, 6 and 7c, 9 (L 305)

If asked how God has spoken to us, most of us would probably say God has done that through the Scriptures. We connect speaking and words, of course. Christians do believe God has spoken this way to us and to the world. The first reading from Hebrews says that God has done this in fragmentary and varied ways, but "in these last days, he spoke to us through the Son"; further on: this Son "is the very imprint of his being" (Heb 1:2, 3). More profoundly, God has spoken to us through the life, death, and resurrection of the Son. This may explain why in today's Gospel the men who were called as disciples were so immediate in their response. Did they see and experience in the living Lord this revelation of God so strikingly that they "left" nets and father to follow him? The overall picture of God that we have in the life and teachings of Jesus is probably more affecting than just the words, important as they are. In Jesus who lives our life, endures our routine and misunderstanding, and went through our suffering and death we see God's tender compassion and closeness to ourselves in a way words could not make clearer. The Eucharist itself works its effect on us more through action than through words alone. We all know how difficult it is to put into mere words what happens here; we recognize within ourselves what it is, just through having shared in it so many times.

Tuesday of the First Week in Ordinary Time—
Jesus and earthly evils

Readings: Heb 2:5-12; Mark 1:21-28
Resp. Psalm: Ps 8:2ab and 5, 6-7, 8-9 (L 306)

To see unclean spirits and demons as behind so much of what is bad in human life (as seems true in Mark) is foreign to most of us today.

But horrendous evil is no stranger to us and to our times. Think of the slaughter in recent years in Rwanda, the attempted extermination of the Jews by the Nazis, the killing of children in schools by madmen or fellow students, or the mass suicides of cult members in Guyana and California. Many more personal evils face us closer to home, in our neighborhood or our own lives: child or spouse abuse, mortal illnesses, mental illness, crippling from birth or brought on by accident. The subjection of everything to the authority of Christ mentioned in the first reading certainly must include a change in such awful situations. Mark must show his readers, as Jesus showed his contemporaries, that the Messiah ultimately overcomes all evil. Possibly the most useful conclusion we can draw from this for our lives is to recognize that there is no evil that can possibly happen that is not material for the power of the Messiah, our Lord. There is no evil that can happen in human life that we cannot put before Christ in prayer or at this Mass with the hope of his help. We cannot dictate the form of that help, but we can with good reason put our trust in him in even the most hopeless situations. He has tasted suffering and death for all of us and become himself their antidote.

Wednesday of the First Week in Ordinary Time—
With us in every terror and ill

Readings: Heb 2:14-18; Mark 1:29-39
Resp. Psalm: Ps 105:1-2, 3-4, 6-7, 8-9 (L 307)

The demons and the devil who appear in both readings today were a more prominent part of everyday thought in the New Testament period than they would be in our own time. We heard this yesterday also. Although we may attribute many of the bad things of human life more to human ill will, neglect, greed, and the like and, consequently, feel less chained by evil spirits, we do feel the weight of sin, suffering, and the many awful things occurring in human life. Today's news tells us of an earthquake killing hundreds; we hear of an accident killing a family of four. But in the midst of all of this, sometimes so overwhelmingly, we have the assurance of Scripture that the Lord is with us: "[b]ecause he himself was tested through what he suffered, he is able to help those who are being tested" (Heb 2:18). Repeated reflection on the word of God and our sharing in the Eucharist solidifies our conviction about this. We are not alone in this often terrifying, depressing world. Realism is not believing that we are left on our own resources in a hostile world; realism is believing that the Lord, come into human life once, is always with each of us in our struggles, depression, discouragement, and sorrow: "[h]e is able to help those who are being tested."

Thursday of the First Week in Ordinary Time—
Today, now is the time

Readings: Heb 3:7-14; Mark 1:40-45
Resp. Psalm: Ps 95:6-7c, 8-9, 10-11 (L 308)

"Encourage yourselves daily while it is still 'today,' so that none of you may grow hardened by the deceit of sin" (Heb 3:13). Today's first reading from Hebrews specifically asks us to help each other avoid a hardened insensitivity to God's word. As the quoted psalm says, "Oh, that today you would hear his voice: Harden not your hearts" (Ps 95:8). But there are many ways in which we can and should encourage one another. The emphasis is on not waiting, not putting it off, doing it now. Even the simple and most welcome encouragement we give others (by a compliment or by commending something good they do) should be done now, today. It must occur to all of us at a funeral to hope that the good things said about the deceased person were also said to her or him while the deceased was still alive. Why not tell Sue today how much her always cheerful and positive attitude is appreciated? Why not thank George with some kind words or a kind surprise for mowing the lawn or shoveling the snow when we were sick? Today, now, is the time to tell our neighbor what a responsible son she has. Today, Thursday, is the time to commend the friend who does her best to speak some Spanish to a new neighbor who is unsure of her English. Now is the time to compliment Harry for always having some little joke or bit of humor to brighten the day. Why not also compliment the receptionist for her patience and good humor? By doing so we encourage people to continue doing good things which, for all we know, may require more of them than is apparent. The time is now, while they and we are living here.

Friday of the First Week in Ordinary Time—
Ever new, ever fruitful

Readings: Heb 4:1-5, 11; Mark 2:1-12
Resp. Psalm: Ps 78:3 and 4bc, 6c-7, 8 (L 309)

It is so easy, especially if we are regulars at Mass, to lapse into a sort of numbness where we may hear the words of Scripture or of the presider but really take nothing in. A moment later or after Mass we cannot for the life of us recall what we heard or what it was about. Some of this, or course, is simply the result of routine and of our difficulty in being present to much of what is before us. More serious, according to the first reading from Hebrews, is the matter of hearing the word of God without faith, that is, without trust in its power and without allowing it to have an impact on our lives. It's a bit like what we hear in James: there the writer says that even the devils believe, that is, they accept that God exists, but it is not a faith which expects good from God or bears any fruit (see Jas 2:19). We just heard in Hebrews: "But the word that they heard did not profit them, for they were not united in faith with those who listened" (Heb 4:2). None of us will probably ever draw out all the meaning of what we hear in Scripture, particularly in a difficult book like the Letter to the Hebrews. And even the Gospel story of the paralyzed man let down before Jesus (see Mark 2:4) always lends new insight to us if we try to listen with an open and receptive heart and mind. Scripture, like poetry and music, always yields something new and, most often, means something slightly different to each of us.

Saturday of the First Week in Ordinary Time—
Jesus came for the sick

Readings: Heb 4:12-16; Mark 2:13-17
Resp. Psalm: Ps 19:8, 9, 10, 15 (L 310)

The high priest of the first reading, an exalted and majestic figure, is still the same person as the Jesus who is so willing to associate with the despised of his world. In the Gospel he calls the despised tax collector, Levi (later called Matthew), and goes to dinner at his house with other unsavory people. "Unsavory" here covers all the people in Jewish society who failed to keep the regulations of the Law. In answer to complaints from the self-satisfied followers of the Law, Jesus says that these unsavory ones are the people he came to save and to help—those who find the demands of religion hard to keep. This is how Hebrews describes Jesus, too. He is not "a high priest who is unable to sympathize with our weaknesses, but one who has similarly been tested in every way, yet without sin" (Heb 4:15). Like the tax collectors and sinners in the Gospel, we too with our failures, weaknesses, laxity, indifference, weariness, and sensuality can come to and call on Jesus here in the Eucharist for understanding and forgiveness. We're just the type Jesus is most comfortable with, those who know they are lacking and want help. "So let us confidently approach the throne of grace to receive mercy and to find grace for timely help."

Monday of the Second Week in Ordinary Time—
Jesus learned obedience

Readings: Heb 5:1-10; Mark 2:18-22
Resp. Psalm: Ps 110:1, 2, 3, 4 (L 311)

Too easily at times we toss off phrases about how suffering teaches patience, courage, compassion, gentleness, etc. It's only realistic to face the fact that suffering leads some to bitterness, negativity, self-pity, or great anger. Suffering is no magic educator in virtue. Much depends on our basic attitude. For our suffering to result in a mature and more Christ-like character requires a fundamental trust in God's ultimate good intentions for us. Given that, we can learn to see how suffering is able to produce some good in us. The first reading from the Letter to the Hebrews sums it up as obedience. Of Jesus we hear, "Son though he was, he learned obedience from what he suffered" (Heb 5:8). Obedience (not a very popular word in our culture) means learning to be attuned to what God deems best for us. Our suffering may go all the way from difficulties and trials resulting from our work environment or from members of the family to enduring the debilitating effects of chemotherapy for months on end or the aching pain of arthritis. Christian tradition does not see obedience as simply rolling over and playing dead before adversity. There's plenty of evidence in Christ and our tradition that we can and must do what is possible to relieve suffering and to get rid of oppression. The suffering which teaches us to be one with God's intentions for us is that which we cannot do much about, that which simply accompanies our life, like it or not. At Mass each day we can join our sacrifice—our suffering and daily difficulties—to the offering of Jesus, our high priest. Through him is all honor and glory to God.

Tuesday of the Second Week in Ordinary Time—*Our anchor*

Readings: Heb 6:10-20; Mark 2:23-28
Resp. Psalm: Ps 111:1-2, 4-5, 9 and 10c (L 312)

The author of the Letter to the Hebrews tells us in his own involved way that we have every reason to trust and hope in God's promises. We're in danger at times of thinking that there is no other virtue than love proper to our life as disciples. Without taking away from the absolutely central place of love, we do need to stress hope. The author uses a nautical comparison here. But instead of suggesting that hope is like an anchor thrown from the ship to lodge firmly in the sea bed, he says hope is like an anchor thrown ahead of and beyond us into heaven: "This we have as an anchor of the soul, sure and firm, which reaches into the interior behind the veil, where Jesus has entered on our behalf as forerunner" (Heb 6:19-20). The hope sustaining us amid the uncertainties, difficulties, and suffering of this present life is anchored in that heaven where Jesus has preceded us and where he prepares a place for us. Our hope flows from our sharing by our lives in the suffering, death, and resurrection of Christ the Lord. We trust that if we have suffered and died with him, we shall also rise with him. Here and now this means that in our prayer and even through our tears we look beyond what our eyes can see and our senses feel to the One who has overcome suffering in our name. In our Lord Jesus Christ we, too, are now overcoming our own suffering.

Wednesday of the Second Week in Ordinary time—
To preserve life

Readings: Heb 7:1-3, 15-17; Mark 3:1-6
Resp. Psalm: Ps 110:1, 2, 3, 4 (L 313)

The Gospel poses another discussion on the Sabbath. Yesterday it was occasioned by the disciples of Jesus picking grain on the Sabbath to assuage their hunger. Today the stage is set when a man with a withered hand is very conspicuous in the synagogue when Jesus enters on the Sabbath. The Pharisees are watching and waiting. But instead of discussing this encounter on the level of his opponents in terms of rules or how much can one do or not do, Jesus raises essential issues: "Is it lawful to do good on the sabbath rather than to do evil, to save life rather than to destroy it?" (Mark 3:4). How different Christian history would have been if Christians of every type had used this criterion for their endeavors! It is still necessary that we evaluate what goes on in the name of religion in terms of whether the activity preserves life or destroys it, enhances life or diminishes it. Suffering and pain are not good in themselves, and we need never feel obliged to continue them, especially for someone else. Deprivation and difficulty are good when they facilitate maturity, improvements, health, and a more productive life. Parents who must miss Mass or attend amid the distractions and needs of little children who compete with the service for their attention are choosing well in giving attention to the little ones. A caregiver in the same situation who stays home with a disabled person is preserving life. Very appropriately, the Letter of James tells us that this is true religion: "looking after orphans and widows in their distress" (1:27).

We can all add to this the poor, the bedridden, the lonely, and those vulnerable in any way.

Thursday of the Second Week in Ordinary Time—
A high priest with and among us

Readings: Heb 7:25–8:6; Mark 3:7-12
Resp. Psalm: Ps 40:7-8a, 8b-9, 10, 17 (L 314)

The first reading from Hebrews describes Jesus Christ our high priest as "holy, innocent, undefiled, separate from sinners, higher than the heavens" (Heb 7:26). One suspects that the writer is so wrapped up in the vision of Jesus as our mediator in heaven that he is willing to sacrifice a bit the picture we have in the Gospels, specifically in today's from Mark. There Jesus is separated from sinners only for the sake of some peace or for the sake of preaching from a boat, but otherwise the picture is of crowds pressing on him, "pressing upon him to touch him" (Mark 3:10). In fact he opens himself so much to sinners that the scribes and Pharisees complain about it. Part of the issue, of course, is that in our Savior we have someone who is truly human and truly divine, as our Creed puts it. Because of his oneness with the Father and the Holy Spirit, Jesus is able to transform us and even make us sharers in divine life; because he is human, he understands and sympathizes with every weakness of ours. The first reading from Hebrews reminds us that this high priest does not offer new sacrifices every day; rather, "He did that once for all when he offered himself" (Heb 7:27). At Mass that offering is re-presented daily under the signs of bread and wine so that we may join ourselves, our lives and our trials, with his as our praise and thanksgiving to God.

Friday of the Second Week in Ordinary Time—
God's law and spirit in our hearts

Readings: Heb 8:6-13; Mark 3:13-19
Resp. Psalm: Ps 85:8 and 10, 11-12, 13-14 (L 315)

Today in the Letter to the Hebrews we hear that God will make a new kind of pact or covenant with the people, and we are to understand this as referring to the followers of Christ. The complaint is that the Israelites of old broke the covenant. In this new period God "will put my laws in their minds and I will write them upon their hearts" (Heb 8:10). The old Israel apparently observed the covenant simply as a set of laws, according to Hebrews, without corresponding interior commitment.

That seems always to be a tendency in religion: to save ourselves the implications of genuine commitment, we tell ourselves we have not broken the letter of the law and that's enough. This, then, does become a purely external observance. But in the time before Christ we have enough evidence of the prophets insisting that the covenant should be interior to question whether it was ever a purely external matter. In any case, what God asks of all of us is internal commitment to our part of the covenant. By dint of prayer, reflection, and awakened observance we make our following of Christ something almost natural, something coming from our hearts sort of like a "second nature." St. Benedict in his "Rule for Monasteries" writes of his hope that observing his way of life involving daily and regular prayer and work produces a monk who "runs the way of God's commandments" (see the Prologue). Our prayer, too, should be that we live and act in all we do out of a genuine heartfelt love of God which determines and directs all we do.

Saturday of the Second Week in Ordinary Time—
Living with misunderstanding

Readings: Heb 9:2-3, 11-14; Mark 3:20-21
Resp. Psalm: Ps 47:2-3, 6-7, 8-9 (L 316)

The Letter to the Hebrews, no matter how much or how little we understand all its references to Jewish rituals, does make us think of sacrifice and priests. We're reminded that the offering of Jesus our high priest was above all interior, although he certainly gave up his body in sacrifice. In actual fact, of course, our spirit and body form the one person each of us is. He "offered himself unblemished to God" (Heb 9:14). Any true giving to God must come from the heart and involve the gift of self. Even in the case of the Son of God, this gift must be made again and again; new moments and new situations require the gift to be confirmed. As the true human being he was, Jesus had to agree to make this sacrifice and had to persevere in it. One can easily imagine that a moment like the one in today's Gospel must have required Jesus to make another interior yes to God. This is a very short and shocking episode. Jesus, besieged by the crowds, is teaching and healing and unable even to eat. Mark says, "When his relatives heard of this they set out to seize him, for they said, 'He is out of his mind'" (Mark 3:21). The misunderstood young person is almost a cliché in our world. Here the man Jesus, in his thirties, has to face the far-reaching incomprehension of his family. That, too, must be accepted and made part of the self-emptying offering to God. Our participation in the offering of Jesus may mean for us, too, an acceptance of the fact that those closest to us may not understand or share our faith or worship.

Monday of the Third Week in Ordinary Time—
More misunderstanding

Readings: Heb 9:15, 24-28; Mark 3:22-30
Resp. Psalm: Ps 98:1, 2-3ab, 3cd-4, 5-6 (L 317)

Just preceding today's reading from Mark was the story, read on Saturday, about how the family of Jesus found his mission so difficult to understand. They had said, "He is out of his mind" (3:21). That was literally forgivable; the Son of the carpenter was attracting crowds so huge that he had no time to eat. Today the misunderstanding of Jesus gets qualitatively worse; in fact, it becomes a blasphemous charge that Jesus castigates in the strongest terms. The scribes have accused him of expelling demons by the power of the devil. Jesus tells them, "Whoever blasphemes against the Holy Spirit will never have forgiveness, but is guilty of an everlasting sin" (Mark 3:29). The limitation on God's mercy, if we can even call it that, refers to this one most specific type of sin: the sin of denying God's goodness toward us and of ascribing Jesus' work to Satan. Most important for us ordinary mortals with our sins of avarice, indifference, envy, slander, sensuality, lying, adultery, dishonesty, or fraud is what precedes these strong words to the scribes: "Amen, I say to you, all sins and all blasphemies that people utter will be forgiven them" (3:28). Despite the language of our translation, it is clear that the Lord is telling us all, women and men, that every sin will be forgiven except the particular one of the scribes. We simply must be willing to be sorry and begin again with the help of the sacrament of reconciliation, prayer, and Mass.

Tuesday of the Third Week in Ordinary Time—
Sacrifice built into daily life

Readings: Heb 10:1-10; Mark 3:31-35
Resp. Psalm: Ps 40:2 and 4ab, 7-8a, 10, 11 (L 318)

Simplified expressions in Scripture sometimes seem to say that God sent his Son to earth with instructions to get himself killed by evil men because that's what God wanted. But the reality is not bloodthirsty and closer to our experience. That first scenario makes God appear cruel and unwilling to give some humans even a chance. Today in the Letter to the Hebrews the writer has Jesus say that God did not want the sacrifices of animals but that he, Jesus, had come, instead, to do God's will. In the Gospel Jesus says that whoever does the will of God is closest to him and is, in fact, his brother and sister and mother. The will of God is not some plan written down way before we appeared on the scene which lays out all we should do; God's will allows for our freedom and cooperation. The will of God for us is to live according to the word of God and after the model God has given us in Jesus above all, but also in other great women and men of the Bible and of our lives. Living this way may well mean confrontation with the world around us and with the powers of this world and perhaps even lead to persecution, suffering, and death. The sacrifice Jesus offers to God and which we offer in our own way is the acceptance of the suffering and difficulty inherent in our attempt to live as God wills. In this sense, we often have some part of that sacrifice to offer daily with our high priest at this altar.

Wednesday of the Third Week in Ordinary Time—
Attentive to what and who is before us

Readings: Heb 10:11-18; Mark 4:1-20
Resp. Psalm: Ps 110:1, 2, 3, 4 (L 319)

Like many another Gospel story, the parable of the sower and the seed is almost too familiar. We find it hard to expect anything fresh and even to listen. Perhaps we're even amazed that, as Mark says, "those present along with the Twelve questioned him about the parables" (Mark 4:10). We think, isn't it obvious? But this line of thought, often unnoticed, indicates that there were, there are some people interested enough to probe more and to reflect and ask questions. Not simply in regard to this parable, but any Scripture we hear or read, there are questions to ask ourselves: Do we close ourselves to anything new by thinking we know it all? How receptive are we really? How much do we take it to heart? Do we look for some application in our own life? Nearly all of us need to listen better and to be more attentive to what we hear, even to those around us. It's related to the matter of avoiding routine. Going to Mass or celebrating Mass, prayer, Scripture, homilies—how do we keep these from being almost meaningless routine? So often we leave the church and for the life of us can't remember anything we heard. We should not easily accept this numbing routine; it can be resisted. Certainly some things should be routine and save us time as a consequence, for example, tying our shoes. But relations with others and with God, prayer, hearing Scripture, and attending Mass—here we're right to fight routine. One way is to intend, anew each day, to put aside all other thoughts and give our full attention to the person to whom we're talking, to the one talking to us, or to the readings we hear. We can all do better than resign ourselves to lifeless routine.

Thursday of the Third Week in Ordinary Time—
Let our hope shine forth

Readings: Heb 10:19-25; Mark 4:21-25
Resp. Psalm: Ps 24:1-2, 3-4ab, 5-6 (L 320)

Today's verses from the Letter to the Hebrews speak (if we look carefully at them) of faith, hope, and love. But in general the emphasis in this Letter is on hope. This may be very timely. We live in a world where increasingly we question what our great scientific and technological ability is doing; are we destroying more than we are saving or improving? Certainly human behavior as seen in wars, conflicts, and crime doesn't suggest that everything is getting better in every way. Progress seems spotty or even false in many areas. The temptation to discouragement and despair is very strong. Our society has a pretty weak—at best—notion of how the Son of God has entered our world to save it. That understanding has disappeared from the hearts of many of our fellow citizens just as completely as December's Christmas carols have from our hearing. To "hold unwaveringly to our confession that gives us hope" (Heb 10:23) is a necessity for ourselves and a duty to our world. Our hope, Hebrews reminds us, is based on our faith in the sacrifice of Jesus for our world. Evidence of hope is a good part of what Christians give to the world; hope is a good part of the Light we are meant to lift up for the enlightenment of the world. We need not be apologetic about our hope, but generous in offering it to those among whom and with whom we live. We probably pray often for an increase of faith and for more love. As we are once again united in and to Christ today, we pray that our hope in him shine forth brightly in our manner and conversation.

Friday of the Third Week in Ordinary Time—
Patience with the unavoidable

Readings: Heb 10:32-39; Mark 4:26-34
Resp. Psalm: Ps 37:3-4, 5-6, 23-24, 39-40 (L 321)

"You need endurance to do the will of God and receive what he has promised," we hear in today's selection from the Letter to the Hebrews (10:36). Endurance in the sense of patience is one of the most down-to-

93

earth qualities of Christian's life. We need it so often and it is so painful to many of us. In its most extreme form, patience is identical with
terrible suffering; even the word "patience" comes from a Latin stem
meaning "to suffer." Patience is involved in everything from waiting for
others, to persisting in tediously slow efforts, to enduring unavoidable
suffering and discomfort in illness. As one of today's parables argues,
the growth of crops seems miraculous in its quietness and inevitability; yet for the farmer it may seem to take ages. Patience is required.
One can imagine the amount of patience the saints needed to stay with
their often disheartening efforts for the neglected and unwanted. Just
to persist in the daily work of being a Christian when there is so little
emotional satisfaction is another exercise of patience. Again, the model
and source of patience for us is Jesus who not only endured death on
a cross but throughout his active ministry put up with the incomprehension of his hearers and of his disciples. The cross we are to take up
daily is in very great part simply a matter of enduring the pains, disappointments, tedium, and the frustration of our jobs, of the sameness
of those jobs, and of the difficult people and circumstances which are
part of the job. Before us here daily on the altar we have set, under the
signs of bread and wine, the suffering, the patience, and death of the
Lord. From it we can draw the strength to be patient and to accept the
unavoidable pains of daily life.

Saturday of the Third Week in Ordinary Time—
Living by what we do not see

Readings: Heb 11:1-2, 8-19; Mark 4:35-41
Resp. Psalm: Luke 1:69-70, 71-72, 73-75 (L 322)

Our coming to this building for this service today, daily, anytime, sets
us apart. It says that we believe there is an unseen dimension to reality
which is even more important than what is seen. Nothing is added to
the GNP (gross national product) by what goes on in this building. No
new products come out of it. We, of course, hope to come out more
committed to the good of all humankind, but our first purpose in being here is basically to testify to and celebrate our belief, trust, and
confidence in the One we do not see. We express that by signs, words,
and a strange ceremony around an altar. By all we do here we express
our confidence that there is more to the world's working and to our
lives than bills in the legislature, price rises at the supermarket, new
car models, the rise or fall of some president, more to it even than our
jobs, families, friends. We are here because of faith, the "evidence of

things not seen" (Heb 11:1). Faith means, among other things, that we believe another force than those mentioned just a moment ago is at work in all of life, and that other force is God. We trust that God initiates and supports our best efforts, that God is on the side of love and goodness, that we are correct in trying to give these (love and goodness) first place, more influence. May our presence here together in worship and prayer strengthen each of us to live by this faith.

Monday of the Fourth Week in Ordinary Time—
Something new in our life

Readings: Heb 11:32–40; Mark 5:1–20
Resp. Psalm: Ps 31:20, 21, 22, 23, 24 (L 323)

Obviously, a story about driving legions of unclean spirits into swine which then stampede over a bluff into a lake could use a lot of explanation and background! That wouldn't be easy and it would take more time than we have. Perhaps we can take away from these readings a reminder about how hard it often is to accept serious deviations from the ordinary. After Jesus had performed this unusual feat of casting out the demon, the locals "began to beg him to leave their district" (Mark 5:17). Undoubtedly the people who owned the pigs, and other pig farmers, were concerned for financial reasons. But in general, people find so unusual a feat to be upsetting or find a person like Jesus to be disturbing. And, if we listen carefully, Christ does disturb us. All of us have reason to be concerned that we too readily accept a rut in many parts of our lives. Very often to open ourselves to new music, new activities, new friends, or new reading could be good for us; it would get us to do some new thinking and experience another part of life. Might we not be in a rut if, when we still have mobility and energy, we spend each evening watching some inane sitcom while munching unhealthy snacks or having a drink? How about a bit of volunteering? How about trying something new, something more stimulating to our minds or hearts?

Tuesday of the Fourth Week in Ordinary Time—
Gratitude for the witnesses in our lives

Readings: Heb 12:1–4; Mark 5:21–43
Resp. Psalm: Ps 22:26b–27, 28 and 30, 31–32 (L 324)

There is a circular-shaped Lutheran church in a little town in Minnesota. Running all along the top of the inside wall are verses from today's reading from the Letter to the Hebrews: "Since we are surrounded by so

95

great a cloud of witnesses, let us rid ourselves of every burden and sin that clings to us and persevere in running the race that lies before us while keeping our eyes fixed on Jesus, the leader and perfecter of faith" (Heb 12:1-2). Below that text are the names of some of these witnesses: St. Paul, the apostles, St. Benedict, St. Francis of Assisi, Martin Luther, John Wesley, Florence Nightingale, Clara Barton, Martin Luther King Jr., and many others. The Letter to the Hebrews, of course, is referring to all the examples we have of biblical characters who kept their faith and their trust in God despite suffering, persecution, delayed promises, etc. Jairus and the woman with the hemorrhage in today's Gospel are further witnesses to trust in God's power. There is no reason why we cannot add to our cloud of witnesses all those dear people, living or dead, who have shown us by their lives and words what faith is. We owe them much and recalling them can strengthen and encourage us in the midst of our daily struggles: a teacher who took pains with us, a mother or father who showed us persevering faith despite serious obstacles, a friend who has always been there to firm up our resolution or hope, a neighbor in ill-health who inspires us. Think of who they are!

Wednesday of the Fourth Week in Ordinary Time—
Only the local carpenter

Readings: Heb 12:4-7, 11-15; Mark 6:1-6
Resp. Psalm: Ps 103:1-2, 13-14, 17-18a (L 325)

"Is he not the carpenter, the son of Mary, and the brother of James and Joseph and Judas and Simon? And are not his sisters here with us?" (Mark 6:3). These words are said by people in Jesus' "native place." They are a way of whittling down the importance of Jesus. In other words, they say, would anyone exceptional or any great person come from our neighborhood? This attitude seems to be an enduring characteristic of many of us. We spend our time (before the TV) and our adulation on overpaid professional athletes and neglect the hard-playing, hardworking boys and girls next door. We look for heroic Christians somewhere across the world and miss the ones we live or work with right here. It's a shocking fact that TV evangelists get incredible financial support from viewers while local congregations and pastors struggle and beg. (As someone has pointed out, the TV evangelist won't be visiting us when we're laid up at home or in the hospital. The local pastor and church workers are the ones who will be there.) Support and encouragement of our neighbors in their work, sport, lives, talents, and achievements are so often neglected in favor of celebrities and famous people. The real heroes are the little people, those around us who are doing good work and living good lives. The big guns get their adulation as well as outsized salaries. Recognizing the talent and goodness right near us, however, builds community and solidarity. That's what we mean when we say that charity (as well as many other good things, if they're genuine) begins at home.

Thursday of the Fourth Week in Ordinary Time—
Traveling lightly

Readings: Heb 12:18-19, 21-24; Mark 6:7-13
Resp. Psalm: Ps 48:2-3ab, 3cd-4, 9, 10-11 (L 326)

As Jesus sends out the Twelve to preach, expel demons, anoint with oil, and cure illnesses, he tells them to take no food, no luggage, no money, no change of clothing—nothing but a walking stick and sandals. The marching orders vary in the Gospels, but the essential is pretty clear. He wants his disciples to rely on God and the good will of others. Traveling lightly is either thoughtless, a way of putting one's confidence in God, or a practical way of living simply and economically. The little kid who decides to run away from home with a couple of items in his lunch box demonstrates the first. People fed up with the complexity of modern life and concerned about the environment often opt for a simple life as a means of lightening their burdens. Jesus commends simplicity and getting along with very little as a sign of confidence in God. This is much more difficult than may appear. Every other person we meet seems to be a financial advisor; many of us are looking for total security. If we're climbing a wall, we want a harness and a soft surface below. If our job looks shaky, we want to be sure there's something to fall back on. As we face old age and its frailties, we plan in hopes of not being caught short. Where and how do we leave some place for God? What does trusting God mean in practice? No simple answers can be given in a few minutes, but we should ask ourselves where in our daily lives can and should we trust in God and be a little less tense and serious about minutely planning everything in advance.

Friday of the Fourth Week in Ordinary Time—
A non-material legacy

Readings: Heb 13:1-8; Mark 6:14-29
Resp. Psalm: Ps 27:1, 3, 5, 8b-9abc (*L* 327)

In Herodias we have an example (as bad as anything in the tabloids) of the wrong kind of parental influence on a child: a mother who tells her daughter to ask for the head of John the Baptist as her reward for dancing! The list of moral reminders in the selection from the Letter to the Hebrews describes the kinds of good example we owe to children and all who are apt to be influenced by us. It can serve well as a check list for the genuineness of our following of Christ. As such, it bears repetition. Love appropriately begins the list; it begins the list and it could also summarize the list. Then we are urged to hospitality, "for through it some have unknowingly entertained angels" (Heb 13:2). What form this hospitality takes depends on our environment—it may mean neighborliness in some cases; it may specifically mean welcoming new people into the neighborhood or condoling with the grieving next door. We are also reminded to "Be mindful of prisoners . . . and of the ill-treated" (13:3). Next we hear a reminder of the high ideal of Christian marriage: faithfulness and commitment. Another staple of Christian moral life follows: "Let your life be free from love of money" (13:5); we must be content with what we have and trust that God will not forsake us. Remember with thankfulness those who have brought the teaching of Christ to us: "Imitate their faith" (13:7). Love, hospitality, sympathy and concern for the suffering, faithfulness to marriage, freedom from greed, and gratitude are ways that each one of us must discern. We owe it to our children and others to treasure and pass on these ideals and attitudes. *You are our helper, Lord; with you we have no need to fear. Be with us to help us follow your example.*

Saturday of the Fourth Week in Ordinary Time—
Prayer and work

Readings: Heb 13:15-17, 20-21; Mark 6:30-34
Resp. Psalm: Ps 23:1-3a, 3b-4, 5, 6 (*L* 328)

The tensions of a Christian's life are apparent in today's readings. First, there is the tension between God's initiative, God's grace, and our activity. Second, there is the tension between work or activity itself and rest and withdrawal. We should not accept easily the oft-heard opinion that Protestants believe they are saved by God's grace and

Catholics believe they are saved by their works. This simple description of convictions does justice to neither Christian stance. Our good deeds, generosity, and doing God's will—all referred to in the first reading—are the fruit of God's gifts to us. As the Letter to the Hebrews says, God carries out in us the good we do. In the Gospel we see illustrated the second tension. Jesus has urged his worn-out followers to get away from the demanding crowds. He and they need prayer, time alone, time to eat, time to center on God in order not to forget why they are working so hard and to be reinvigorated for this work. As we see in the story, others may prevent this. Jesus, out of pity, interrupts his effort to get away and responds to the insistent crowds who would otherwise be without a shepherd. We cannot put off the immediate needs of others for our own comfort, but we will not serve them well if we do not nourish our activity with prayer, quiet, and solitude. Such is the tension with which we Christians live.

Monday of the Fifth Week in Ordinary Time—
Care for creation

Readings: Gen 1:1-19; Mark 6:53-56
Resp. Psalm: Ps 104:1-2a, 5-6, 10 and 12, 24 and 35c (L 329)

We begin reading today the endlessly fascinating book of Genesis. This first book of the Bible is concerned with the fundamental issues of our life: the riddle of death, the nature of evil, the place of faith, and the value of our world. This book doesn't deal with scientific or historical matters, but with matters important to how we are to live in this world. Today's opening verses stress that this world we see around us came from God. The moon, sun, and stars are not themselves gods, but they come from God. Another very important teaching in this reading is that everything God made is good. We may take this for granted, but we shouldn't; there have been people who believe that matter, earth, and flesh are all bad. The environmentalists remind us in their own way of this basic truth: this world and everything in it has value and purpose in the larger scheme of things. We all live interdependently with every other element in our world and this is essential for a truly good and safe life. Creation is not to be worshiped, but certainly it is to be reverenced much more than modern people have done or more than we do when we waste its resources or contribute to fouling and polluting the world around us. Caring for the earth, our world, follows from the lessons of Genesis.

Tuesday of the Fifth Week in Ordinary Time—
More than productivity

Readings: Gen 1:20–2:4a; Mark 7:1-13
Resp. Psalm: Ps 8:4-5, 6-7, 8-9 (L 330)

In the past, some of the human and cultural traditions which surrounded the Sabbath, our Sunday, made it very unattractive to many.
The idea that Sabbath rest meant making sure that nothing we did
that day was enjoyable or anything that involved physical exertion,
may be an example of the kind of tradition Jesus rejected. In our day
the whole idea of the Sabbath, of Sabbath rest, has practically disappeared. A good number still keep the day by going to Mass, by worship. It seems irrelevant to many to imitate God's rest and put aside
the activities and work by which we make a living. But setting aside
a day on which we particularly honor God in worship and turn aside
from the activities occupying us the other five or six days is still most
desirable. It is desirable from the standpoint of our relation to God
and for the health of our spirit. For the man or woman who works
hard all week in an office or at a machine or computer, a little garden-
ing on Sunday may be a really contemplative and refreshing activity.
So much modern technology seems aimed only at making us "more
productive," as the contemporary expression has it. Isn't the business
of having a phone or beeper always at hand, of not simply driving
somewhere but eating breakfast and making phone calls while doing
so—doesn't all this assume that materialistic adage, "time is money"?
We can't, so the thinking is, let any bit of time be lost to profit. Simply
enjoying and living in the moment without thought of productivity,
making money, or getting ahead is to rest and allow for a genuine appreciation of God's good creation. Our spirit is only open to God if we
let it be still at times and empty of plans for making a living. What
sets us aside from animals is freedom from having to scrounge for our
livelihood every single minute.

Wednesday of the Fifth Week in Ordinary Time—
Formed from clay

Readings: Gen 2:4b-9, 15-17; Mark 7:14-23
Resp. Psalm: Ps 104:1-2a, 27-28, 29bc-30 (L 331)

Chapter two of Genesis gives us another story about our origins. The
first story stressed the place of the human being in creation by leading
up to the creation of man and woman as the climax of all God did. This

story puts the creation of humans in the first place and then speaks of God's making our environment. While the other story made the legitimate point about our supervision of creation, this one stresses that we are one with the world around us: "The Lord God formed man out of the clay of the ground" (Gen 2:7), that is, out of the same ground of which God makes the rest of creation. Here our stewardship of the earth is stressed more and related to our oneness with all of creation. We are "to cultivate and care for it" (2:15). We have many ties to the animal and plant world; we are all interdependent. If there is going to be anything bad in all this, it comes from the human being. As Jesus stresses in the Gospel, "Nothing that enters one from outside can defile that person; but the things that come out from within are what defile" (Mark 7:15). Mysteriously, we alone in all of creation can be the source of trouble, sin, and disaster. What comes out of us—our minds, hearts, and imaginations—is so all important.

Thursday of the Fifth Week in Ordinary Time—
Finally, a friend

Readings: Gen 2:18-25; Mark 7:24-30
Resp. Psalm: Ps 128:1-2, 3, 4-5 (L 332)

The picture we get from today's first reading is another unforgettable one from Genesis. We can just picture Adam sitting on a rock with the animals coming before him in a long file while he gives them names: giraffe, gerbil, tiger, cat, koala, and so on. If we took this image too literally, we'd have to imagine someone (but who? Eve is not on the scene) recording the names. The point, of course, is that it is the human who has intelligence and the ability to classify and distinguish. But most important in today's story is the emphasis on our need for other people and for human companionship: "It is not good for the man to be alone" (Gen 2:18). A dog may be a man's best friend, according to some, but we human beings need companionship on a deeper level. And so God makes the woman and Adam rejoices: "This one, at last" (2:23), is what he had been waiting for. Further on, the author describes the origin of the woman from the man's rib as an argument for the drive toward marriage. The two parts desire to be one again. Scripture does not offer very many opportunities to reflect on friendship and love. Today's story is one such opportunity. We need other people; we need friendship and love. None of us can really be too busy for friendship or love.

Friday of the Fifth Week in Ordinary Time—
We need each other

Readings: Gen 3:1-8; Mark 7:31-37
Resp. Psalm: Ps 32:1-2, 5, 6, 7 (L 333)

"And people brought to him a deaf man who had a speech impediment," we read from Mark's Gospel today (7:32). The words take for granted what is such an important part of our lives: our dependence on others for many things, whether we're deaf or not. But the word "dependence" has a very negative and unacceptable resonance for many in our society. Our world prizes standing on our own, being independent, really making something of ourselves. After instances such as mass suicides in obedience to a religious leader like Jim Jones, for example, people rightly stress the importance of thinking for ourselves. But in reality we are all dependent upon God for our existence, upon parents and medical people for nurture and health, upon farmers for food, and upon the courtesy of others for our safety in traffic. One reading of today's story from Genesis sees giving in to the serpent as typifying our human unwillingness to accept dependence. Genesis is always speaking of us and of our lives, and here the message touches a most enduring temptation: that to self-sufficiency. It almost seems that we only learn to accept dependence graciously and not see it as a dirty word when we're buffeted by illness, tragedy, and the deaths of those close to us. Probably only in grief, loneliness, or physical or emotional helplessness do we come to embrace our dependence as a good. We express dependence every time we come to worship, to this table. So much of life is only endurable because of the kindness of others and the help of God. So much of life becomes truly happy once we accept and actually embrace the help of others and the lasting love of God.

Saturday of the Fifth Week in Ordinary Time—*Who? Me?*

Readings: Gen 3:9-24; Mark 8:1-10
Resp. Psalm: Ps 90:2, 3-4abc, 5-6, 12-13 (L 334)

When we have misused our abilities or opportunities, we are like Adam and Eve: we hope to be invisible to God or to those we have offended. "Where are you?" God calls. And we say "Who? Me?" before finally admitting we are here. The author of Genesis may have been aware of all the excuses we can come up with for not accepting responsibility for our actions. The tendency, Genesis says, is always there. In response to God's query, Adam points to the woman and she, in turn, points to the serpent. Passing the buck has a long history. Accepting responsibility for our actions, especially when they have been publicly foolish and clearly erroneous, is often very, very difficult. Unfortunately, our national leaders have illustrated most clearly what we all do. Instead of lying, they "misspeak"; indifference to serious issues is usually an "oversight." Or, "my wife was handling my checkbook." Or, someone takes "full responsibility" and it's only words. A good beginning for taking to heart this first reading would be to pray for honesty, self-knowledge, and the courage to admit our responsibility.

Monday of the Sixth Week in Ordinary Time—
Cain and Abel are here and now

Readings: Gen 4:1-15, 25; Mark 8:11-13
Resp. Psalm: Ps 50:1 and 8, 16bc-17, 20-21 (L 335)

While full of intriguing mysteries like the mark on Cain, the well-known story of Cain and Abel has probably earned its fame because it speaks of genuine and lasting aspects of our daily lives. For one, it concerns the painful reality of hurt and quarrels within families. Is there any family that has not known a situation where son and mother have not spoken for years, where siblings have cut each other off, where husband and wife bicker, or where spouses have bitterly separated? Or, to take another element from this story, are any of us unfamiliar with the seeming injustices of human life like the way the offerings of Abel and Cain were received? All these difficulties mark human life: estrangement from others; difficulty in living with those closest to us; misunderstandings; questions about how the world, God, and nature treat us. We must find a place between a too easy resignation to these difficulties and an unrealistic expectation that somehow we and our families are exempt from them. Family hostilities and problems may be helped by counseling, but often what's needed is for one of us to swallow his or her pride and forgive and be willing to start anew. The inequalities which cause resentment or envy may be best treated by turning our attention to more positive elements of our life and not dwelling on what is simply unchangeable. Usually what the Lord does within us and for us at Eucharist is not to give extraordinary signs to comfort, convince, or strengthen. Instead, he responds to the least bit of prayerful faith on our part with peace, hope, a deep assurance, and, often, even offers new approaches to old problems.

Tuesday of the Sixth Week in Ordinary Time—
A good person is not hard to find

Readings: Gen 6:5-8; 7:1-5, 10; Mark 8:14-21
Resp. Psalm: Ps 29:1a and 2, 3ac-4, 3b and 9c-10 (*L* 336)

Yesterday we heard of the sigh from the depth of the spirit of Jesus and how disheartened he was by his opponents' words and actions. Today we hear something similar from God: "When the Lord saw how great was man's wickedness on earth . . . he regretted that he had made man on the earth, and his heart was grieved" (Gen 6:5, 6). But, humanly speaking, God was saved from despair by finding one good person, Noah. Isn't that what we can and must also do in the face of our discouragement? If we look around, we can find not just one but often many good people who give us and our world hope. Think of the Noahs in our own experience, in our neighborhood, and among those with whom we work. Couples have dedicated themselves with little fanfare to being good parents and spouses without great material reward. There's the widow who has lost her husband to early death and suffered other tragedies, yet is always on hand to share others' grief. There's the stranger who came to our aid in an unhappy time. There's the always helpful and pleasant co-worker. Most of us can balance all the horror stories we hear with examples of people who manifest God's goodness all around us.

Wednesday of the Sixth Week in Ordinary Time—
Improved vision

Readings: Gen 8:6-13, 20-22; Mark 8:22-26
Resp. Psalm: Ps 116:12-13, 14-15, 18-19 (*L* 337)

The Gospel of Mark often seems to readers to be simple and naïve. A bit of study, however, reveals much more. Today's cure of a blind man opens the second major part of the Gospel, which ends also with the cure of a blind man. In yesterday's reading Jesus complains with exasperation to his disciples that they are simply blind to what he is doing and who he is. Oddly, Jesus seems to have trouble curing this blind man; after the first touch by Jesus the man only sees dimly. It takes another laying on of hands for him to see perfectly. This is a picture of what happens to the spiritual blindness of Jesus' disciples; as we move on in the Gospel we see that they come to more clarity and their blindness likewise is overcome in stages. The fact that the disciples took such a long time to catch on to what Jesus was about is, in a way, comforting to us; it tells us they were not a bunch of gullible guys ready to believe the latest guru. Most importantly, their experience of gradually learning to see and to have faith in Jesus as the Savior teaches us that faith for any one of us is a progressive affair. It is never complete at any one moment. Experiences and changes in our lives all bring up new demands and make new requirements of faith. To say that we really have faith in the Lord as our Redeemer and Savior means a lot more when we are still able to say it after a life-threatening illness or the devastating loss of a son or daughter or the breakup of a marriage. Faith grows and deepens partly by more knowledge, but most of all through experiences, good and bad, that we have lived through and accompanied with prayer.

Thursday of the Sixth Week in Ordinary Time—
Human and divine ways of thinking

Readings: Gen 9:1-13; Mark 8:27-33
Resp. Psalm: Ps 102:16-18, 19-21, 29 and 22-23 (L 338)

The ups and downs of faith and the steps forward in faith and the falling back are illustrated vividly in Peter. It is Peter who professes his faith by telling Jesus, "You are the Christ" (Mark 8:29). A moment later, after hearing that this Christ, this Messiah, will go to glory only through suffering and death, he objects vehemently to this path. He who had called Jesus the Christ, Jesus now calls "Satan" for his blindness and incomprehension. Messiah, king, the one who will save his people—all this Peter can understand just like his contemporaries. But that this Messiah should save us by undergoing death at the hands of human beings, that Peter and they cannot and will not understand. We can understand well why Jesus told them after Peter had called him Messiah not to tell anyone. If those closest to him did not understand, how much more inconceivable would it be to those expecting a conquering hero! The paradox that life comes out of death, glory out of suffering, and victory out of defeat is one we begin to glimpse only by our having the experience itself. Logic or thinking cannot make this mystery reasonable. Like Peter, our faith seems to advance at times and seems so clear, so obvious, and so satisfying. Shortly after, in changed circumstances, our faith makes no sense; we're close to despair. Perhaps the person who is brought down—crushed by cancer, chemotherapy, and radiation and then has come back to health—perhaps such a person knows what Jesus is talking about. *Give us, Lord, a faith founded on rock that will weather the storms of life; help us to see your light and love beyond the tears, pain, anxiety, and fears of the present.*

Friday of the Sixth Week in Ordinary Time—
We cannot know all the implications

Readings: Gen 11:1-9; Mark 8:34–9:1
Resp. Psalm: Ps 33:10-11, 12-13, 14-15 (L 339)

It was bad enough when the Messiah insisted that he would only save his people and come to victory by going through suffering and death; but today Jesus tells the disciples that to follow him means the same thing: "Whoever wishes to come after me must deny himself, take up his cross, and follow me" (Mark 8:34). Instead of joining a victor's triumphal procession, Jesus' followers are, it seems, to follow his hearse. Like most of us entering the larger commitments of life such as marriage, children, or a new position, we seldom are able to see at first all the implications. But few of these other things we sign up for carry with them anything as ominous as what Jesus promises his followers. Other commitments may carry with them the possibility of suffering and death, but hardly of crucifixion and total rejection! Still, it may be good to reflect that we would probably never undertake any of these good things such as marriage, rearing children, or public office if we could foresee every hardship which comes along. We need, perhaps, to enter our great commitments with the abandon and generous idealism of youth and trust that God and maturity prepare us for and sustain us in the harsher aspects of life.

Saturday of the Sixth Week in Ordinary Time—
If God has been so faithful . . .

Readings: Heb 11:1-7; Mark 9:2-13
Resp. Psalm: Ps 145:2-3, 4-5, 10-11 (L 340)

Despite how spare the narrative in Mark is, he manages to convey well the impression of the spiritual yo-yo which is the life of the disciples. After the harsh realities of the preceding verses about the Cross and suffering, three of the disciples now are jerked in another direction by seeing Jesus transfigured. And not only this, but a voice reassures the embattled disciples, "This is my beloved Son. Listen to him" (Mark 9:7). If they received this reassurance in such a vivid way, we might surmise that this experience would help them through the dark days to come. Such experiences are rare. If we've ever been on the receiving end of an encouraging, energizing, and reassuring experience of any kind in our spiritual life, we should be grateful and use it to help us maintain equilibrium in harsher times. More often our reassurance comes not so much from one isolated and glorious experience of God and God's love, but from repeated experiences of how God has helped us through difficulty after difficulty. This gives us courage for the ones yet to come or that face us now. If God has been so faithful for so long, assuredly this will continue.

Monday of the Seventh Week in Ordinary Time—
Everything is possible

Readings: Sir 1:1-10; Mark 9:14-29
Resp. Psalm: Ps 93:1ab, 1cd-2, 5 (L 341)

A man asks Jesus for the cure of his son who has convulsions and has been thrown down by a mute spirit; it sounds like what we might call epilepsy today. He begs Jesus, "If you can do anything, have compassion on us and help us" (Mark 9:22). Jesus questions the "if" and says, "Everything is possible to one who has faith" (9:23). Perhaps we need to point out that the "possible" doesn't include circus-type wonders or something amusing and useless like making a turkey perch on our shoulder and say, "Tommy wants a cracker." The sixteen-year-old boy who prays for a Harley-Davidson probably doesn't come under this "possible," either. Jesus is not encouraging us to test God and see what odd things God can do, but is assuring us that within the context of God's will everything is possible, even cures of deadly illnesses. The petitions we are encouraged to make in the Our Father are all conditioned by our accompanying prayer, "Thy will be done." If "[e]verything is possible to one who has faith," "everything possible" must be understood to be anything that fits in with and advances God's loving intentions for our world. It is clear enough from Scripture that God does not will mortal illnesses, suffering, oppression, torture, or whatever else might cause human grief. Our best prayer is always accompanied by our willingness to trust God's intentions and the manner in which God may fulfill our prayers. We only know what is possible by trusting prayer to God.

Tuesday of the Seventh Week in Ordinary Time—
Our preoccupations

Readings: Sir 2:1-11; Mark 9:30-37
Resp. Psalm: Ps 37:3-4, 18-19, 27-28, 39-40 (L 342)

One could argue that the most constant temptation of the followers of Christ has been pettiness. Like students more interested in a basketball tournament or their weekend activities than anything their teacher has to teach, we Christians easily concern ourselves with frivolous non-essentials, if not with downright selfish preoccupations. Religious leaders can concern themselves with who stands where in the sanctuary or what gender the server is, while people question the very purpose of Christianity. We file our nails while Christ asks us to see him in the poor. Any of this seems pretty petty compared to the large heart, broad concerns, and serious issues occupying our Teacher and Savior. While Jesus tries to prepare his followers for his suffering and death, they are busy arguing about who is the most important, who is the big shot among them. Jesus in response stresses that the hallmark of his followers is service rather than position. The model he gives them is not a corporation tycoon or CEO, but a child. The same lessons have to be learned over and over again by all of us who claim to follow Jesus.

Wednesday of the Seventh Week in Ordinary Time—
Humans first of all

Readings: Sir 4:11-19; Mark 9:38-40
Resp. Psalm: Ps 119:165, 168, 171, 172, 174, 175 (L 343)

"For whoever is not against us is for us" (Mark 9:40). That's quite different from saying that whoever is not with us is against us. The words of Jesus give us a model for accepting all those who do good, who work to better the world, who serve others, who cooperate in combating the power of greed and exploitation and of hatred and prejudice. The important thing in the long run is not whether an action or good deed is labeled Catholic or Christian or Buddhist, but whether, like the deeds of Jesus, others' actions do good for poor and suffering humans. The teaching and example of Christ are powerful in motivating people to the service of others. But it remains true that many, without accepting Jesus' teaching and example, still put to shame those of us who claim Jesus. This is a reminder to us that God's grace works in many places and under many names. Like Jesus who says, "Do not prevent him" (9:39), we should rejoice in the good others do and cooperate whenever possible. Seeing how much good our neighbors do—neighbors of no religious belief or of quite different beliefs—is a wakeup call for us Catholic believers. Others' actions may simply encourage us or challenge us to continue the good we do. If all the good things being done for the poor, the addicted, the suffering, and the homeless around us are being done by others, why are we failing? We're back to the reminder we all need so often: what we do and celebrate here at the altar together, our solidarity with Christ and each other, must show itself beyond the church doors.

Thursday of the Seventh Week in Ordinary Time—
The eternal Now

Readings: Sir 5:1-8; Mark 9:41-50
Resp. Psalm: Ps 1:1-2, 3, 4 and 6 (L 344)

"Delay not your conversion to the Lord, put it not off from day to day" we hear in the first reading from the Book of Sirach (5:8). It sounds like an Advent or Lenten message! But if we know ourselves well, we realize that, like the church itself, we all need constant reform and not simply during some special season. For one thing, there is always some persistent, nagging fault still needing work. Our temper needs control; our mood needs to be more predictable; our materialism needs to be checked; and so on. Or, more positively, we need to reaffirm our commitment to some good work we agreed to at one time—some volunteering or neighborly act, some faithfulness to prayer or to the needs of a sick or lonely friend or parent. Procrastination or excusing ourselves from some commitment is so easy. We all need the energizing power of the Holy Spirit, the force which can drive us to make a difference in our world and our immediate surroundings. We who make the effort to come to daily Mass receive so much; we are exposed here to so much; we are touched by such good influences, by such power for good: "Delay not your conversion to the Lord, put it not off from day to day." *Come, Holy Spirit, fill our hearts and through us renew the face of the earth.*

Friday of the Seventh Week in Ordinary Time—
Friends, new and old

Readings: Sir 6:5-17; Mark 10:1-12
Resp. Psalm: Ps 119:12, 16, 18, 27, 34, 35 (L 345)

Today Sirach speaks of friends, a topic close to our hearts whether or not we talk about it much. In this first reading we hear a variety of viewpoints on friendship and we hear about a number of aspects of friendship. The author tells us to test friends, that some are fair weather friends, that a faithful friend is a great treasure, that we make friends by our own graciousness and our own friendliness, and other such comments. While Sirach has many positive comments, the text also suggests friendship is a minefield. In the Gospel Jesus speaks of that great friendship or love we call marriage and of how a man and a woman by marriage become a new entity in one flesh. Both readings are about, in modern parlance, relationships—something most important to all of us. Listen to the young especially and the conversation goes, "Where did you meet him?" or, "I'm bummed; I can't seem to find or keep a girl friend." The greatest accolade is always that so-and-so is my best friend. After that ardent period of youth, it's easy to take our friends for granted and cease to make new ones. The excesses and sentimentality of our youthful loves may have caused a too-sober reaction in us. To be able to "fall in love" or be swept off our feet by someone suggests a persistent and desirable youthfulness. Friends, loves, and good neighbors all are the most concrete signs of God's love for us. Do we do enough to preserve them, to save them, to develop them?

Saturday of the Seventh Week in Ordinary Time—
Receptivity and responsibility

Readings: Sir 17:1-15; Mark 10:13-16
Resp. Psalm: Ps 103:13-14, 15-16, 17-18 (L 346)

Today Jesus reminds the impatient disciples that little children are a model of how receptive and how open we should be to the kingdom of God and to all God wants to give us. Mary, the great model of how a Christian responds to God's grace, said to the angel, "May it be done to me according to your word" (Luke 1:38). Sirach beautifully details some of what God has given us humans: life, strength, power, understanding, a covenant, and commandments. The implication in all this is strong and clear: we have received from God in order to be able to give and to be good stewards of all this. We are not merely puppets of God, but we have been given freedom and responsibility. Sirach says God has given us a strength of our own and power over all other things on earth. Environmental concerns and the difficulties of maintaining peace all tell us daily how genuinely serious is this responsibility. Our stance before God every day is a mixture of receptivity to the abilities and opportunities given us and the obligation to do what we can with all this. The Eucharist daily confirms that the awesome responsibilities we have with respect to our families, neighborhoods, and our own selves are supported by our union in Christ. We are not alone with this huge task. The life of Christ pulsates in us.

Monday of the Eighth Week in Ordinary Time—
Dangers of walking

Readings: Sir 17:20-24; Mark 10:17-27
Resp. Psalm: Ps 32:1-2, 5, 6, 7 (L 347)

Health experts continually promote walking; most of us could benefit from it, they say. In a big city one of the spiritual advantages of walking a few blocks to a restaurant or to a play or a sports arena is that we inevitably have to pass a few homeless or poor people. Sometimes they ask for a handout; if we're out late enough, we see them lying in makeshift cardboard shelters or doorways. We can, of course, make the assumption that all of these are frauds, con artists too lazy to work for a living. But that seems a bit too broad a generalization. As we walk in comfort to our good time, their presence makes unavoidable the issues of wealth and poverty. The inequalities of our world are clear in the relative wealth of many of us over against the appalling poverty of homeless children on big city streets or of whole nations living in sub-human conditions. The constant reminders from Jesus in the Gospels about the dangers of wealth and the need to use it responsibly must make us stop and think. That puts it mildly; the words of Jesus actually shocked the disciples. Jesus' words prod us to act when opportunity presents itself either through political action, neighborhood action, or cooperating with larger movements to ease poverty. Our solidarity in the Body of Christ tells us we can't simply sweep under the carpet the problem of the poor. What we can do, of course, varies depending on our situation, our position, our means, and our obligations. May the presence of the poor at least alert us to whatever we *can* do.

Tuesday of the Eighth Week in Ordinary Time—
Giving and how

Readings: Sir 35:1-12; Mark 10:28-31
Resp. Psalm: Ps 50:5-6, 7-8, 14 and 23 (L 348)

In the Catholic Church when we hear today's Gospel we tend to think of nuns, brothers, and priests who have given up ordinary family life to serve God's kingdom. Both "giving" or "giving up" are frequently used words in any talk about discipleship. Some think of the season of Lent almost exclusively in terms of "giving up" something. Our first reading today from Sirach encourages us to think about how we give or give up. A priest or religious who has become bitter or crabby as a result of giving up things is certainly a poor advertisement for ordained or consecrated life. At times giving up Chivas Regal or choco-late or dessert means also that we give up civility and good humor. What Sirach tells us (and common sense tells us the same thing) is that giving, giving anything, which is not accompanied by good cheer, generosity, and real kindness is better left undone. Gifts and giving are soured by stinginess, bad humor, regret, or self-seeking. We've all been around to hear a compliment given, only to be accompanied by an unkind word which undoes the whole thing. Giving a greeting, a gift, our time, or a word of advice or encouragement only have value if given, as Sirach says, with "a cheerful countenance." Grudging and forced giving is no giving at all. Ungenerous giving may flow from an unfounded fear on our part that any true giving we do might diminish us. But giving simply makes us more Christ-like.

Wednesday of the Eighth Week in Ordinary Time—
Perseverance with or without signs

Readings: Sir 36:1, 4–5a, 10–17; Mark 10:32-45
Resp. Psalm: Ps 79:8, 9, 11 and 13 (*L* 349)

"Give new signs and work new wonders. . . . Give evidence of your deeds of old; fulfill the prophecies . . . ; [r]eward those who have hoped in you" (Sir 36:5, 14, 15). Sirach's prayer speaks for the tendency in all of us. We'd like God to show with some splash that serving God is right or, even better, prove God's existence and presence by signs or by some visible evidence. For centuries the writers of the Old Testament held to the belief that God justified our faith by always doing what was best for believers. In one of the psalms the writer says that he has never seen a good man begging or in bad straits (see Ps 37:25). If that were always true, we would have to believe that every poor and suffering person was in that situation because of his or her fault. The writers of the Bible eventually realized this was not a true generalization. And, of course, Jesus, a model of obedience to God, came to a terrible death at an early age. No, we believe in God without always having visible assurances that God is intervening. We may pray for years for the sick and suf-fering and see no change in the situation. Have not parents and others prayed often and much for a disabled child? And many still fill beds in hospitals! As Jesus told Thomas: "Blessed are those who have not seen and have believed" (John 20:29). Persevering prayer and closeness to God do not necessarily change the outward aspects of misery and suf-fering for us or those for whom we pray, but over time we experience a deeper, more inward assurance that God is with us.

Thursday of the Eighth Week in Ordinary Time—
The gift of seeing and hearing

Readings: Sir 42:15-25; Mark 10:46-52
Resp. Psalm: Ps 33:2-3, 4-5, 6-7, 8-9 (L 350)

The references to hearing and seeing in today's readings underscore both how important these are to human life *and* the deeper symbolic meaning of these two physical senses. Possibly only those whose hearing and sight are impaired fully appreciate what it means really to hear and really to see. The blind Bartimaeus, upon hearing that Jesus was passing by, asks him for the gift of sight. Once he receives it, he begins to follow Jesus. Genuinely to hear is to be receptive and open to what is being said, being open to what is. Really to see is to penetrate reality and go beyond appearances to full understanding. For Bartimaeus it would mean eventually to comprehend fully who this Son of David is. We close ourselves off from genuine hearing and seeing by being certain we already know and understand everything. Someone has said that too many people too early believe they know too much. In a most general sense, to be open to hearing and seeing what is means having a sense of awe and wonder. The first reading from Sirach models some of this for us. It sees the glory of God in creation; it sees the beauty of creation and signs of God's purpose everywhere. When we look at our universe and life itself as gift, we are acting more as creatures than as masters evaluating and judging the whole. It brings us back to what we heard our Lord say the other day about receiving the kingdom like a little child. "God, give us the gift of seeing all as gift and taking nothing for granted." How this prayer would enliven our participation here at the Eucharist if we would remind ourselves more often that Eucharist, above all, is a gift.

Friday of the Eighth Week in Ordinary Time—
Fruit in winter

Readings: Sir 44:1, 9-13; Mark 11:11-26
Resp. Psalm: Ps 149:1b-2, 3-4, 5-6a and 9b (L 351)

What a strange story! Jesus curses a fig tree for not having figs, yet Mark tells us, "It was not the time for figs" (Mark 11:13). We may be accustomed to mysteries in Scripture and things difficult to understand, but this seems so defiantly irrational! Even Luke, who like Matthew relies on Mark for much of his material, omits this story. Mark attempts to put the best spin on the story by turning it to some advice on trust and belief. Possibly some details of the story were lost in transmission; possibly we need more background. We do know that Old Testament writers frequently refer to God's chosen people as a fig tree in the Lord's garden. Cursing it for not having fruit as Jesus does could be a picture of God's judgment on his unresponsive people, the indifferent, even the enemies Jesus finds around him. God has a right to expect some fruit from his people, so long cared for and nurtured. Mark here turns our thoughts to greater trust in prayer. Is it perhaps that prayer expects and produces humanly impossible results, like figs out of season? No matter how little we can figure out the story of the fig tree, we all profit from reinforcing our trust in prayer, never giving up on asking for what we need, and continuing to pray for the suffering and sick among us and the discouraged and despairing. Not to continue praying for "impossible cases" could be itself a form of despair. *Lord, we know you can act in ways beyond our understanding; hear our prayers for those whose situation seems so hopeless. We put our trust in you.*

Saturday of the Eighth Week in Ordinary Time—
Becoming wise

Readings: Sir 51:12cd-20; Mark 11:27-33
Resp. Psalm: Ps 19:8, 9, 10, 11 (L 352)

Today we finish the readings from Sirach, one of the longest books in the Bible. It is part of a body of biblical writings called "wisdom litera-ture." Pretty generally in these writings wisdom is depicted as a wom-an and the seeker for wisdom at times seems to be wooing this elusive woman. Today's reading is typical: "When I was young and innocent, I sought wisdom openly in my prayer. I prayed for her before the temple, and I will seek her until the end" (Sir 51:13-14). Finally, he says, he came to know her secrets. For us Christians, seeking wisdom must mean, among other things, a willingness to ponder repeatedly on the sometimes obscure elements of the Scriptures. Stories like that of Jesus cursing the fig tree tease our minds endlessly; the teaching of Saint Paul, although given with confidence, seems to us sometimes so impenetrable. Wisdom is not the same as knowledge; wisdom seems to involve something more profound: learning about how to live and think by being rooted in study, for sure, but also attentive to what life's experiences tell our heart. What have we learned from growing up, from illness, from disappointments, from relationships amicable or hostile? What happens in our lives (sometimes quite apart from any plans of ours) often illuminates some of the teachings we hear or read.

One of the titles given to Mary has been that of "seat of wisdom"; we might say she is one place where wisdom lives. Like Mary reacting to the prophecies made regarding her infant Son, we owe the depth of our own belief in the Gospel and our spiritual reflection on it to being fed by what others say and teach and by our own experience. In many of the wise elderly we meet, their wisdom seems to have come primarily from their willingness to learn and to hear what God, the world, experience, and others have to say.

Monday of the Ninth Week in Ordinary Time—
The mystery of the suffering of the good

Readings: Tob 1:3; 2:1a-8; Mark 12:1-12
Resp. Psalm: Ps 112:1b-2, 3b-4, 5-6 (L 353)

The Old Testament book we begin reading today, Tobit, deals with a topic which we still find wrenching: the suffering of the innocent and the ill-treatment of the good. On TV and in the news generally, it's ever present: the misery of abandoned, homeless, or abused children; the exploitation of the poor; or the accidental or criminal death of parents. Jesus himself took his place among the unjustly tried and his suffering and death are put before us at this altar, a daily reminder of his solidarity with those who suffer. Tobit tries to do all the good deeds of his faith: he invites the poor to eat with him and he buries the dead left in the street. For the latter, as an exile in a foreign land, he is liable to execution. The good he does seems at times only rewarded with disaster. More will follow as we hear the book proclaimed. Jesus, the well beloved of his Father, is rejected by the people he came to save. Although in Jesus' resurrection we see the triumph of the poor and rejected, this doesn't immediately wipe away the tears of mothers with starving children or of those who have lost spouses or children to tragedy. We can't easily or flippantly console others without deep faith. Like Jesus, the best we can often do is show our solidarity with the suffering, be present with them in their agony and horror, and simply hold our tongue.

Tuesday of the Ninth Week in Ordinary Time—
The human heart

Readings: Tob 2:9-14; Mark 12:13-17
Resp. Psalm: Ps 112:1-2, 7-8, 9 (L 354)

So often the Gospels and Scriptures in general demonstrate how rooted they are in genuinely human people and situations by their honest depiction of the human heart and its complexity. Yesterday our first picture of Tobit indicated a compassionate and even heroically obser-vant Jew. We saw this in his concern for the poor and for the sacred duty of burying the dead. Today, after some years of blindness result-ing from what we would call a freak accident, he is pictured in a sharp dispute with his wife. Perhaps his blindness has led him to imagine what he cannot see or be sure of, and he seriously misunderstands his wife Anna. In response to his anger, she throws up several unkind phrases of her own. It isn't so important that we are able to name all these defects of character as it is important that we recognize ourselves in some of this: so often we misunderstand and judge prematurely; we lose our equanimity under adversity; we say bitter things we quickly regret but which are hard to obliterate. And, of course, in the Pharisees and Herodians who try to ensnare Jesus, we see another unlovely as-pect of the human heart which may also be familiar to us: a hypocriti-cal effort to destroy or cut down another. We can look at this Gospel in a larger framework of relations between government and church, but taken with Tobit the Gospel selection offers us a moment to reflect on how complicated and twisting are the movements of our heart, our desires, and our mind. How much we need self-knowledge and, as a corollary, how much we need compassion and understanding for the hearts of our fellow human beings! We are all in this together; we all need forgiveness and encouragement.

Wednesday of the Ninth Week in Ordinary Time—
At the end of their rope

Readings: Tob 3:1-11a, 16-17a; Mark 12:18-27
Resp. Psalm: Ps 25:2-3, 4-5ab, 6 and 7bc, 8-9 (L 355)

Limitations of time don't allow us to hear in church all the details of this well-crafted and absorbing story of Tobit. But today we see something of the parallel stories which make up the book. Two people, very far from each other and for different reasons, are depicted as so desperate that they long for death; one even thinks of suicide. Again, in the extremities of Tobit and Sarah, we can recognize ourselves. At some point in our lives most of us feel we've hit rock bottom and are hard pressed to keep up our zest for living or are tempted to despair. Tobit's surrender to God's will is all the more impressive when we realize that his faith held no hope for reward in another life. Sarah, too, although reluctant to crush her father with her suicide, asks for death from a God in whom she still believes—again, with no hope of a better life. In today's Gospel Jesus clarifies the resurrection for some of his opponents. Even our hope for new life with God, we must understand, cannot at times help genuine believers to ignore their feelings of desperation. Despairing and desperate people need our understanding and patience, not some over-simple advice to "cheer up." Perhaps our prayer for them and for ourselves might help lead us to some practical help for the despondent.

Thursday of the Ninth Week in Ordinary Time—
There is no God but God

Readings: Tob 6:10-11; 7:1bcde, 9-17; 8:4-9a; Mark 12:28-34
Resp. Psalm: Ps 128:1-2, 3, 4-5 (L 356)

No matter what we reflect on today, we shouldn't miss the ironic, almost black humor in the words of Sarah's father as he tells Tobiah to "Eat and drink and be merry" (Tob 7:10), for no man is more entitled to marry his daughter. The Gospel is almost too large to get a handle on, but perhaps we could think for a moment about the First Commandment, which commands that we love God with all our heart, soul, mind, and strength. The scribe paraphrases it by saying, "He is One and there is no other than he" and this commandment taken with the commanding love of neighbor "is worth more than all burnt offerings and sacrifices" (Mark 12:32, 33). By now in our multicultural world the scribe's words remind us of the daily Muslim prayer which says, "There is no God but Allah." Allah, it's interesting to note, is related to a common word for God used by the Jews, *El*. Doesn't this tell us that we Christians (Orthodox, Catholic, Anglican, Protestant) all have great belief in common with many other fellow human beings, the belief that there is one God? And that this one God is of supreme importance? Over against the indifference and/or hostility of some of our contemporaries, we have an important belief to proclaim by word and deed. Many other religions of the world, too, while they may use a variety of names, often proclaim one God. In our zeal to demonstrate properly our love for God by genuine love and concern for others,

117

it is possible to neglect the simple, direct worship of God. There are moments (regular ones, it is to be hoped) of prayer and worship in a Christian life devoted directly to God. Our relation to God necessarily comes to the service of others but, no matter how important that is, it also finds expression in words and actions intent on God alone.

Friday of the Ninth Week in Ordinary Time—
Light of my life

Readings: Tob 11:5-17; Mark 12:35-37
Resp. Psalm: Ps 146:1b-2, 6c-7, 8-9a, 9bc-10 (*L* 357)

It would take something more in the nature of an hour-long academic lecture to get across the point in today's Gospel about the Messiah. It is an obscure passage, one that is so far out of our experience as to be intelligible only with great difficulty. Our belief that Jesus is the Messiah, the Christ, stems from more comprehensible matters. In the first reading, Tobit, the man who longed for death in Wednesday's reading, is ecstatic at regaining his sight and at seeing his son Tobiah. This great story of the lives and sufferings of several people comes to its happy ending. Tobiah has returned safely with the father's money; he has come back with a wife whose bad fortune has been turned around; and he has come back with a cure for his father's blindness. Before Tobit's cure, Raphael says he will be able again "to see the light of day" (Tob 11:8). Tobit, after the cure, calls his son "the light of my eyes" (11:14). Both the natural light of sun and moon as well as the light of a loved person are vital ingredients in our own ability to survive life's darker moments. Many Hindus begin the day with a prayer to the sun. We can at least be thankful for natural light and for man-made light but, above all, for the people in our lives who literally light up our life. Like Raphael, they are God's messengers to us.

Saturday of the Ninth Week in Ordinary Time—
Gratitude and attitude

Readings: Tob 12:1, 5-15, 20; Mark 12:38-44
Resp. Psalm: Tob 13:2, 6efgh, 7, 8 (*L* 358)

The happy conclusion of the book of Tobit is accompanied by an exhortation from the angel Raphael, now revealed as such, to Tobit's family to give praise to God for all the good which has come about. The good works of God should be made known, he says. It is often only in such extremities as had overtaken Tobit and his family that we understand how little we should take anything for granted. When life looks like it will stretch on forever and our health, vigor, and prosperity seem to guarantee this, it is often difficult to think of everything as gift. But when all seems lost or gone awry, we often awake to the truth. If only we could see every day and hour, every good in our life—spouse, children, friends, work, health, care, and all the other wonderful things that may accompany these; if only we could see these as all undeserved gifts, what a difference it would make in our attitude. We would probably be more generous, gentle, loving, patient, and just plain happy. We can rightly suspect that recognition of everything as gift propelled the poor widow in today's Gospel to give of the little she had. *Blessed are you, Lord, thank you, our God, for . . . .* For what? Anyone of us can fill in the blank.

Monday of the Tenth Week in Ordinary Time—
What we do with the unavoidable

Readings: 2 Cor 1:1-7; Matt 5:1-12
Resp. Psalm: Ps 34:2-3, 4-5, 6-7, 8-9 (L 359)

When everything goes well in our lives, we think that others who talk about suffering are being melodramatic. When we ourselves are suffering, of course, it's a different matter; we pretty well expect the world to stop. Our first reading in this series from the Second Letter to the Corinthians begins with Paul speaking of his suffering. For some, Paul's talk about this is one of the less attractive traits of a prickly personality. But that may, again, be just another indication of our impatience with others' suffering. Paul does his best to point out the values found in the suffering which in some form (physical or emotional) strikes all of us. For one thing, suffering in Christ—that is, suffering where we find consolation in being made like to Christ in this way—can prepare us to encourage others "who are in any affliction with the encouragement with which we ourselves are encouraged by God" (2 Cor 1:4). On an even more basic, human level, suffering gives us an insight into something we often think happens only to others; it can enable us to be more sympathetic and more understanding. Paul also says that his suffering (ours, too) can be some encouragement to others; it confirms for them when their time comes that suffering, indeed, is a part of Christian life and another aspect of our imitation of Christ. Only the actual personal experience of suffering in some form can justify to us the blessings pronounced on it by Jesus: "Blessed are the poor in spirit . . . they who mourn . . . who are persecuted"

(Matt 5:3, 4, 10). None of us need look for suffering; it is inevitable. And something so inevitable Jesus makes a part of our way to God. At this altar we learn its value and find its significance.

Tuesday of the Tenth Week in Ordinary Time—*Learning Yes*

Readings: 2 Cor 1:18-22; Matt 5:13-16
Resp. Psalm: Ps 119:129, 130, 131, 132, 133, 135 (*L* 360)

We enter today's words from Paul in the first reading at a point where he responds to the charge that he has been unable to make up his mind or be consistent. Somewhat hurt by this complaint, Paul says he follows the example of Christ who was never anything but "yes." Christ always and totally fulfilled the promises of God: to everything God said, the answer of Jesus was "yes." We're all amused and generally tolerant of the many times a two-year-old says "no." They're cute even when they say no to the pureed spinach, no to help with walking, no to having the applesauce wiped off their foreheads. Forty or sixty years later a response of no to everything is much less appealing. A willingness to say yes more often to life itself, to its challenges, to the needs of others, and to the demands of the moment makes for a positive and generous person, someone who is an encouragement to the rest of us. All of us are helped, even inspired in our daily struggles by people around us who are positive in their outlook, who see, as we say, "the bright side." We are all brought down, find the atmosphere poisoned by the complainer or the person who finds fault with everything, the person who has nothing but critical remarks to make about others and all of life's moments. How much more of a help to any of us is the person who commends the good in others, who sees the positive side of a situation, who is able to laugh at petty annoyances, who enjoys all the good which is around us! They (and we, if we share their yes to life and circumstances) are truly the light of our world and salt for its blandness.

Wednesday of the Tenth Week in Ordinary Time—
Jesus and Paul were Jews

Readings: 2 Cor 3:4-11; Matt 5:17-19
Resp. Psalm: Ps 99:5, 6, 7, 8, 9 (*L* 361)

The Second Vatican Council urged Christians to greater respect and understanding with regard to the Jewish people. The Council participants emphasized that the Jews cannot be blamed for the death of Jesus. All in all, it was the beginning of an effort to reverse the centuries of sporadic persecution of Jews by Christians. Jesus and Paul were both products of a Jewish background and show the respect and reverence we should share for Judaism, the "parent" religion of Christianity. The very term we use for our relation to God, "covenant," comes from an earlier usage by the Jews. Jesus speaks in most reverential terms of the covenant with the Jews: "Do not think that I have come to abolish the law or the prophets. I have come not to abolish but to fulfill." Our appreciation for the teaching of Jesus and Paul advances significantly when we pay more attention to their Jewish background. Being mindful of their reverence for Judaism makes us respectful of the religion of our Jewish neighbors and ready to counter ugly anti-Semitism. It would help a great deal if Christians were the first to rebut the oft-heard stories that blame the Jews for every calamity or see some Jewish conspiracy behind every bad happening. At the very least the Christian does not tolerate such talk in his or her presence.

Thursday of the Tenth Week in Ordinary Time—
Elements in our transformation

Readings: 2 Cor 3:15–4:1, 3-6; Matt 5:20-26
Resp. Psalm: Ps 85:9ab and 10, 11-12, 13-14 (L 362)

For many of us, St. Paul offers serious challenges. We find it so hard to enter into his thinking and into his argumentation. It is often an accomplishment if we can find something in St. Paul that seems to touch our life and our way of thinking. The words about freedom and transformation near the beginning of today's first reading offer some possibilities to us. And in the Gospel today we begin a section of the Sermon on the Mount in which Jesus points to the transforming power of the Jewish Law when his hearers carry out the internal spirit of this Law, not simply the external words of the Law. It is not simply murder that is condemned, but the anger and abusive language which we permit and which is the source of murder. Although Jesus does not use here the language, we could say that he wants us to be free from anger and, in later readings, free from other crippling passions. St. Paul speaks of the Lord who is the Spirit transforming us into the image of the Lord. Practically speaking, this transformation occurs to the degree that we are freed from the chains of our desires, passions, and self-seeking. An essential aspect of St. Paul's teaching is that Christ is the image of the invisible God and that we are transformed by grace into the likeness of Christ; by putting on Christ we become more Godlike.

121

Our part consists in removing obstacles to God's transforming grace and opening ourselves to the freedom which comes through grace. The Bread we receive at this altar is not only our nourishment; it has the power to transform us into the One we receive.

Friday of the Tenth Week in Ordinary Time—*Surrender*

Readings: 2 Cor 4:7-15; Matt 5:27-32
Resp. Psalm: Ps 116:10-11, 15-16, 17-18 (*L* 363)

Paradoxically and often in the New Testament, the recognition of our frailty and our powerlessness opens the way to freedom and strength. To see this we have to surmount St. Paul's piling up of prepositional phrases. The power and the grace that God has given us is carried around in very breakable containers. This tells us that the power of grace in us does not come from us and is not something about which we may boast. Referring to his own life, St. Paul illustrates this by pointing out that although he has been afflicted, in doubt, persecuted, and struck down, he continually comes up alive and well. God brings him through all this. In St. Paul's thought, this is a liberating idea: because the important things in life, like survival itself, depend on God, we can be free from worry, anxiety, and struggle. This undoubtedly seems beyond the power of most of us, beyond even our ability to surrender ourselves to God. But the Apostle is trying to teach a lesson which perhaps only some experience like his can ever teach us. We might nod our heads in agreement with what he says, but at the same time we realize that we are just not there. We simply cannot let go of ourselves enough to allow God to work this way. But we can see the ideal and pray for more trust and more willingness to surrender ourselves so completely into God's hands.

Saturday of the Tenth Week in Ordinary Time—
No longer for self but for the Lord

Readings: 2 Cor 5:14-21; Matt 5:33-37
Resp. Psalm: Ps 103:1-2, 3-4, 9-10, 11-12 (*L* 364)

Tuesday of this week we heard Paul say that in Christ there was not yes and no but always yes. Today we hear Christ urge that we be direct in our speech: "Let your 'Yes' mean 'Yes' and your 'No' mean 'No.'" The context of this part of the Sermon on the Mount again speaks to our intentions; they should ideally be simple and pure, not requiring a lot of provisos and qualifications. In our world of never-ending litigation and the need to protect ourselves against manipulative language, such simplicity is hard to come by or preserve. As we probably know from experience, simple matters are not necessarily easy matters. For instance, St. Paul gives us a wonderfully basic statement today of what our life in Christ should be: "He [Christ] died for all, so that those who live might live no longer for themselves but for him who for their sake died and was raised" (2 Cor 5:15). What is more central to our following of Christ than this: to conform our own thoughts and actions to the model he has given? Just as he died for all and rose for our sakes, we are to live no longer for ourselves but for him. In a sense what is said is simple and direct: to be a follower of Christ means living no longer for ourselves but for him who died and rose for us. A little reflection, however, shows us that this direct and clear injunction is by no means easy or attained overnight. But it is the ideal which can unify and simplify our lives. It's what we celebrate day after day here at the altar. If it were an easy, once-for-all matter, it could have been accomplished within us long ago and we wouldn't need to stand here at this altar before the Cross day after day. But as it is, we pray daily: *Help us, Lord, to live no longer for ourselves.*

Monday of the Eleventh Week in Ordinary Time—
Having it all

Readings: 2 Cor 6:1-10; Matt 5:38-42
Resp. Psalm: Ps 98:1, 2b, 3ab, 3cd-4 (L 365)

Our language and environment seem to be so susceptible to standardization. Is it due to TV or advertising? Whatever the answer, clichés and a narrow range of language seem to take over and then fade away almost as quickly. "Show me the money." "That's cool." Unthinkingly, we accept and use many of these phrases. So often in our consumerist society, we hear as the highest praise for someone, living or dead, another one of these expressions, that he or she was or is "competitive." What different ideals come through today's readings! The words of Jesus in the Sermon on the Mount must strike modern ears as absurd, incomprehensible or, as we'd say, "off the wall": "Offer no resistance to one who is evil." And Jesus goes on with the familiar lines about turning the other cheek, giving not just your shirt but your coat as well. Similarly, Paul speaks of his hardships, hard work, and unwillingness to fight the world around him on its terms and concludes: we seem as those "having nothing and yet possessing all things" (2 Cor 6:10). Are these words just a lot of bluff? No, both Paul and Jesus are reminding us that genuine values do not get the publicity or the advertising money. We can find words for some of the important values in Paul: patient endurance, sincere love, hard work, innocence, and truth. Implicit are values like a good conscience, integrity, and generosity. With all these we may seem to have nothing, yet possess all things.

Tuesday of the Eleventh Week in Ordinary Time—
There are no undeserving

Readings: 2 Cor 8:1-9; Matt 5:43-48
Resp. Psalm: Ps 146:2, 5-6ab, 6c-7, 8-9a (L 366)

As we hear in some of the words and cries of St. Paul, the early Christians were as familiar as we are with the gap between verbal commitment and actual performance. In the background of the next few days' readings from St. Paul's Second Letter to the Corinthians is a collection of money for the Christians in Jerusalem. The Corinthians apparently have not been as forthcoming in their contribution as Paul expected. The Macedonians, on the other hand, have given freely: "the abundance of their joy and their profound poverty overflowed in a wealth of generosity" (2 Cor 8:2). Now there's a line which certainly questions ordinary logic! Part of the difficulty may be that we generally like to have limits. That's why a law about not having meat on some day of the week is so much easier to keep than the kind of injunctions we hear from Jesus in today's Gospel: "love your enemies and pray for those who persecute you" (Matt 5:44). There seems to be no end to the demands! We'd like some limits. We'd like to draw the line. Our preference is captured when we hear the familiar expression, the "deserving" poor. Jesus says that God does not distinguish deserving and undeserving; the Father "makes his sun rise on the bad and the good, and causes rain to fall on the just and the unjust" (5:45). And we're supposed to do the same. That's how we share the "perfection" of the Father—by not discriminating among those whom we love or for whom we do good. There's plenty to pray for here!

Wednesday of the Eleventh Week in Ordinary Time—
Without thought of reward

Readings: 2 Cor 9:6-11; Matt 6:1-6, 16-18
Resp. Psalm: Ps 112:1bc-2, 3-4, 9 (L 367)

He just doesn't let up, does he? The Lord continues in the Sermon on the Mount to ask of us a profound self-forgetfulness: "Take care not to perform righteous deeds in order that people may see them . . . when you pray, go to your inner room, close the door, and pray to your Father in secret" (Matt 6:1, 6). And St. Paul in the first reading from the Second Letter to the Corinthians is no slacker, either! He continues to push a similar generosity: "Whoever sows sparingly will also reap sparingly, and whoever sows bountifully will also reap bountifully" (2 Cor 9:6). Today's words in the Sermon on the Mount recall Lent with the talk about prayer, fasting, and charitable giving. Again, the emphasis is on not doing good things for commendation or reward, but doing them solely for God and with total trust in God. This ideal is, judging from the teaching of other religions as well, one of the highest ever proposed for human beings. The most popular religious work of India (*Bhagavadgita*) has a similar refrain: do your works without desire for reward. The ideal of living in the present, so frequent in various religions, also means doing what one does now without thought of recompense. These ideals propose a kind of purity of intention, an intention to do such things as prayer, fasting, and charitable giving without expecting that these will give us something in return. If there are good by-products, okay, but we pray, fast, and give for God, not for self. Do we ever learn this? Can we train ourselves in this? Possibly somewhat. God gives this lesson to us as we learn to share more in the self-giving of Jesus at this altar.

Thursday of the Eleventh Week in Ordinary Time—
The quality of our prayer

Readings: 2 Cor 11:1-11; Matt 6:7-15
Resp. Psalm: Ps 111:1b-2, 3-4, 7-8 (L 368)

The prayer we call the "Our Father" was, it seems, given to the disciples by Jesus as a model of how to pray and a pattern for prayer's priorities. It has become, of course (with the wording from an older translation of Matthew's version), the most popular prayer among Christians. But by praying this prayer we are in danger of offending against the warning given by Jesus which precedes it. He says we shouldn't rattle on in our prayer as if we think that the number of words or the repetition of a prayer guarantees success for our requests. Do not do that, he tells us; our Father knows what we need. Praying is not a matter of informing God or getting the attention of a very busy universal executive. Prayer must be an expression of trust, a matter of genuine statement of our needs and hopes, and a way of preparing our heart for what is or will be. We need to put the emphasis on quality. How many of us have gotten into the habit of requiring of ourselves that we say certain prayers each day and in the process have ended up rattling them off in a mechanical manner? Hearing our Lord's words about prayer is an opportunity to review and evaluate how we pray. Do we let that collection of prayers which we think we must repeat each day get in the way of heartfelt expression of our needs and hopes? Do we really get to asking God earnestly in our own words for help and care for a friend's marital problems, for that family member with cancer, or for our own adjustment to some painful aspect of our work?

Friday of the Eleventh Week in Ordinary Time—
What we treasure

Readings: 2 Cor 11:18, 21-30; Matt 6:19-23
Resp. Psalm: Ps 34:2-3, 4-5, 6-7 (L 369)

Why did St. Paul go through all the trials and harrowing experiences he enumerates today in the first reading? It wasn't by any means simply so that he would have an impressive resume to offer prospective converts! It was because of the urgency of bringing Christ to many. In the process of giving everything to this mission, St. Paul underwent and accepted all these hardships. Jesus says, "where your treasure is, there also will your heart be" (Matt 6:21). We are led to hard work, suffering, sacrifice, and the expenditure of time and thought and means by the strength of our devotion to someone or to some cause. What we are willing to work for, to sacrifice for, even to suffer for indicates what we regard as important, what has the center in our lives, where our treasure is. Any one of us can gauge the strength of our devotion to God or anything else by our willingness to do all these things. For what do we give up our own comfort and schedule? To what do we devote our time and thought? What drives us, motivates us, even gets us out of bed in the morning? New parents know what gets them up from their sleep over and over again during the night. Our Lord's words say that it is our treasure which draws us, what counts most for us, to which we give everything. It might be a bit uncomfortable questioning what truly is our treasure, but this is the direction of Jesus' teaching.

Saturday of the Eleventh Week in Ordinary Time—
Here and now with confidence

Readings: 2 Cor 12:1-10; Matt 6:24-34
Resp. Psalm: Ps 34:8-9, 10-11, 12-13 (L 370)

Yesterday we heard the words of Jesus questioning what our treasure really is, what earns our strongest devotion. Today's beautiful passage, unfortunately never read on Sunday, continues the emphasis on putting all our trust in God. Do not worry about food, shelter, and clothing. See how well God takes care of the birds of the air and the flowers of the field. Can't we presume God cares for us, too? God knows we need all these things. "Seek first the Kingdom of God and his righteousness, and all these things will be given you besides" (Matt 6:33). Today's passage clarifies the fact that seeking God's way and putting God first does not mean that we must forget about or despise the concerns and needs of everyday life. The issue is one of priorities. As is clear in Jesus' teaching throughout the Gospels about material things and about wealth, he does not consider (any more than the rest of the Bible) that these things are bad. What could be bad would be our putting them before everything else. A decent concern for food, shelter, and clothing is not opposed to loving and serving God. It is never the material things of our world that are bad; it is only our desperate pursuit of them, our putting them before God and our fellow human beings that is bad. Even apart from such an extreme situation, today's beautiful Gospel passage encourages us to a great and consoling trust in God. Pondering these words could help reduce the worry which so often prevents us from living generously in the present.

Monday of the Twelfth Week in Ordinary Time—
Judging others

Readings: Gen 12:1-9; Matt 7:1-5
Resp. Psalm: Ps 33:12-13, 18-19, 20 and 22 (L 371)

The next three weeks bring us readings from the second part of the book of Genesis that accentuate the blessings promised to Abraham and all humankind. While this is basically hopeful, the wrinkles and warts of our race show up vividly. Jesus pinpoints one of these, our excessive willingness to judge others. Our education and our ability to live in the day-to-day world both require that we evaluate matters, test, and decide between this and that, in other words, that we make judgments. Employers, public officials, parents, and teachers all must make judgments. Judging becomes habitual, and to get out of the judging mode becomes difficult. We catch ourselves, when we think of it, judging everything and everyone around us: hairstyles and opinions, ways of walking and vocabulary. Here are a few suggestions. Whenever we're tempted to judge others in matters not our business or when we have insufficient knowledge, why not turn the judging back on ourselves? How do I fare in the same matter? Our Lord admonishes, "remove the wooden beam from your eye first; then you will see clearly to remove the splinter from your brother's eye" (Matt 7:5). Further, we could look upon not judging another as giving ourselves a rest. Why not leave it up to God? Take a rest; remind ourselves that our knowledge of others' motives, personal problems, limitations, or strengths is generally too limited to make valid judgments. One final suggestion: couldn't we look at others' actions and appearance as instances of the wonderful variety in the world? Instead of judging, we could see what goes on around us in many cases as some of the amazing diversity of God's world.

Tuesday of the Twelfth Week in Ordinary Time—
No limits here

Readings: Gen 13:2, 5-18; Matt 7:6, 12-14
Resp. Psalm: Ps 15:2-3a, 3bc-4ab, 5 (L 372)

"Do to others whatever you would have them do to you" (Matt 7:12). We're so used to hearing various forms of what is called "The Golden Rule" that we rarely analyze it. Deep down, there is probably little we couldn't get used to as our due, "whatever you would have them do to you." Let someone bring the car around to the front door and shield us with an umbrella from either the sun or the rain as we move to the car. Let someone wave a fan over us as others serve us our favorite meal. Let someone do the cooking just as we like it. Let someone pick up clothes, newspapers, and wrappers after us. Let someone do all the errands. The TV we can handle; we have the remote. But let someone else bring in the ice cream or the popcorn. In fact, we've very likely already gotten used to much of this. And we often do not find it too unusual. We like ourselves; shouldn't others also? Some of this may be a bit exaggerated, but we're often pretty willing to take any amount of favors and service. A big romance with ourselves goes back to our infancy. We got a lot of attention and service then and may still miss it. So, treating others as we'd like to be treated really opens the door to a lot of kindness and service from us. If we're going to treat others as we'd like to be treated, there's really no limit to what we might do for others!

Wednesday of the Twelfth Week in Ordinary Time—
Judging rightly

Readings: Gen 15:1-12, 17-18; Matt 7:15-20
Resp. Psalm: Ps 105:1-2, 3-4, 6-7, 8-9 (L 373)

Warning against false prophets and spiritual con men, Jesus says, "by their fruits you will know them" (Matt 7:16). We're back to that unavoidable judging about which Jesus warned in Monday's Gospel. One can tell a tree by its fruit, he says. Judging, discriminating, is definitely involved. And the implication of the words of Jesus is that some judging is unavoidable. Today's teaching, taken in conjunction with the text the other day about judging, tells us, too, that what Jesus teaches needs to be understood in its context. In most cases, we cannot simply take a phrase and take it as the only thing to be said on the topic. In this part of the Sermon on the Mount, we turn to a legitimate and necessary bit of judging. We may have an obligation stemming from our position as a parent or teacher or pastor to warn against phony gurus, false evangelists or misleading teachers. We can only do this, of course, from the stance of someone who is informed. As we've seen in scandals involving well-known religious figures, often their deeds have betrayed them. In cooperation with other concerned Christians, we cannot neglect this kind of judging; too much is at stake. Nevertheless, even this kind of judging is to be done conscientiously and not casually. No one else can do that for us. *Be with us, Lord, and direct our consciences.*

Thursday of the Twelfth Week in Ordinary Time—
Faulty families

Readings: Gen 16:1-12, 15-16 or Gen 16:6b-12, 15-16; Matt 7:21-29
Resp. Psalm: Ps 106:1b-2, 3-4a, 4b-5 (L 374)

There's very little in our Scriptures that could qualify as escapist or never-never-land material. Some critics of religion like to imagine for their own comfort that people go to church and take part in worship to escape from the realities of everyday life. There, they imagine, we enter a world of sweet-smelling incense, quiet, love and peace, where "never is heard a discouraging word." But the reality is that we continually run into the same problems besetting our families and us; Scripture deals with real people. The stories surrounding Abraham are good examples. Today's reading relates abuse within a family, a runaway, and a prickly personality. Earlier we've heard disputes about money and property. A good and problem-free family life is probably rare or a dream. The middle section of today's Gospel is occasionally used at a wedding Mass; it suggests to the couple that their marriage and their home must be built on the rock of faith in the word of the Lord. Undeniably, a strong, shared faith in the word of the Lord is a central element for any real family stability. We ensure as much as any of us can a good foundation for a family or a home by hearing the word of the Lord, putting it into practice, and trusting his help from this table and coming here for forgiveness in times of failure.

Friday of the Twelfth Week in Ordinary Time—
A light touch

Readings: Gen 17:1, 9-10, 15-22; Matt 8:1-4
Resp. Psalm: Ps 128:1-2, 3, 4-5 (L 375)

"I am God the Almighty" and "Abraham prostrated himself" (Gen 17:1, 17)—such phrases from today's first reading embody the Hebrew Scriptures' sense of awe and reverence for the great God. We are pretty accustomed to them. They have made such an impact that to many the God of the Hebrew Scriptures is only a mighty and remote being who demands obedience. But there is another aspect of the relation to God of even such a great figure as Abraham. After hearing about the impending birth of a child to a hundred-year-old man and his ninety-year-old wife, the text says: "Abraham prostrated himself and laughed" (17:17). And in tomorrow's reading from Genesis Sarah laughs at overhearing the same promise. When asked about her laughter, she tries to deny it, only to be told by the Lord: "Yes, you did" (18:15). Whether because there is little humor in Scripture or because we do not recognize it, the issue of humor gets little attention in our faith. But there's a value in laughter, in a sense of humor, and in being able to look at some things in a light way. Not everything in human life need be on the same level of somber seriousness. Sarah and Abraham both laugh at the incongruity of the situation, at the idea that two such elderly people will have a child. There are odd and unlikely aspects of human life that we do better to smile at than take too seriously. Some things that happen, especially to ourselves, are simply funny. A sense of humor can often take care of aspects of life that do not deserve tears or rage. Also, humor puts into perspective many of the lesser irritations and problems of daily life.

Saturday of the Twelfth Week in Ordinary Time—
Hospitality

Readings: Gen 18:1-15; Matt 8:5-17
Resp. Psalm: Luke 1:46-47, 48-49, 50 and 53, 54-55 (*L* 376)

The Church has us use the words of the centurion in today's Gospel before receiving Communion, words expressing humility and great trust: "Lord, I am not worthy to have you enter under my roof; only say the word and my servant will be healed" (Matt 8:8). Hospitality can link together both of today's readings: our hospitality to the Lord in Communion and Abraham's to the three strangers. The story of Abraham greeting three strangers who are out in the scorching noontime heat of the desert is endlessly fascinating. Do they represent God? Is Abraham receiving them like the Lord? Notice he wants to give them a bit of refreshment and ends up killing a steer and baking bread. In any case, hospitality is a good term for our overall relation to God. Our growth as followers of Christ is in many ways a growth in receptivity and generous hospitality to the God who comes to us in the sacraments and in other people. Learning the Lord's wishes and eagerly responding to them is hospitality.

Monday of the Thirteenth Week in Ordinary Time—
Deeds which make the difference

Readings: Gen 18:16-33; Matt 8:18-22
Resp. Psalm: Ps 103:1b-2, 3-4, 8-9, 10-11 (*L* 377)

Abraham's bargaining with God about sparing Sodom and Gomorrah is another example of a somewhat humorous bit of biblical dialogue. Basically the point is made how even the smallest bit of innocence (we might say moral decency) is of great value in God's eyes. We've all had the experience on a particularly bad day on the job or just being in the city, of coming across a person or a deed that makes up for all the hassle, argument, brutality, and coarseness that has otherwise characterized the day. We stop for coffee and are served by a gracious and smiling person who stands out against the backdrop of insensitivity and anger. Or a colleague on the job senses worry or discomfort in us and shows concern. In traffic or in the checkout lane someone waves us on or ahead. For a moment we are reassured in our belief that not everyone in our world is looking for a confrontation. It's such a relief and this may be enough to restore our confidence in the human race and our hope for a better world. We experience the same thing when we come home from a day of painful meetings and sometimes even rude people to the loving embrace of husband or wife, of children, and of friends. It is enough to make it all worthwhile. And, of course, it works the other way around. Any one of us can be that light and restorative grace for others who may be experiencing life and other people as simply combat or cross. Let Abraham's bargaining with God remind us that we can go from this Mass to be that saving bit of refreshment and encouragement that bring hope and joy to some of those we meet.

Tuesday of the Thirteenth Week in Ordinary Time—
Where we put our trust

Readings: Gen 19:15-29; Matt 8:23-27
Resp. Psalm: Ps 26:2-3, 9-10, 11-12 (L 378)

As always, the behavior of the disciples in the Gospel stories is not merely of historical interest but, more, of relevance to our own lives. In today's incident the disciples who had followed Jesus into the boat become frightened by the storm threatening to swamp the boat. They turn, appropriately, to Jesus: "Lord, save us! We are perishing!" (Matt 8:25). Although the account is brief and clipped, it seems apparent that Jesus is disappointed with the depth of their trust. He wakes to quiet the storm, but says to the disciples: "Why are you terrified, O you of little faith?" (8:26). Faith is tested and shows its true character in difficulties, in crushing disappointment, in sorrow, or in betrayal. The demeanor of the disciples in their trial tells the rest of us that our faith is never to be taken for granted. How do we know ours will hold up? What can we do to prepare ourselves for the times which try our faith? Since faith is initially God's gift, paradoxically, we must trust that God sustains our faith. Much of a Christian's spirituality is working and praying for a deeper and more pervasive faith. *Lord, we know from the Gospels your power and loving care; help us truly to trust you above all other powers and securities, and more and more to put our deepest trust in you rather than in our own power and plans.*

Wednesday of the Thirteenth Week in Ordinary Time—
Chosen and responsible

Readings: Gen 21:5, 8-20a; Matt 8:28-34
Resp. Psalm: Ps 34:7-8, 10-11, 12-13 (L 379)

The story of Hagar and Ishmael shows God's solicitude for those who are not the stars of the story and who are not the chosen in this great saga of Abraham and his family. Abraham himself apparently did what he could to ease the expulsion of Hagar and Ishmael, but eventually it is not enough. God hears the cries of Ishmael and the fears of Hagar. He provides water in the desert, says he will also make of him a great nation, and "was with the boy as he grew up" (Gen 21:20). The fact that God has chosen Abraham and his son Isaac as bearers of the promise for all the nations of the world obviously does not entail damning those not so chosen. The status of chosen people does not imply the exclusion of others, but is a responsibility conferred on certain individuals or a group that, in a sense, is also a burden. By our baptism we, too, have been chosen and with the maturing of our faith come to realize that this adoption by God entails living up to this dignity. This is why we are justified in regarding Christian life more as a response in love to God's goodness than a matter of obeying a book of rules. We have been chosen; gratitude is our response.

Thursday of the Thirteenth Week in Ordinary Time—
Total trust

Readings: Gen 22:1b-19; Matt 9:1-8
Resp. Psalm: Ps 115:1-2, 3-4, 5-6, 8-9 (L 380)

The Abraham-Isaac story is deceptively familiar and even obvious. We see it through the traditional lenses as a foreshadowing, a picture, of that love for us by which God allowed his only begotten Son to endure death for our sake. But considered from a psychological viewpoint, it raises many questions. For example, some would say: "None but an evil demon can ask of a father to sacrifice his only son" (see David Cotter, *Genesis*, Berit Olam [Collegeville: Liturgical Press, 2003]). Others ask: how could Abraham ever forgive God for this trial? Or, how could Isaac ever endure his father after this? Scripture commentators point out that human sacrifice had been practiced not only by Israel's neighbors but by the Hebrews themselves, and this story in its original form meant to show Yahweh's *rejection* of such a practice: "Do not lay your hand on the boy" (Gen 22:12). If we can abstract from the psychological horrors seen in this story, we can find a profound lesson about faith and trust. In his willingness to obey God, Abraham would not only be killing his son but also committing a kind of suicide by ending all his chances for hoped-for descendants. As he once gave up his past when he left his homeland in Haran, now he's asked to give up his future. Can't we see in this a model of radical trust willing to leave all security and look beyond disaster and even beyond death? As the Letter to the

Hebrews says: "[Abraham] reasoned that God was able to raise even from the dead, and he received Isaac back as a symbol" (Heb 11:19).

Friday of the Thirteenth Week in Ordinary Time—
Proving ourselves

Readings: Gen 23:1-4, 19; 24:1-8, 62-67; Matt 9:9-13
Resp. Psalm: Ps 106:1b-2, 3-4a, 4b-5 (*L* 381)

The story we have today from Matthew's Gospel tells us again a truth so difficult for us: people do not have to prove themselves worthy to be disciples of Jesus. He comes, rather, to call those who exhibit only faith and the trust that he can cure or help them. This is all we can offer and all God expects. Yet this is very difficult for us. We cannot help thinking there is some merit, some great merit, in showing God by our good deeds, hard work, suffering, and perseverance that we are worthy of God's blessing. We find it so hard really to believe everything begins with God and not with us. It may be this ingrained attitude which makes us judgmental in the sense that we think of certain people of less probity as unworthy. We don't think they have worked hard enough or suffered enough or shown enough by their lives that they are worthy. The attitudes of believers over the centuries have probably given color to the image so many have of "church people" as self-satisfied, stuffy, stodgy, and, worse, as hypocrites. The "church lady" of TV fame is so recognizable because of a prissy self-satisfaction which, unfortunately, has marked churchgoers in the eyes of many. Possibly we identify middle class customs too easily with the demands of the Gospel. Do we need to make the unconventional, those of questionable customs, more welcome at our sacred table?

Saturday of the Thirteenth Week in Ordinary Time—
Jesus Christ today

Readings: Gen 27:1-5, 15-29; Matt 9:14-17
Resp. Psalm: Ps 135:1b-2, 3-4, 5-6 (*L* 382)

The evangelist Matthew was especially concerned with the relation of the Jewish Law and faith to the teaching of Jesus. It's in Matthew that we hear Jesus say that not the slightest bit of the Law shall be undone; all must be fulfilled. For Matthew the old (the Jewish observance) and the new (the following of Jesus) are not contradictory. Instead he sees Jesus preserving the old in his teaching. We touch matters that are always to some degree the concern of living religion in ever-changing situations. How does the church preserve and pass on intact the teaching of Jesus in a world which is changing so quickly? There must be a way, Matthew's Gospel suggests, of preserving the core of Christian faith while presenting it in ways which mean something to people immersed in the electronic age and in a world so different from that of the first century. Matthew tells us that there must be ways for us today to tell the world the old story of God's enduring love and to celebrate this in a manner that means something to our contemporaries. Whether more inclined to keeping old ways of doing things or to adapting to new circumstances, we all need to face honestly the difficulties of showing our world that Jesus Christ is relevant to its problems. As we leave the church today or any day, once more confirmed in our union with Christ and his whole Body, we ask ourselves how to make that meaningful for others.

Monday of the Fourteenth Week in Ordinary Time—
The Lord in every spot

Readings: Gen 28:10-22a; Matt 9:18-26
Resp. Psalm: Ps 91:1-2, 3-4, 14-15ab (L 383)

"Truly, the Lord is in this spot, although I did not know it! . . . This is nothing else but an abode of God, and that is the gateway to heaven!" (Gen 28:16, 17). These are Jacob's words after God's appearance to him in what came to be called "Bethel," a sacred place for the Israelites. And the woman in the Gospel believes that a sacred power resides in even the tassel of Jesus' cloak. Although we may have a strong belief that God is everywhere, we still celebrate that presence in particular places at particular times. Sacraments are all about highlighting at particular moments and in special actions the presence and power of God which we know exists even apart from these sacred moments. We should know that God's love and power are present for us in any place, at any time; but without sometimes making a point of it, we tend to forget it. "Out of sight, out of mind" is truly descriptive of how we act. Our "too, too solid flesh"—Shakespeare's words—requires that we point to God's presence with and through visible and tangible things. Jesus himself, as the woman with the hemorrhage knew, was the walking embodiment of God's presence. Theology calls Jesus the original sacrament. In him all God's grace is available for us. Since his resurrection and ascension, his grace and love are available to us in signs and words, in sacraments. At this Eucharist we hear daily the words: "Do this in memory of me." Celebrating his memory with

135

bread and wine reminds us of the broader truth that God is present in all the ordinary matters of life.

Tuesday of the Fourteenth Week in Ordinary Time—
Crisis in the Church

Readings: Gen 32:22-33; Matt 9:32-38
Resp. Psalm: Ps 17:1b, 2-3, 6-7ab, 8b and 15 (*L* 384)

Part of today's Gospel is more immediately suggestive for us than the strange story yesterday of Jacob's wrestling. Jesus' cures have awakened hostility in the Pharisees, and amazement and hunger among the crowds. Moved with pity and concern to minister to them, Jesus says to his disciples, "The harvest is abundant but laborers are few; so ask the master of the harvest to send out laborers for his harvest" (Matt 9:37-38). In our more consumerist world, it may be difficult to arouse this same hunger in people, but many within and without the fold need and want the ministering and message of the Lord. Generally speaking, we are short of ministers of the word and sacrament in the Catholic Church. Priests are spread thin; congregations become larger and more impersonal; the number of services is reduced. One of the greatest casualties is the loss of a sense of community in a parish and even the possibility for parishioners to feel at home and know many of their fellow worshipers. While we await some genuine solutions, what do we do? We pray, of course; we ask the Master of the harvest to send us the necessary laborers. We can join small prayer and Bible study groups which at least connect us with some of our fellow Christians. And we can volunteer our services as helpers with the readings, Communion distribution, welcoming others, or instruction of children and new members. What will have to change in order for us to have more laborers in the field? "The harvest is abundant but the laborers are few."

Wednesday of the Fourteenth Week in Ordinary Time—
Listening

Readings: Gen 41:55-57; 42:5-7a, 17-24a; Matt 10:1-7
Resp. Psalm: Ps 33:2-3, 10-11, 18-19 (*L* 385)

The fifth-century founder of monasteries and a guide for many others, St. Benedict wrote a little manual for monasteries now called "The Rule of St. Benedict." The first line is, "Listen carefully, my son, to the master's instructions." A very little bit of reflection tells most of us that truly to listen is not easy. Genuine listening is not just for monks; we all need to do it. How many of us even remember hearing the first reading for today? Or the Gospel we just heard? We are so distracted; our minds are so scattered. It's not just the little kid out playing who can't hear his mother calling; it's all of us. Even when we're ostensibly listening (in a conversation, for example), so often we're not really listening. We're just waiting for a chance to say something ourselves, not necessarily related to what the other person has been saying. At Mass on weekdays like today it's rare that the presider can cover more than one point in the Scriptures. Some real listening on our part must make up for the fact that the homilist is only able to touch a bit of the texts. Further, listening in a much broader sense is vital to our whole interior life. We need to learn to listen to others, to circumstances, to the world around us, to nature (especially our own nature), and to our bodies; God speaks to us through all of creation. Finally, listening allows God and others to have a chance at affecting us. "Be still," we hear God say in Psalm 46:11, "and confess that I am God!"

Thursday of the Fourteenth Week in Ordinary Time—
Go and give as you have received

Readings: Gen 44:18-21, 23b-29; 45:1-5; Matt 10:7-15
Resp. Psalm: Ps 105:16-17, 18-19, 20-21 (L 386)

For Christians the key to the Scriptures is our Lord Jesus Christ. His life and mission shed light on so much that otherwise remains simply impenetrable. And these other parts of the Bible often do New Testament events the same favor. Often it is that the significance and mission of the Lord is hinted at in some figure like David or Moses. The whole story of Joseph in Egypt is an obvious example. The parallels between Jesus and Joseph are many and offer good material for our reflection. In each case there is a betrayal by his brothers, the repentance by some of them, and a great good coming out of the suffering and persecution of the principal character. Joseph's words to his brothers at the end of today's first reading point to Christ: "It was really for the sake of saving lives that God sent me here ahead of you" (Gen 45:5). The self-sacrifice which was, in a sense, pushed on Joseph, becomes a gift for his family in dire times. In both Jesus and Joseph we see a self-giving offered for the salvation of others. We have this self-giving put before us every time we join in this celebration in order to lead us to greater self-giving ourselves. Everything we have been given only comes to its full measure when poured out in selflessness learned at the foot of the cross. The Gospel reminds us, "Without cost you have received; without cost you are to give" (Matt 10:8).

Friday of the Fourteenth Week in Ordinary Time—
Christians and governments

Readings: Gen 46:1-7, 28-30; Matt 10:16-23
Resp. Psalm: Ps 37:3-4, 18-19, 27-28, 39-40 (L 387)

From the biblical viewpoint our government or the state is never an unmixed blessing. Undoubtedly, the state can do good for Christians just as it can for many of its citizens. Many apparently essential benefits flow from it: sanitary conditions, good highways, some care for the poorest and weakest, etc. On the other hand, the state can drag us all into a war and fail large segments of the population with regard to health and safety. In Joseph we might see a good man using an exalted office for much good. But the same state which makes that possible has brought believers to judgment for their beliefs and killed them for their beliefs: "You will be led before governors and kings for my sake" (Matt 10:18) and brought to trial before them, Jesus says. Christians cannot put all their hope or trust in government or politics. The Christian's attitude toward the state requires distinctions, care, and caution. At this date in human history, it must be evident that no state or government deserves simply blind approval of all it does. "So be shrewd as serpents and simple as doves. But beware of men" (10:16-17). We must be on our guard with respect to the state. We must question it, be intelligently involved, vote, and do our part.

Saturday of the Fourteenth Week in Ordinary Time—
Persecution and praise

Readings: Gen 49:29-32; 50:15-26a; Matt 10:24-33
Resp. Psalm: Ps 105:1-2, 3-4, 6-7 (L 388)

Confucius said that if everyone speaks well of a person, there is cause for concern and that if everyone speaks ill of a person that, too, is cause for concern. The Christian vocation requires a willingness to speak up when basic human values are threatened and, therefore, risk being spoken of badly. Pleasing everyone cannot be the final goal of Christians. Further, there is a time and place for Christians to encourage various movements and initiatives among our fellow citizens. At times we will be commended, but our Lord warns us that neither the commendation of others nor their hatred is the goal in itself. Neither persecution nor praise is the end. One can be opposed by others because one is wrong, just as one can be praised by others for the wrong reasons. Speaking up for what we believe and for the Lord to whom we have committed ourselves often brings repercussions. But the Lord says: "Even all the hairs of your head are counted. So do not be afraid" (Matt 10:30-31). So often throughout the Gospels, Jesus tells us not to fear. As we grow in closeness to the Lord and in faithfulness to his way, we should find trust and fearlessness also increasing within us. If the Lord is for us and we are with him, what should we fear?

Monday of the Fifteenth Week in Ordinary Time—
Radical demands

Readings: Exod 1:8-14, 22; Matt 10:34–11:1
Resp. Psalm: Ps 124:1b-3, 4-6, 7-8 (L 389)

Today's journalists would probably call the section of Matthew which we have been hearing for a couple of days "hard hitting." It is a collection of relentless sayings from Jesus about discipleship. Today, for simplicity's sake, we might single out three radical injunctions of Jesus. The first takes a view contrary to our ordinary view of family; the second argues against the usual view of suffering and pleasure; the third turns our idea of fulfillment on its head. In place of our usually comfortable view of the ideal family life, Jesus tells us that if we love father, mother, son, or daughter more than him we are not worthy of him. It must make us think at least about how and when this could be an issue in our lives. Second, Jesus tells us that if we do not take up our cross and follow him we are not worthy of him. It's pretty rare that healthy people are motivated to displace pleasure with suffering. Jesus tells us that following him will necessarily entail suffering, difficulty, and pain. Finally—and this is perhaps the most shocking to our age—Jesus says that the way to discover who we are is to risk losing ourselves for his sake. In other words, we find true fulfillment when we are not seeking self or self-fulfillment, but in giving ourselves to others in service. These are three radical demands giving us all something to think about. Maybe one of them would be enough to take away with us today for further reflection. A hint: all of these make most sense when related to the life, suffering, death, and resurrection of Christ.

Tuesday of the Fifteenth Week in Ordinary Time—
Our activism

Readings: Exod 2:1-15a; Matt 11:20-24
Resp. Psalm: Ps 69:3, 14, 30-31, 33-34 (L 390)

We can certainly see early signs of Moses the activist in today's passage from Exodus, story of Moses and the Israelites. The oppression
of his fellow Israelites early on leads Moses to decisive and dangerous
action. Those of us who live in heavily populated areas may see daily
on the way to our job or to shopping examples of people who at the
very least are not sharing in prosperity. We see the poor, the homeless,
the demented, and the unemployed and unemployable. All of us see
even more of the same plus pictures of the oppressed and starving and
the victims of war and hatred on our TV screens. There is so much of
this visible to us that we speak of "compassion fatigue," our inability really to get excited or concerned about the suffering around us.
The follower of Christ probably never is able to completely forget or
obliterate images of suffering humankind. Our "compassion fatigue"
is a pretty small thing compared to the genuine emotional and physical fatigue of the victims of war, poverty, and disease. While there are
certainly limits to what most of us can do about the world's problems,
we cannot simply harden our hearts against them. As we think about
what we can do, we can at this Eucharist at the very least place these
problems before God and ask help for the disadvantaged and generous
courage for ourselves.

Wednesday of the Fifteenth Week in Ordinary Time—
Not masters but children

Readings: Exod 3:1-6, 9-12; Matt 11:25-27
Resp. Psalm: Ps 103:1b-2, 3-4, 6-7 (L 391)

By his life and example Jesus shows us how the paradox of life from
death is realized. Today he makes a similar point about his teaching: it
is not the intellectuals or scholarly who have most insight, but those
who are most receptive: "Father, . . . although you have hidden these
things from the wise and the learned you have revealed them to the
childlike" (Matt 11:25). Reason would say that we get most insight
into ancient documents like the Scriptures by knowing the original
languages, studying the earliest texts, and knowing a lot about the
historical background of the writers. We cannot deny that all of this is
of value; the church requires, for instance, that priests have so many

years of study of the Scriptures and theology. But Jesus says that there is wisdom here which is open only to those who allow God to give it to them. Reason favors a process where we "master" a subject and figure it out, something reassuring to our egos. But the paradoxical way Jesus proposes to become wise is that we allow God to give us the understanding; instead of mastering it, we are given it—which may be something much less satisfying to our self-esteem. Much of the teaching of the New Testament is all about the fact that we owe everything to God's gift. This is what we mean by that sometimes fuzzy term "grace." Knowing how to receive this gift is crucial. We benefit most from coming before God at Mass with open hands ready to receive, with a heart aware of how much it needs, with a spirit hungering for God's food.

Thursday of the Fifteenth Week in Ordinary Time—
Rest in a person

Readings: Exod 3:13-20; Matt 11:28-30
Resp. Psalm: Ps 105:1 and 5, 8-9, 24-25, 26-27 (L 392)

The first phrase of the words of Jesus today comes as close as we can to being universal. Who hasn't felt "burdened" at some time or other? We look for all kinds of ways to be refreshed, be it from a coke or a coffee or a vacation or buying a new sweater. "Come to me," Jesus says, "I will give you rest" (Matt 11:28). His yoke, his teaching and demands which often sound so tough are, he says, easy and light. They are easy and light compared to the legalistic demands of the Pharisees and their successors down the ages who have tried again and again to make life consist of a collection of rules and regulations. We may have enough regulations regarding recycling, parking, and our insurance. Our life as disciples is built not around laws but around our personal commitment to Christ the Lord, to a person, to *The Person*. Most of us know from experience, especially that of falling in love, how demanding and satisfying at the same time are the requirements flowing from devotion to a person. Christian life, too, is above all faithfulness to the person of Jesus. In prayer and at this Eucharist we are devoting time and attention to deepening this relationship.

141

Friday of the Fifteenth Week in Ordinary Time—
Persons first

Readings: Exod 11:10–12:14; Matt 12:1-8
Resp. Psalm: Ps 116:12-13, 15 and 16bc, 17-18 (*L* 393)

Today's story of the disciples of Jesus pulling off heads of grain on the Sabbath to assuage their hunger illustrates the primacy of persons, of human beings, over things and laws. Jesus reiterates this principle in his response to the Pharisees who complain about this infringement of a law. The welfare of a human being is more important than a law, and the Son of Man is superior to any such law. We heard yesterday the call to loyalty to the Lord rather than to laws; today we hear more of this. Persons and their welfare are more important than laws; we moderns perhaps also need to be reminded that persons are more important than TV, money, business, games, and things in general. It is always refreshing to meet people who are financially very secure but whose whole concern in conversation and action is with persons, with people. We may say, of course, that it's easy enough for them to do this; their needs are taken care of. But, too, we may see it even more in the very poor and financially strapped who similarly show primary concern for other impoverished and suffering people. In this day of technology's reign and the dominance of the Internet, we may need more reminders that persons, the people in this room with us, are the focus of God's activity in this world, as illustrated in the Exodus of the Chosen People. As someone said in Yogi Berra style, "People are more important than anybody."

Saturday of the Fifteenth Week in Ordinary Time—
Alert, awake, up before the dawn

Readings: Exod 12:37-42; Matt 12:14-21
Resp. Psalm: Ps 136:1 and 23-24, 10-12, 13-15 (*L* 394)

With a very human description, today's first reading from Exodus speaks of a "night of vigil for the LORD" (Exod 12:42) as he protects the departure of the Israelites from Egypt. God takes no rest but stays awake the whole night, vigilant for the safety of the people, alert to any danger to them. Because of this the Israelites are told that on this same night they "must keep a vigil for the LORD throughout their generations" (12:42). Taking this more broadly, we hear an echo of a frequent message of Scripture to us about being awake, alert, and vigilant against evil and ready to take opportunities for doing good; this is quite contrary to being awake primarily to every chance to make a profit. One of the psalms has the same refrain which we might make into a theme for our lives, today and any day: "My heart is steadfast, God, my heart is steadfast. I will sing and chant praise. Awake, my soul; awake, lyre and harp! I will awake the dawn" (Ps 57:8-9). What a refreshing and inspiring way to face each day, each opportunity! *I am ready, Lord, to take advantage of all the day brings to praise you and serve others. I will do it joyfully, with a song on my lips. Not only am I ready, I am so ready that I am up and willing to move even before the dawn breaks.* This prayer may be quite beyond us at the moment, but it offers a refreshing and generous goal at which to aim. "My heart is steadfast, God . . . I will awake the dawn."

Monday of the Sixteenth Week in Ordinary Time—
Miracles are everywhere

Readings: Exod 14:5-18; Matt 12:38-42
Resp. Psalm: Exod 15:1bc-2, 3-4, 5-6 (L 395)

In the college classroom it is refreshing to hear (and it seems to happen more frequently) students showing less interest in magician-style miracles and more willingness to see other genuine miracles. In a discussion of miracles, there is usually a good deal of support for the idea that, as one young lady put it, "miracles happen all the time." By this she meant that in her life there were many signs of God's love and extraordinary care in the people she met and things that happened. We have some of this implied in Jesus' rebuke of the scribes and Pharisees who were looking for signs. Signs from God require some willingness to be open and to see God working in human life. The signs are there; it is up to us to see them, even to do our part. As the Lord says to Moses in today's first reading: "Why are you crying out to me? Tell the children of Israel to go forward" (Exod 14:15). Miracles in our daily life are the result of God's love, our receptivity, and our willingness to cooperate with God's grace in our lives.

Tuesday of the Sixteenth Week in Ordinary Time—
Misunderstood

Readings: Exod 14:21–15:1; Matt 12:46-50
Resp. Psalm: Exod 15:8-9, 10 and 12, 17 (L 396)

Is there anything more disheartening than to find that those closest to us do not understand or appreciate what we are doing? We usually expect that family members, spouses, and dear friends will understand what we are doing and regard it favorably. To find them really puzzled, angered, or shocked hurts probably more than the direct opposition of those who don't mean so much to us. Along with everything else, Jesus shared in this most heartbreaking experience. We have echoes of it in both Matthew and Mark where his family members cannot figure out what he is doing and wish to pull him back from whatever it is. Further, throughout the Gospels we have plenty of evidence that his closest followers displayed a mixture of trust in him and much incomprehension. This suggests, for one thing, that we can all stretch ourselves more to try to understand even the more bizarre behavior around us. And, conversely, we, for our part, can hardly expect that every interest, project, or concern of ours is going to get the support of those closest to us. Endeavors done in faithfulness to conscience have the support of the Lord and this is reaffirmed in the Eucharist.

Wednesday of the Sixteenth Week in Ordinary Time—
When to speak, when not

Readings: Exod 16:1-5, 9-15; Matt 13:1-9
Resp. Psalm: Ps 78:18-19, 23-24, 25-26, 27-28 (L 397)

A journey is probably the most frequently used image in any kind of literature for the human being's effort to understand life and to find one's purpose. As we hear of the Israelites' wanderings in the Exodus account, we should be sure to make all this meaningful for ourselves by comparing it to our own journey through life. Like the Israelites, we're often afraid of the next stage on the trip; we, too, would often rather stay put than grow; we grumble and complain; we're confused and fearful of the future. Although this may be true of all of us at any time of life, it's especially true with adolescents—young people who are often very confused and worried about their future. We ourselves may believe that the answer to many of our questions is found in the teaching of Jesus and in the seed he sows in our hearts. But we need patience with those, whether younger or not, who don't appreciate this and whose faith in the Word is not so sure or is undeveloped. The young, maybe even our children, need space to move, even to make mistakes, and they need patience and love from parents, teachers, clergy. Those who have been on the journey longer and have reached some certainties about how to live may have to restrain themselves from giving it all to the younger set. Just because we know (or think we do) how life should be lived doesn't mean it's always helpful to pour it all into ears and hearts not ready for it. We may all be going in the same direction on the journey, but there are many different ways of traveling. Our patience and gentleness with the less sure may be the most effective help.

Thursday of the Sixteenth Week in Ordinary Time—
Puzzled for progress

Readings: Exod 19:1-2, 9-11, 16-20b; Matt 13:10-17
Resp. Psalm: Dan 3:52, 53, 54, 55, 56 (L 398)

We've all heard of those phrases in certain strands of Buddhism used to startle people into thinking differently, seeing things anew. The most famous is probably, "What is the sound of one hand clapping?" Yesterday in the regular cycle of readings Matthew began recounting a series of parables of Jesus which form chapter thirteen of his Gospel. These parables continue for the next few days. Parables are a bit like these Buddhist phrases, called "koans." Parables are simple yet mysterious. When hearing or reading them we need, perhaps, to avoid two extreme reactions. In one case we may say to ourselves, "Well, that's pretty simple and clear." In the other case we might say, "That makes no sense whatsoever." The parables of Jesus are comparisons meant to open up some new facet of understanding for us. The comparison is taken from nature or ordinary life and for that reason may strike us at first as obvious. We know that seed sown in the ground, for example, needs rain and cultivation, etc. But there is enough oddity in the parable to make us wonder if it isn't simply absurd. Scholars say that parables are meant to leave us unsure of what they mean so that they will badger our minds into untried ways. We can all afford to let our minds be teased into more thinking, into some more wide-ranging dimensions. Just as we human beings are too complicated and rich to be completely understood by another person, so many things in life and religion are similarly without a discoverable depth. Not everything by any means is clear and defined like a memorized catechism answer. We should be happy that there are such things—that we can let our minds freely wander around trying to figure out what this parable might mean to me and my life at this moment.

Friday of the Sixteenth Week in Ordinary Time—
Requirements of a relationship

Readings: Exod 20:1-17; Matt 13:18-23
Resp. Psalm: Ps 19:8, 9, 10, 11 (L 399)

Referring to what is often termed our "permissive" age, we hear people say that God gave us Ten Commandments, not "Ten Suggestions." Well, neither one may be right on. We've probably all noticed that among Christians there are differences of numbering with respect to the Ten Commandments. For example, we refer to the Sixth Commandment as having to do with adultery; for others that would be the Fifth Commandment. For the Jewish tradition, however, the First Commandment actually is that first sentence uttered by the Lord in today's first reading, "I, the LORD, am your God, who brought you out of the land of Egypt, that place of slavery" (Exod 20:2). That's neither a commandment nor a suggestion; it's a statement. It's probably better to call them the Decalogue (as they often are called), a term meaning the "Ten Words." With this in mind, we might emphasize that the Decalogue is presented in terms of a relation to God; these ten words are the conditions to be fulfilled by those who have become God's people. They are the consequences spelled out of such a relation to God. Similarly for us Christians, moral standards are seen in much of the New Testament as the only fitting response to God's love. Our dignity as God's daughters and sons requires that we do not bring dishonor on the One who has chosen us.

Saturday of the Sixteenth Week in Ordinary Time—
God's patience and ours

Readings: Exod 24:3-8; Matt 13:24-30
Resp. Psalm: Ps 50:1b-2, 5-6, 14-15 (L 400)

Moses splashed the blood of the sacrificed bulls on the altar and on the people, a ritual that may seem quite exotic to us, but which is not all that incomprehensible. Splashing the blood on people and altar was a way of signifying their union now through the agreement they have made, the covenant. Regulations and laws such as what we call the Ten Commandments are among the conditions of the agreement on the part of the people. In today's Gospel Jesus envisions the people of the New Covenant, his followers, in their life in the church. While all by baptism and faith are committed to new life in Christ, it is obvious that not all are equally fervent or even observant regarding its conditions, that is, living like members of Christ. If we have any knowledge of history, we know that not all the members of the church are by that fact saints. Even without history, our own personal experience probably tells us how we have failed, sometimes seriously, to live as daughters and sons of God. In Monday's first reading from Exodus we will see a famous example of unfaithfulness to the covenant on the part of the Israelites. In the farmer who lets the weeds and wheat grow side by side until harvest time, we see the patience of God toward us and our sins. Further, the story calls on us to be patient, forgiving, and understanding with those who seem less faithful than ourselves. Others must be patient with us. *Lord, may we meet your patience with us with more generosity in the way we live our lives as disciples.*

Monday of the Seventeenth Week in Ordinary Time— *The force of example*

Readings: Exod 32:15-24, 30-34; Matt 13:31-35
Resp. Psalm: Ps 106:19-20, 21-22, 23 (L 401)

Within a little over four hundred years after the death and resurrection of Jesus, Christianity had become the official religion of the Roman Empire, covering much of present-day Western Europe and parts of North Africa and the Middle East. What a change! From being an oft-persecuted small sect, Christianity had become a state religion. It became fashionable to be a Christian; it was a way to advancement. Laws were made to promote the faith. It all sounded good to many Christians and such an arrangement continued in many places until modern times. Unfortunately, this often meant that Christians did not feel very much individual responsibility for their faith. Being a Christian was more a matter of where one was born than of genuine personal commitment. Believers depended on laws to enforce Christian belief and practices. The temptation to do this is still with us occasionally. But with a longer view and distance, most have come to see the bad aspects of this arrangement. The brief parable we hear today about how yeast is able to permeate and transform a large amount of flour suggests a better way to influence our society than by laws. People who believe in Christ and his announcement of God's love can often spread his Good News by quiet lives of faithfulness, joy, and genuine love. Studies and observation again and again tell us how powerful individual example can be, how people are led to Christ not by argument and talk, but by good example. The life of Christ in his members, reinforced at this table, makes this example possible.

Tuesday of the Seventeenth Week in Ordinary Time—
Aspects of God

Readings: Exod 33:7-11; 34:5b-9, 28; Matt 13:36-43
Resp. Psalm: Ps 103:6-7, 8-9, 10-11, 12-13 (L 402)

Scholars see in these early books of the Bible (such as Genesis and Exodus) good examples of how the final author or editor put together current stories from different sources. We should be a bit surprised to read today that the Lord spoke to Moses face to face. Elsewhere we've undoubtedly heard words about how no one can see God and live and how God did not show his face to humans. We'd probably understand more and get more spiritual help from the Bible if we didn't think of these passages as describing matters literally. The various authors are giving us their own insights into the relations of God and human beings. One says God and Moses were so close that it was like two friends speaking face to face. Another emphasizes that God is so different from us and our experience that we cannot see or conceive of God in this existence. Both make helpful points. One, God does choose to come very close to those who open themselves to God's presence and are attentive to what God asks. Two, on the other hand, in this life we cannot see God as God is. Terms like "friend," "face to face," and others are merely our efforts to describe something beyond us. In Jesus we have, of course, the more perfect picture of how our God acts.

Wednesday of the Seventeenth Week in Ordinary Time—
Giving all for the pearl

Readings: Exod 34:29-35; Matt 13:44-46
Resp. Psalm: Ps 99:5, 6, 7, 9 (L 403)

One wonders if the huge variety of anything and everything available in our world today, coupled with the ease of communication and transportation, doesn't contribute to making commitment so difficult for many. In good economic times, if one job doesn't please, there's always another. If one place is unsatisfactory, moving is not out of the question. Further, through the media and by travel we see so many different possibilities that "tying oneself down to one," as some describe it, seems too limiting. People have more trouble making a decision or a commitment. Yet, suspending our judgment and never coming to a conclusion makes real growth impossible. Without roots the plant can not mature to the point of producing its fruit. Without giving ourselves to something or someone, we waste our talents and time. Today's parables about the buried treasure and the really valuable pearl tell us that there is something to which we should give ourselves wholeheartedly: helping to establish the reign of God and keeping God central in our lives. The parables do not urge an unthinking gift of ourselves to whatever comes along, but a wholehearted dedication to what is most important. To forever hesitate and weigh possibilities can be simply a way of avoiding the generosity which commitment requires. Life is too short to spend most or all of it trying to figure out whether there is anything to which we should give ourselves. It's like marriage: at some point we decide that this is the person and give ourself to him or her without forever looking over our shoulder to see if someone better is coming along. The lesson is the same whether it's regarding a commitment here and now or that commitment which grounds our life and all else we do. The complete gift of ourselves to God is justified by the results.

Thursday of the Seventeenth Week in Ordinary Time—
Truly to understand

Readings: Exod 40:16-21, 34-38; Matt 13:47-53
Resp. Psalm: Ps 84:3, 4, 5-6a and 8a, 11 (L 404)

"Do you understand all these things?" Jesus asks his disciples, and they answer, "Yes" (Matt 13:51). Matthew is intent on contrasting the disciples with his opponents who refused to understand and were obstinate. If we think of the experience of all the evangelists and of other incidents in John and Mark especially, we cannot help but feel a little hesitant about accepting the disciples' yes as definitive. In Mark the disciples are shown as much less comprehending, in fact, they are generally quite at a loss. We who hear the words of Jesus at Mass and read them for meditation or study them for comprehension probably know by now that the agreement and understanding we come to in our armchair or at a desk is one thing. Accepting the words of Jesus in daily life, in suffering and disappointment, in cancer or a divorce, in aggravation and drudgery, or in old age is quite another. To take up our cross and follow the Lord is one thing; sitting in our La-Z-Boy reading the Scriptures is quite another. Grave illness, heartbreak, and false accusations are something else. *"Yes, we have understood all this" needs to be followed, for most of us, by something like: "Help me to accept everything this may entail today."*

Friday of the Seventeenth Week in Ordinary Time—
Nothing is too ordinary

Readings: Lev 23:1, 4-11, 15-16, 27, 34b-37; Matt 13:54-58
Resp. Psalm: Ps 81:3-4, 5-6, 10-11ab (*L* 405)

"Is he not the carpenter's son?" (Matt 13:55). Wisdom and miraculous powers are supposed to come in more elegant packaging, we often think, or at least come from a person in formal dress with some academic degrees behind the name. Certainly these powers don't come from the local carpenter's Son. But the teaching of the incarnation, the coming to earth of God's Son, is just this: God is to be found in someone as ordinary as this neighbor's son, someone who used no flashy displays to get our attention. We so easily forget the presence and availability of our God in the everyday events and people of our lives that we must remind ourselves of God's presence in other ways. Basically, this is why we dramatize God's presence in the sacraments and feasts of the church. In these special moments, we recall and put before ourselves what is always true: God is always present. Even the minute regulations we read in Leviticus today were concerned with coming to the same realization for the Jews: God is everywhere. We celebrate God's presence and recall it by highlighting it in particular places and at particular times. We find God's presence in ordinary bread and wine offered on this altar.

Saturday of the Seventeenth Week in Ordinary Time—
Cost of being a disciple

Readings: Lev 25:1, 8-17; Matt 14:1-12
Resp. Psalm: Ps 67:2-3, 5, 7-8 (*L* 406)

To varying degrees we all want to be liked; we want to live in peace and even in warm comfort with other people. Some of us carry this to the point of avoiding all confrontation and ignoring things really bothering us. Each of us faces the question of how to balance the desire to be liked and to live in peace with the need to stand up for something. In presenting the life and death of John the Baptist as such a complete parallel to that of Jesus, the Gospel writers tell the reader that opposition and serious differences are inevitable; for most of us they constitute a major part of our share in the Cross. Both John and Jesus were regarded as prophets, were taken into custody for shaky reasons, and were finally executed because of leaders unable to stand up for anything. Both were buried by their followers and believed to have risen from the dead. The point? Strengthened by participation at this table, the Christian at some time must face opposition if not downright persecution for following Christ. This is the Cross built into any conscientious Christian life. That other great model of Christian life, Mary, also had her heart pierced with sorrow.

Monday of the Eighteenth Week in Ordinary Time—
In this desert

Readings: Num 11:4b-15; Matt 14:13-21
Resp. Psalm: Ps 81:12-13, 14-15, 16-17 (L 407)

We read from the book of Numbers for the next several days. Like Leviticus, it's another book of the Bible that seems so far at times from our own experience. Yet it does speak to us. The book is about the Israelites' wandering in the wilderness or desert before finally entering the Promised Land. They are shown, as in today's first reading, as a crowd of grumpy old men, grumpy old women, grumpy kids. They are bored, angry, and resentful as they move through the often inhospitable wilderness. They grumbled and complained, despite signs of God's favor and care. Their experience in the wilderness is like aspects of ordinary life for many: difficult, boring or dreary, full of worry and danger. As we all know from personal experience, not all the grumpy people are in the Old Testament or the movies; a good number live in Decatur, New York, Edmonton, Newcastle, or Cairo. Yet if we're alert to the signs, we are able to recognize that God is among us, too, and that the heart of God is shown in Jesus who pitied the crowds which had followed him to a deserted place. Sometimes going through life can be a beautiful, exhilarating experience; at other times we feel like the Israelites: angry, resentful, and just plain grumpy. We would like something more dramatic than the Eucharist to show us that God is present; we want some sign, some God-given high. But, ordinarily, God is going to be with us and help us in much more simple ways: in our meals with others or through our contacts with good and encouraging people. The Eucharist reminds us to look for God in this life we live, in this place, with these people.

Tuesday of the Eighteenth Week in Ordinary Time—
"It is I. Do not be afraid"

Readings: Num 12:1-13; Matt 14:22-36
Resp. Psalm: Ps 51:3-4, 5-6ab, 6cd-7, 12-13 (*L* 408)

"It is I. Do not be afraid" (Matt 14:27). Along with the action of calm-ing the storm, these words in another way confirm for the disciples that this man Jesus has a special relation to God. They said after that event: "Truly, you are the Son of God!" (14:33). "It is I" was a frequent reference to God, for example, in the prophet Isaiah. The use of it by Jesus here is a way for his Jewish hearers to see a reference to Yahweh. Because this man who comes to the disciples during the storm is so closely related to God, they can and should have trust, not fear. Fear, it is true, is a reality of human life. If we are in a situation where we need to do something dangerous to help another (for example, save a child drowning in a pond), we rightfully have some fear and it makes us careful. The realities of life in our big cities, of life in a world where there are constant nationalist and other tensions also cause us to have fear. After seeing the weather report, we may fear that a storm will hit our locale. But if there are so many nature-given and human-made things to fear, does that mean we should expect to live in constant fear of God? Reverence for God and awe of God's greatness and power is understandable and appropriate. But being scared of God? How can that fit in with a Christian belief about God? Should we expect that God delights in keeping us scared? The miracle stories of the New Testament again and again encourage us, instead, to honor God's greatness by having trust and confidence. Because God is so great and so powerful, we put all our trust in God and we expect all good from God.

Wednesday of the Eighteenth Week in Ordinary Time—
The new immigrants

Readings: Num 13:1-2, 25–14:1, 26a-29a, 34-35; Matt 15:21-28
Resp. Psalm: Ps 106:6-7ab, 13-14, 21-22, 23 (*L* 409)

The story of the Canaanite woman and her treatment by Jesus shocks us. It defies our image of a more open and all-embracing Lord. And his language to her certainly strikes us as pretty rough. It reflects the in-sistence, especially in Matthew's Gospel, on the priority of the mission of Jesus to his fellow Jews. In other matters towards which we have a different attitude today (an issue like slavery, for example), Jesus and the apostles did not make any revolutionary moves. They probably

realized that changing such customs would only happen when believers saw the implications of belief in the Lord. Similarly, the Jewish
contemporaries of Jesus found it difficult to overcome their negative
estimation of non-Jews. Instead of bemoaning their deficiencies, we
might turn the spotlight on ourselves and our society. In our country
and among us there is at times a great reluctance to accept recent immigrants whether they are Hispanic or Asian or from various third-
world countries. There's a great deal of work for all of us to do in our
own neighborhood, town, or country to open the church and our society to these newcomers who have such different customs and practices. In many first-world countries most of us are the descendants of
immigrants. Many of those early settlers experienced harsh prejudice
and great sufferings to make possible the life we now live. Acceptance
of new immigrants is a very practical way of carrying out the Lord's
command to love our fellow human beings; it's doing to others as has
been done to us—in our ancestors. We can look around at the situation
in our own parish or neighborhood and then draw some conclusions
about what needs to be done.

Thursday of the Eighteenth Week in Ordinary time—
Our thirst satisfied in living

Readings: Num 20:1-13; Matt 16:13-23
Resp. Psalm: Ps 95:1-2, 6-7, 8-9 (L 410)

The Israelites' thirst in the desert is a prophetic picture of the universal
human longing for fulfillment, joy, peace or, as Christian tradition
calls it, salvation. What better name than thirst can there be for the
emptiness and ache in our hearts for perfect love and perfect bliss?
The way we go through life expecting to find all these things in some
person, some experience, some feeling, or some teaching or technique
is certainly like one huge thirst. People, especially in affluent societies, go from one fad or therapy to another; it almost seems, weekly.
What people look for so often is the easy fix, some all-effective cure
for everything from our pain to our dissatisfaction and boredom. The
buildup in the Gospels about who Jesus is (the Son of God, the revelation of God's wisdom in word and act) encourages us to look to him
for all this. What he gives is not an easy fix, not an overnight release
from illness or painful confrontations, but an invitation to follow him
on the path of death and resurrection. As companions of the Lord, we
discover a way of getting through, of not avoiding all that life may
bring. This way tells us that the self-emptying and self-forgetting we

undergo in life's pains and onslaughts is a sharing in the passion and death of Jesus. And it leads to new life, resurrection, not only in the world to come but here and now in more patience, love, compassion, and sympathy for the rest of suffering and hurt humanity. Here at the altar we renew our commitment to live according to this pattern.

Friday of the Eighteenth Week in Ordinary Time—
The paradox of surrender

Readings: Deut 4:32-40; Matt 16:24-28
Resp. Psalm: Ps 77:12-13, 14-15, 16 and 21 (*L* 411)

For the next several days our first reading will be from Deuteronomy, another Old Testament book which seems so foreign and even repugnant to modern readers. A thorough reading of it provokes a huge variety of responses. To simplify: it seems to have been written to recall the Israelites to loyalty to their agreement with God (the covenant) or, put another way, to call the Israelites to obedience. It was written during a time of confusion and doubt among the people because of the awful things that had befallen them. Does this mean, as many a television evangelist tells us, that if we do obey God, God improves our finances, removes cancer from us and family members, and gives the kids higher grade point averages? Do cancer, pain, bankruptcy, or unemployment happen only to those who disobey God? The answer to both of these questions is no, despite the fact that such was Israelite belief for quite a long time. Deuteronomy—and the Christian message gleaned from it—tells us that trusting acceptance of God's way means that we are in God's hands, no matter what happens. In ways we cannot easily foresee or recognize, God is working good in us and our lives if we but put our trust in God. For us the obedience we owe God is summed up in our willingness to accept and enter into the pattern described in today's Gospel and put before us on the altar: surrendering our life into God's care ultimately means more abundant life.

Saturday of the Eighteenth Week in Ordinary Time—
Deeds not feelings

Readings: Deut 6:4-13; Matt 17:14-20
Resp. Psalm: Ps 18:2-3a, 3bc-4, 47 and 51 (*L* 412)

The first reading today gives us the original passage cited by Jesus in the New Testament when explaining which is the greatest commandment: "You shall love the LORD, your God, with all your heart, and with all your soul, and with all your strength" (Deut 6:5). Today we think of love so often with a romantic connotation and always stress how love cannot be commanded but arises almost inexplicably. For example, "You shall love Harry or Lisa" spoken to a son or daughter would strike us as very authoritarian, maybe the beginning of an arranged marriage. But love in this passage from Deuteronomy means something more like loyalty and the consequent obedience which should follow. We're talking about the love between parent and child, not the love between adolescents or people who are dating. The love meant here can be commanded because it should be an obvious conclusion from the fact that God has rescued the Israelites from slavery in Egypt and brought them into their own land. Loyalty to him, avoidance of any allegiance to other gods, and obedience to what God asks in return should be understood. Knowing this should help us realize that we serve God primarily by how we live and act rather than by how we feel. Love as understood here doesn't carry with it any suggestion that our hearts must palpitate upon hearing God's name; rather, we work with God's help to live in accord with God's plan for us humans.

Monday of the Nineteenth Week in Ordinary Time—
Scandal and sensitivity

Readings: Deut 10:12-22; Matt 17:22-27
Resp. Psalm: Ps 147:12-13, 14-15, 19-20 (L 413)

True to his impulsiveness, Peter tells the tax collectors that, of course, his master Jesus will pay the Temple tax. Jesus tries to refine Peter's understanding and finally gives the same answer as Peter, but for a different reason. Peter presupposes that as a faithful Jew Jesus will pay the tax. Jesus, by his dialogue with Peter, makes clear that the Son of the Most High should hardly be expected to pay taxes for his Father's house. But in order to avoid scandalizing others, he will pay the tax. We avoid scandal by not creating obstacles to another's belief or efforts to live a good life. Probably the most obvious cases of scandal occur when Christians who profess love of neighbor show indifference to others' need or suffering. When a clergyman abuses the trust and respect of others, we have scandal. When Christians attack other Christians, we have scandal. Disagreeing with other Christians in a reasonable and civil way is not a scandal. And there are many things which are "just not done" in a particular society; but doing them is not scandal. Using the wrong fork at dinner, for example, or wearing the wrong kind of clothing to some event—such matters do not cause real scandal. They may offend someone's idea of propriety but scandal concerns serious moral or religious matters. Sensitivity to the feelings and beliefs of others is probably the key principle in avoiding true scandal. As in Christian life in general, our growth in this area is really a growth in greater sensitivity.

Tuesday of the Nineteenth Week in Ordinary Time—
True greatness in the kingdom

Readings: Deut 31:1-8; Matt 18:1-5, 10, 12–14
Resp. Psalm: Deut 32:3–4ab, 7, 8, 9 and 12 (*L* 414)

In yesterday's Gospel Jesus told Peter how he could miraculously produce the necessary money to pay the Temple tax for both Jesus and himself. Right after that Matthew tells us the disciples asked Jesus, "Who is the greatest in the Kingdom of heaven?" (Matt 18:1). There may be a hint that they are jealous of Peter's privileged position; there was no mention of Jesus' providing for their payment of the Temple tax! Their preoccupation with self provides a good opportunity for instructing them about genuine greatness in the kingdom among Jesus' followers. Jesus points to little children; in that society they were not doted on as they are often among us today. They were simply very dependent beings who had to receive everything as a gift from some adult. They were lowly and of no weight or significance. The great people among the disciples are those who know that they have no claims and must receive everything as a gift. Jesus or Matthew is already, at this early stage in the history of Christianity, warning against ambition and the seeking of prestige and power among the people we might call "clergy" today. Ambition and the struggle for power are not much younger, if at all, than the beginnings of Christianity. For all of us, whether priests or lay people, our greatness in the kingdom consists in our receptivity to what God alone can give us or do in us.

Wednesday of the Nineteenth Week in Ordinary Time—
Lay initiative

Readings: Deut 34:1-12; Matt 18:15-20
Resp. Psalm: Ps 66:1–3a, 5 and 8, 16–17 (*L* 415)

Too strong an emphasis on the organizational or institutional aspect of the following of Christ can (and probably has over the centuries) diminish the initiative of lay people. Despite improvements since Vatican

II, we still wait too often for "Father" or the bishop or the church to act. Jesus encourages more initiative by ordinary Christians with his words: "Where two or three are gathered together in my name, there am I in the midst of them" (Matt 18:20). It may just be another way of reminding ourselves that we are the church, not only clergy but lay people as well. The responsibility for the Christian faith belongs to all of us; the organization of hierarchy, dioceses, boards, conferences, etc., should not steal the thunder of lay people. In the Gospel context Jesus especially speaks of prayer: "If two of you agree on earth about anything for which they are to pray, it shall be granted to them by my heavenly Father" (18:19). And this is certainly an area where Catholics, for example, might easily join with other Christians or simply those who believe in God to pray in times of tragedy or difficulty. Fortunately, we do see and hear of Christians of various denominations consoling and helping each other. But there are times when we Catholics seem to be waiting for someone "higher up" to speak or act when we have that ability and duty by our baptism.

Thursday of the Nineteenth Week in Ordinary Time—
Growing toward wholeness

Readings: Josh 3:7-10a, 11, 13-17; Matt 18:21–19:1
Resp. Psalm: Ps 114:1-2, 3-4, 5-6 (L 416)

We see and expect certain kinds of exemplary behavior in others—mercy, for example, as shown by the king in today's Gospel parable. On the other hand, like the servant whose debt was written off, we so easily fail to see or are unwilling to carry out the implications of the kindness shown ourselves. Our blind spots are legion. By some curious trick within our minds and hearts, we are able to mouth moral lessons about mercy and forgiveness all the while failing to show them in our own lives. We clamor for honesty in our elected officials, while we are unable to practice it toward a business partner or family members. We espouse hospitality toward visitors and travelers, but are unwilling to be personally inconvenienced to carry it out. We can and probably should accuse ourselves in these and other areas, maybe even be a bit discouraged. After all, if our actions and ideals were all of one piece, we'd be about ready for canonization. The light certainly has to shine within our consciences to show us where we fail and how we can improve. There is no substitute for self-knowledge and for a willingness to hear in the criticisms we get from others some idea of our genuine if unrecognized failings. This lack of wholeness in our following of

Christ is one of the reasons we pray and approach his table so often. We only become whole by finally trusting in the grace of God and allowing it to work in us.

Friday of the Nineteenth Week in Ordinary Time—
Maybe it's better not to commit . . .

Readings: Josh 24:1-13; Matt 19:3-12
Resp. Psalm: Ps 136:1-3, 16-18, 21-22 and 24 (L 417)

There seems to be quite a degree of agreement that commitment is particularly difficult in our world and for people today. Religious orders have in many cases concluded that young people are not ready to make any lasting commitment until later in their twenties. It does seem that commitments today often hinge on whether or not something better comes along. People are fearful of missing something desirable by making a too-early gift of themselves to what may prove to be less desirable. The response of the disciples to Jesus' words about the indissolubility of marriage suggests that commitment was a problem then, too. They say: "If that is the case of a man with his wife, it is better not to marry" (Matt 19:10). Perhaps the time of Jesus was like ours in this regard. Or, the fact may be that commitment is always tough. Whatever our own experience suggests to us, commitment is a serious topic and one which touches all of us, married or unmarried, in some way. Our age gives us a particular perspective on the subject. If we've been married for forty or fifty years, we know a great deal about commitment of which twenty- and thirty-year-olds are ignorant. In order to make most life-long commitments, we probably need a bit of innocence or ignorance. If we knew everything a commitment would entail, we'd probably be paralyzed in our tracks. Giving ourselves generously is something we learn at home and at the Cross.

Saturday of the Nineteenth Week in Ordinary Time—
Re-committing ourselves

Readings: Josh 24:14-29; Matt 19:13-15
Resp. Psalm: Ps 16:1-2a and 5, 7-8, 11 (L 418)

What the Israelites do in terms of religion after Joshua's death reinforces the truth of the old saying about protesting too much. At least four times in today's first reading the Israelites have affirmed their determination to serve the Lord. Their subsequent history is one of infidelity to the Lord, return to the Lord, more infidelity, etc. As with

many of our affirmations (especially those involving some obligations), we state them repeatedly, hoping to really convince ourselves.
The first reading shows a way in which we adults are often willy-
nilly, like children; we seem to have a short attention span or quickly
move from one interest to another. In this case, it's from fidelity to
the covenant to infidelity. Fidelity, faithfulness, does not get much re-
inforcement in our society or in our media. We're more likely to see
spontaneity or a readiness to try something new commended, often at
the expense of a prior obligation or promise. The Mass places before us
daily the selfless offering of One who, St. Paul tells us, became obedient
to death. Being obedient to death is another term for the faithfulness of
Jesus to the mission the Father gave him. This might be a good subject
for our prayer at this Eucharist: to ask Christ to strengthen our faithfulness to God and to those to whom we are committed.

Monday of the Twentieth Week in Ordinary Time—
The pursuit of wealth

Readings: Judg 2:11-19; Matt 19:16-22
Resp. Psalm: Ps 106:34-35, 36-37, 39-40, 43ab and 44 (L 419)

Just this past Saturday we heard the firm sounding and repeated commitment of the Israelites to the one God, Yahweh. Today as we begin
reading the book of Judges, these same people have gone back on their
word; they are worshiping other gods. In the Gospel story the plight of
the rich young man highlights the idolatry of wealth which is probably the greatest competition today to belief in the God of Jesus Christ.
What we hear or know of the injustices of our world's societies (our
own included) is often traceable to someone's greed or cheating others of just recompense for work or services. Neglect of families and of
people to whom we are committed is often related to the relentless pursuit of wealth. The shady deals making us so unfortunately suspicious
of people in government seems due so often to the lust for wealth. It's
no accident that the Gospels record so many more admonitions against
desire for wealth than they do against sexual desire. Sexual sins are bad
enough; they often involve exploitation of another person. But the teaching of the Gospels points the finger consistently at the lure of wealth. An
obsession in the Christian churches with sex often has served to protect
our more general obsession with wealth and the comfort it brings. Even
we ordinary mortals, probably not among the country's top ten percent
in income, need to check on how the pursuit of our livelihood impacts
our faith and relation to others and to our families.

Tuesday of the Twentieth Week in Ordinary Time—
Trusting not impressing

Readings: Judg 6:11-24a; Matt 19:23-30
Resp. Psalm: Ps 85:9, 11-12, 13-14 (L 420)

We unthinkingly repeat many stereotypes about the Bible and Christ's teaching. We talk sometimes as if the God of the Old Testament only wanted people to fear him, whereas the God of the New Testament relates to us in love. This is an insufficient summary. We talk as if Peter were set up as a full-fledged pope in the New Testament; this is just not true. We talk sometimes as if the idea of reward and punishment were completely foreign to our God. Or, on the other hand, as if God had a crew of accountants keeping track of all we did and adding it up so as to give us the exactly equivalent reward or punishment. Both attitudes are too simple. The New Testament repeatedly stresses that life with God, salvation, is a gift. On the other hand, Jesus does speak of reward. But reward in Jesus' dictionary is not something determined by how impressive God has found us, but by how good God is. God rewards us because God is good, loving, and generous, not because we have twisted God's arm by showing our extraordinary virtue. The point for us in such readings as today's from Matthew is that salvation is God's gift. And the good we do is because of God's grace, which is also God's gift. Human boasting in the presence of God is completely ruled out. Our relation to God comes down, finally, to trusting God's goodness and not simply trying to impress God.

Wednesday of the Twentieth Week in Ordinary Time—
The generous God

Readings: Judg 9:6-15; Matt 20:1-16
Resp. Psalm: Ps 21:2-3, 4-5, 6-7 (L 421)

Today's Gospel puzzles us because it seems to justify unfair labor practices, that is, not paying individuals according to how long they work, but arbitrarily. The problem may be in understanding the nature of parables. These frequently bizarre stories intend to make one point and one only. For other balancing points we need other parables or common sense and reason. All the workers in this parable get the same pay, a full day's wages, no matter when they started to work. The point is that God gives eternal life, entrance into the kingdom, to all and any who turn to God. The strength and grace to turn to God is, in the first place, always God's gift no matter how much we credit ourselves. This turning to God (conversion) opens us to receiving all God has to give. Another parable or story would have to make a point to balance this one. It would need to stress that there are differences of fervor among us and that God must certainly recognize that. We single out extraordinarily generous people as saints and presume, rightly it seems, that their closeness to God prepares them to receive more of what God has to give. We don't have any detailed information on how God does this. Common sense suggests that we have different capacities for happiness. A four-year-old may find happiness in unlimited visits to the Dairy Queen; a person matured by a variety of experiences may find happiness in a profound love. Again, as yesterday, we trust God's love, not our own achievements.

Thursday of the Twentieth Week in Ordinary Time—
Spotty development

Readings: Judg 11:29-39a; Matt 22:1-14
Resp. Psalm: Ps 40:5, 7-8a, 8b-9, 10 (L 422)

"The spirit of the LORD came upon Jephthah" we hear as today's first reading opens. A bit later: "The LORD delivered them [the enemy] into his [Jephthah's] power" (Judg 11:29, 32). And then we hear of this man Jephthah, apparently God's instrument to deliver Israel, ready to have his daughter put to death to fulfill his vow. Such vows were part of the local religion surrounding Israel, but not a part of the religion of Moses. It looks like Jephthah's religion is spotty: part, the religion of Yahweh and part, more primitive and cruel. It may not be so starkly exemplified in our lives, but our religion, too, is most likely a bit spotty. We have heard and tried to answer the invitation of God to the wedding banquet, but we bring to it some unredeemed behavior. We may show genuine love for family members and the neighbors, but we are perfectly willing to leave out of our love a whole race or group of people. We are basically honest, but allow ourselves more leeway when money is involved. We are faithful to Sunday worship, but may spend our time there grumbling within about some little slight. Or, we are generally sensitive to others' feelings, but allow ourselves an exception in the case of the wife or husband. While all this may be reason for some self-reproof, it also tells us that we cannot expect total consistency and thoroughgoing Christlike behavior in everyone else, either. Rightly we preface our worship with a request for forgiveness and a willingness to forgive the same behavior in others.

Friday of the Twentieth Week in Ordinary Time—
Being an example is unavoidable

Readings: Ruth 1:1, 3-6, 14b-16, 22; Matt 22:34-40
Resp. Psalm: Ps 146:5-6ab, 6c-7, 8-9a, 9bc-10 (L 423)

This first of our readings from the Book of Ruth is used quite often as the first reading at weddings. Couples see in Ruth's declaration of commitment to her mother-in-law and her God a statement of their own mutual commitment: "Wherever you go, I will go, wherever you lodge I will lodge, your people shall be my people, and your God my God" (Ruth 1:16). Ruth's dedication is, first, to Naomi and then to Naomi's God. Doesn't that reflect the way things actually go so often? We come to God, to love, to faithfulness and a sense of loyalty, to responsibility, and to an appreciation of commitment first of all through our admiration of or love for some person, his or her example. In fact, to get back to marriage, aren't husband and wife supposed to mirror for each other the eternal love and faithfulness of God? Don't most of us learn of these matters through other people, friends, people we love and who love us? Other people, Ruth's commitment tells us, are so important to us and, vice versa, we are so important to others' faith and hope, whether we realize it or not. This is another way of reminding ourselves that our faith, hope, and love are intrinsically bound up with others. We depend on each other; we influence each other; we support each other—or, on the other hand, discourage or weaken each other. Someone somewhere is dependent on us for help, inspiration, and encouragement whether in word or example. United to Christ in this sacrament, we are other Christs to each other.

Saturday of the Twentieth Week in Ordinary Time—
To profit others rather than to preside over them

Readings: Ruth 2:1-3, 8-11; 4:13-17; Matt 23:1-12
Resp. Psalm: Ps 128:1b-2, 3, 4, 5 (L 424)

The sayings of the Lord which Matthew has collected in today's Gospel selection cover many topics and suggest a variety of reflections. Mostly they are cautions to Christians (Christian leaders especially) to avoid the sins and errors of the scribes and Pharisees that Jesus has so roundly condemned. The sins of these religious leaders of Jesus' time are the occupational hazards of religious leaders anywhere, anytime. And, further, to make all this applicable to all of us, they are temptations for those who lead others, whether it be the family, business, education, or government. Leaders are warned not to make the perks of being a leader the goal of their leadership. Leading should be for the benefit of those we lead, not for our comfort. Genuine leaders, according to Jesus' teaching, are servants of those they lead. They are more concerned to profit those they lead than to profit from being leaders. They are more concerned with service than with dignity and power: "The greatest among you must be your servant" (Matt 23:11). Here at Mass we have before us the self-emptying and sacrifice of our leader Jesus, in order that we learn to practice the same.

Monday of the Twenty-First Week in Ordinary Time—
Harmony of ideals and deeds

Readings: 1 Thess 1:1-5, 8b-10; Matt 23:13-22
Resp. Psalm: Ps 149:1b-2, 3-4, 5-6a and 9b (L 425)

In a short homily it's impossible fruitfully to go into all the background of today's Gospel. It should be stressed, though, that the picture of the Pharisees we get here is very one-sided. In their origins the Pharisees were a movement within Judaism to encourage devout following of the Law. The abuses condemned in Matthew point up a danger for all religious people: Christians, Jews, any group. The danger is the temptation to present a religious appearance which lacks substance or reality. Put another way, it's the problem of the split between what religious people say and what they (we) do. Our translation has Jesus call the Pharisees "hypocrites." Inevitably our religious ideals are going to be above and ahead of what we actually do. This is to be expected. The problem comes in our trying to give the impression that we are perfectly fulfilling religious demands when, in fact, we lack the humility to recognize our failures. When our behavior corresponds with our beliefs and ideals, we have what we call "integrity." Integrity is derived from a Latin word meaning "whole"; the person with integrity is unified around a central focus. Reaching complete integrity is sanctity. Until we get there, honesty requires that we don't make false claims for ourselves in our talk or behavior; and that we recognize our shortcomings, ask forgiveness, and put our trust in the One who alone can make us whole. Every time we gather at this altar, this desire is part of what we bring here.

Tuesday of the Twenty-First Week in Ordinary Time—
The weightier matters

Readings: 1 Thess 2:1-8; Matt 23:23-26
Resp. Psalm: Ps 139:1-3, 4-6 (L 426)

"Trivial Pursuit" might be a name for the game Jesus denounces in today's Gospel. "Woe," he says to his opponents, "You pay tithes of mint and dill and cumin and have neglected the weightier things of the law: judgment and mercy and fidelity" (Matt 23:23). In this behavior condemned by Jesus, we see yet another temptation of all people serious about religion. In our quest for faithfulness to God, we try to be sure about it and secure in it by making regulations and mandatory practices to safeguard it. We think that somehow a collection of practices carried out carefully assures the inner spirit. It must be admitted that specific practices can help focus our spirit. For most of us, a purely inner religion, never expressed or made concrete in and through the body, can become entirely unreal. But our practices also can become ends in themselves, with the result that we really forget why we initiated them. We must think of this sometimes when we think how we, congregations, so often whip through our common prayers as if the bare recitation, at no matter what speed, is magic. And we can make so much of a deal about specific practices that they become distracting fetishes. We must say this prayer so many times, for so many days; the priest must not deviate from some exact formula. More of this probably exists in church regulations about which most of us are better off ignorant. Over the centuries Catholicism picked up a great deal of this legalism and petty regulation. Fortunately, we have been moving away from it and, we hope, toward concentration on weightier matters like justice, mercy, good faith, love, and union with God.

Wednesday of the Twenty-First Week in Ordinary Time—
Encourage, support, compliment

Readings: 1 Thess 2:9-13; Matt 23:27-32
Resp. Psalm: Ps 139:7-8, 9-10, 11-12ab (L 427)

One can't help but be impressed by the positive, encouraging, and hopeful tone of the readings from the First Letter to the Thessalonians which we hear this week. Scholars agree that this is most likely the first written work of the New Testament, written down as we have it before the other letters of Paul or the Gospels. Throughout it we hear a Paul who is gratified by how well the Thessalonians have responded to his preaching, how well they have carried it out, and what an example they are to the rest of the world. Elsewhere in the New Testament we hear the same writer rebuke, complain, reprobate, and feel misunderstood. In the Gospel selection from Matthew today we hear a different tone, one to which people like Paul are driven at times. People in authority in whatever field (parents, priests too) all face the issue of what tone to use with those they are trying to help and lead. To find and encourage the positive good in others is sometimes difficult; if possible, it is always the better approach. To give hope is better than to denounce and depress. Many a parent like Saint Monica, faced with a son, Augustine, dissipating his life away, has resisted the temptation to denounce and excommunicate with good results. Her silent and persistent prayer was effective. Many of us would profit from asking the help to follow Monica and Paul's example in praying for and encouraging those for whom we feel responsible. The power to do so is found in the Lord whose patience and victory we commemorate here daily.

Thursday of the Twenty-First Week in Ordinary Time—
Stay awake!

Readings: 1 Thess 3:7-13; Matt 24:42-51
Resp. Psalm: Ps 90:3-5a, 12-13, 14 and 17 (L 428)

One is struck on hearing passages from many parts of the New Testament at how prominent in the writers' minds is the coming of the Lord at the end of time. This is certainly not at the forefront of the thought of most of us. When it is at the forefront in our day among Christians, it's usually with some group which is intent on setting the day and the hour of that coming. All this is in flat indifference to what we hear from Jesus: "Stay awake! For you do not know on which day your Lord will come" (Matt 24:42). And, "For at an hour you do not expect, the Son of Man will come" (24:44). In writing to the Thessalonians, Paul likewise prays that they be kept "blameless in holiness before our God and Father at the coming of our Lord Jesus with all his holy ones" (1 Thess 3:13). Maybe the deaths of friends around us from cancer and accidents remind us of the fact that the Lord's coming is always imminent. The death of a classmate—always so young—for a high school student or a college student shakes them up and makes the living young feel their fragility. But it doesn't last long. How do we keep a sense of the end of things, the end of life, before ourselves without doing something like contemplating a skull? How do we do it and still maintain a hopeful and even cheerfully encouraging stance in

165

daily life? This is something for all of us to think about and to come to an appropriate solution in our own lives.

Friday of the Twenty-First Week in Ordinary Time—
Trust and good sense

Readings: 1 Thess 4:1-8; Matt 25:1-13
Resp. Psalm: Ps 97:1 and 2b, 5-6, 10, 11-12 (L 429)

Just yesterday we heard the same message that ends today's Gospel: "Therefore, stay awake, for you know neither the day nor the hour" (Matt 25:13). We might emphasize today another aspect of this Gospel about the foolish and sensible bridesmaids. This message is, we might say, one of common sense and prudence. The point is that faith and trust in God and the Christian life in general do not dispense us from using the little God-given abilities we have. Prudence, forethought, and careful preparation are not ruled out or replaced by the more exalted virtues of trust and hope. A problem develops if we presume by our careful planning to more or less take over God's governance of the world and life itself. In a number of places in the Gospels Jesus commends prudence and forethought. These are simply the good use of the intelligence and skill God has given us. The temptation to bypass our intelligence and the ordinary means in conducting life's affairs comes sometimes to genuinely religious people. They believe that it honors God more to expect God directly to settle issues and problems than to use, for example, medicine and human ingenuity. We see this in extreme form when a family refuses proven means of cure for a sick child in order to rely on direct intervention by God. Again, as in so many matters of the Christian life, we are left to strike a balance within our own consciences between trust in God and the use of ordinary human means.

Saturday of the Twenty-First Week in Ordinary Time—
Getting to know you

Readings: 1 Thess 4:9-11; Matt 25:14-30
Resp. Psalm: Ps 98:1, 7-8, 9 (L 430)

Again, today's parable sounds a theme we've heard several times recently about preparedness for the Lord's coming by using well what we have received from God. It may be helpful and less repetitious if we limit ourselves to a more specific theme. In the parable we hear that the servants received varying amounts of the master's resources "to each according to his ability" (Matt 25:15). What is important is not how much talent we have received or what kind of talent we have, but how we use it. In some phases of our life we are often tempted to wish we had someone else's talents. Many a young person seems to feel that if he or she had so-and-so's height and ability at basketball, that would be the key to a successful life. Other people seem willing to languish in mediocrity because they don't have another's mathematical or musical ability. Part of the problem is that our society, our culture, and our media tend to define success or fulfillment in very narrow ways, that is, in terms of net income, fame, athletic, or financial success. But there are many, many different talents spread among us all which, if well used, can do so much for the world around us. A talent of worth to God and the world certainly doesn't have to be athletic, financial, or one used in the entertainment industry. A gift for consoling and encouraging others, an ability to be patient and understanding with children, a talent for bringing some humor and lightness to the too serious and grim, a gift for bringing out the talents of others—these are all much under-appreciated and much needed. To discern and use well our own special talents is a task for prayer and self-reflection.

Monday of the Twenty-Second Week in Ordinary Time—
Food for reflection

Readings: 1 Thess 4:13-18; Luke 4:16-30
Resp. Psalm: Ps 96:1 and 3, 4-5, 11-12, 13 (L 431)

"And all spoke highly of him and were amazed at the gracious words that came from his mouth." And then, "They also asked, 'Is this not the son of Joseph?'" (Luke 4:22). And finally, "they were all filled with fury. They rose up, drove him out of the town, and led him to the brow of the hill . . . to hurl him down headlong" (4:28-29). These passages gleaned from reading Luke illustrate many reactions to Jesus and give us a pattern for reactions to him throughout his life. It's probably healthy for our faith to put ourselves back in the time of Jesus and think of how we would have reacted. We have the distance of centuries, which has smoothed over the difficulties and made worship of Jesus and belief in him seem almost obvious to some of us. The reactions of admiration, doubt, and outright opposition which we heard in today's Gospel are good material for our reflection. Do we take seriously the implications of belief? Have we ever reflected on what we mean when we say we believe that Jesus is true God and true man? Do we take seriously the demands he makes on his followers? on us? Does our belief that Jesus died and rose again truly affect our hope for our deceased family members and friends? If nothing else, some reflection on these questions might lead us to ask more earnestly that God increase and deepen our faith.

Tuesday of the Twenty-Second Week in Ordinary Time—
Free to serve

Readings: 1 Thess 5:1-6, 9-11; Luke 4:31-37
Resp. Psalm: Ps 27:1, 4, 13-14 (*L* 432)

Hardly a day goes by that some passage in our Scripture does not speak of our salvation by Christ or his works of power in those he touched. The preparation in the Hebrew Scriptures for the work of the Lord was above all the liberation of the Jews from slavery and their new life in the Promised Land. We present our faith in all its positive attraction when we see it in similar terms—as deliverance, freedom, and new life. The Gospel presents this repeatedly in vivid stories of Jesus' freeing those suffering from disease and the power of evil. To present the following of Christ as a matter of laws and regulations, or of fear and a punishing God waiting to pounce on sinners, certainly doesn't do our discipleship justice. In a letter to a friend about to become a Catholic, Flannery O'Connor wrote that she should not enter the church unless she felt it would be an enlargement of her freedom. The legalism and narrowness of which Jesus accused the Pharisees so often persists as a danger in Christianity. But there are many reasons for seeing the following of Christ as liberation. Putting the emphasis on love frees us from smallness of mind and heart and from substituting conventional customs for Christian generosity. As our life in Christ grows in depth, it frees us from fear. United to Christ and each other at this table, we pray to be freed from the limitations of a merely this-worldly perspective.

Wednesday of the Twenty-Second Week in Ordinary Time—
Proclaiming good news

Readings: Col 1:1-8; Luke 4:38-44
Resp. Psalm: Ps 52:10, 11 (*L* 433)

"To the other towns also I must proclaim the good news of the Kingdom of God, because for this purpose I have been sent" (Luke 4:43). This is the first mention of the reign or kingdom of God in Luke. Expulsion of the devil and curing of illnesses characterize the reign of God in us. Earlier, without using this term, Jesus had proclaimed in the synagogue at

Nazareth that prophecies about Good News for the poor, release of captives, sight for the blind, and freedom for the oppressed were all fulfilled in him. Looking around our world at any given moment, we are likely to be discouraged about just such things. Oppression replaces oppression, the poor we always have with us it seems, and there are always blind people and sick people present in the most disheartening ways. The good news of the reign of God is both a message of hope and a spur to our faithfulness and generosity. Through Jesus God promises that every tear will be wiped away and that suffering and death will have an end. And the strong implication throughout the Gospel is that the good we do out of thankfulness for God's love is a necessary element in the coming of the reign of God. The urgency in Jesus' words—"To the other towns also I must proclaim the good news"—must resonate in us, his members, as we face each day. How can, how do we announce and evidence the reign of God in what we say and do?

Thursday of the Twenty-Second Week in Ordinary Time— *The art of fishing*

Readings: Col 1:9-14; Luke 5:1-11
Resp. Psalm: Ps 98:2-3ab, 3cd-4, 5-6 (L 434)

When we look at it carefully, the Lord's words to Peter about "catching men" (or women, any human being) do not sound all that great. Catching a fish means we take the fish out of its element—nothing very congenial to the fish. And then we fry, broil, or bake it—something congenial to us but, again, not to the fish. In the background of Jesus and his contemporaries the sea was a place of terror and chaos (see Gen 1:1). The last book of the Bible, The Revelation to John, in telling us that in the end there will be a new heaven and a new earth tells us also there will no longer be any sea; its terrors will be over. In other words, Peter is called by the Lord to share in the work of saving human beings from all the evils that threaten: sin, disease, suffering of all kinds, and death. The time and care Jesus took in assembling the apostles tells us that the work of human salvation and deliverance is both God's work and ours. It's a paradox that we will never figure out mathematically how God and we work together in such matters. But the lesson for us is that God does not accomplish apart from our generous cooperation and our hard work. We can even push the picture further about "catching men." Just as the fisherman uses various lures and approaches to catching the fish, so those (ourselves) who share "in the inheritance of the holy ones in light" (Col 1:12) use all the resources of human ingenuity as well as prayer and faith to bring the Good News to the world.

Friday of the Twenty-Second Week in Ordinary Time—
God above and within

Readings: Col 1:15-20; Luke 5:33-39
Resp. Psalm: Ps 100:1b-2, 3, 4, 5 (*L* 435)

As we hear a passage like today's from the Letter to the Colossians, we might wonder what picture of the universe the author had. Only within the past century has modern astronomy with the help of powerful telescopes shown us new and hitherto unimaginable dimensions of the universe. People at the time of the writing of Colossians thought that the Gospel would be preached to the whole world within a few years. They thought of the lights of the heavens as jewels hung out each night. Both in terms of how old the universe is and how far it extends, our concepts have been stretched immensely. Modern observation tells us the universe is at least ten to twenty billion years old and of a physical vastness requiring such terms as "light years." When we hear that in Christ "all things in heaven and on earth, the visible and the invisible" (Col 1:16) were created, the picture we have today makes that sound even more awesome. "He is before all things, and in him all things hold together" (1:17). When we stare into the skies on a clear night, we have even more reason to be awestruck than did the ancient peoples. We have some idea at least of how vast it is. We are left to marvel at the God who is the source of all that is in this huge universe and at the same time is able to appear among us in the shape of a human being. Not only that, but this same God is willing to be made present in the Body and Blood of Christ under the forms of ordinary bread and wine. Our God is both the creator of this immense universe and the one who listens to us in our worries and pains.

Saturday of the Twenty-Second Week in Ordinary Time—
Christ, Lord of space and time

Readings: Col 1:21-23; Luke 6:1-5
Resp. Psalm: Ps 54:3-4, 6 and 8 (*L* 436)

The selection from the Letter to the Colossians once again stresses all that Christ means for us and for human life. Through the Cross and Gospel we are at peace with God and assured of even more to come.

Colossians exhorts us to "persevere in the faith, firmly grounded, stable, and not shifting from the hope of the Gospel that you heard" (Col 1:23). The temptation, though, is to see this world and this life as all there is and as a pretty dismal picture—one that further tempts us to despair. Despite the good will and heroic actions of which we hear, the overwhelming picture is often discouraging. Pick up the morning newspaper and we read of a festering war between two peoples, of a grandmother killed by the crossfire of two warring gangs, of a flight diverted because of a bomb threat, of a government agency suspected of drug dealing, of a fourteen-year-old dying of leukemia, or of a disgruntled employee killing fellow workers. A pessimistic philosopher goes so far as to say that those who laugh haven't heard the news. No matter how much heroism there is or how much unselfishness or how many good ordinary people, it seems at times as if evil and sin inundate us all. The justice, peace, and love for which we long are only realized here in fits and starts and in little pieces. Our ultimate trust and hope are rooted in the saving power of Christ working here and now through many people, but bringing final peace and joy only beyond this troubled world. Our daily prayer, our daily attendance here at Mass is a statement that we put our hopes for the world in God's power. "The Son of Man is lord of the sabbath" (Luke 6:5) and of all else.

Monday of the Twenty-Third Week in Ordinary Time—
The Body of Christ

Readings: Col 1:24–2:3; Luke 6:6-11
Resp. Psalm: Ps 62:6-7, 9 (L 437)

Whoever wrote the Letter to the Colossians in the name of St. Paul says something here that seems contrary to the main drift of Paul's teaching. The author writes that "in my flesh I am filling up what is lacking in the afflictions of Christ on behalf of his Body, which is the Church" (Col 1:24). Repeatedly Paul speaks of how all-sufficient is Christ's grace and work for our salvation. To suggest that Christ got off the cross too soon or that he did not drink the full cup of suffering also goes against New Testament teaching. That line in today's first reading can, however, be a stimulation for our life in Christ. We might think of it as referring to what St. Augustine called the "whole Christ," that is, Christ united with all the members of his Body over the centuries. Jesus tells us in that parable of the sheep and goats in Matthew 25 that any good we do to the imprisoned, the thirsty, the hungry, the naked, etc., is done to him. The suffering people of the world are in solidarity with

Christ. We might say that the suffering of Christ that saves the world from sin and death includes the suffering of all his members over the centuries. In them he continues that suffering before our eyes or in our own lives. In those who suffer, we serve and comfort Christ. Our own pains and sufferings can be joined to Christ's as we share in his offering here at this altar. And, in coming to the aid of those suffering around us, we are giving worship to Christ himself.

Tuesday of the Twenty-Third Week in Ordinary Time—
Risen but still wounded

Readings: Col 2:6-15; Luke 6:12-19
Resp. Psalm: Ps 145:1b-2, 8-9, 10-11 (L 438)

The Letter to the Colossians is strong on our sharing now in the resurrection of Christ by baptism. Resurrection is not just a future but a present reality; it has already begun in us. Recalling this often is a great way of preserving a sense of our dignity as Christians. And that should spur us on to live accordingly. This doesn't, of course, mean that all risk is gone from Christian life or that we can't sin or fail or make serious mistakes. The Gospel story about Jesus praying all night and being in communion with God tells us more about this. First, that the Son of God needs to spend the night in prayer should make us think. If he is so close to God, one with God, why this need? And then the story suggests that he did this in preparation for the selection of the twelve apostles, one of whom eventually betrayed him. That Jesus needed to pray and that one of those he chose should turn out so badly point to the fact that he did not cease to be a full human being. Christian life for us, too, although we have already risen with Christ by baptism, also carries with it the need to pray and strengthen our union with God. Further, it does not remove from us, either, the possibility of failure or sin. Our faith and union with Christ do not provide a security for us that removes the need to pray, to think, and to be careful and vigilant. Strengthening our union with Christ at this altar means that we have the power and the endurance to deal with and eventually come through the hardships and pains of daily life.

Wednesday of the Twenty-Third Week in Ordinary Time—
Sorrowing but saved, despised but risen

Readings: Col 3:1-11; Luke 6:20-26
Resp. Psalm: Ps 145:2-3, 10-11, 12-13ab (L 439)

You were raised with Christ, the Letter to the Colossians tells us, and "your life is hidden with Christ in God" (Col 3:3). This provides a helpful framework for looking at the so-familiar Beatitudes which we hear today in Luke's version. If we are poor and hungry, lacking many things necessary for a good human life, still "the Kingdom of God" is ours; we are nevertheless already sharing in the risen life of Christ. If we are sorrowing because of enduring disagreements in the family, because of pain and illness, or because of difficult financial circumstances, we can still have a deep-down confidence that God enables us to live through this. If our faith makes others ignore us or consider us out of touch or even attack us, this is all a sharing in the Cross of Christ which always precedes a full resurrection. Being risen with Christ, in other words, is no simple cure-all for serious, even desperate human situations. But the resurrection encourages us to hope and trust that God does not mean this desperate situation to be the end—that God can help us through this and even bring good from it. Faith in Christ and our share in his risen life do not take us out of the messiness and misery of ordinary human life. Rather, faith offers us a way to go through our difficulties with hope and strength. Each time we share at this altar we are reminded by the so-ordinary-looking signs of the presence of Christ that in the agony, discouragement, and hard work of daily life our God is with us.

Thursday of the Twenty-Third Week in Ordinary Time—
Singing with gratitude

Readings: Col 3:12-17; Luke 6:27-38
Resp. Psalm: Ps 150:1b-2, 3-4, 5-6 (L 440)

Act and live worthy of people risen with Christ. So the Letter to the Colossians exhorts. The emphasis is very positive and concludes on a lyrical and large-hearted note: "Singing psalms, hymns and spiritual songs with gratitude in your hearts to God. And whatever you do, in word or in deed, do everything in the name of the Lord Jesus, giving thanks to God the Father through him" (Col 3:16-17). One cannot help but think how much more attractive and inspiring this kind of spirituality is than the negative and legalistic approach which many blame for alienation from Christian life and faith. Additionally, another strong note in Colossians' exhortations is the emphasis on the community—Christian life is life with others. The virtues commended pertain to living with each other, to life in community. Our two readings today echo each other. Luke gives us his version of the Sermon on the Mount. Again, as in Colossians, the words of the Lord ask behavior which is expansive, generous, and self-forgetting: "Love your enemies and do good to those who hate you . . . Give to everyone who asks of you, and from the one who takes what is yours do not demand it back. . . . Be merciful. . . . Stop judging . . . Give and gifts will be given to you; a good measure, packed together, shaken down, and overflowing, will be poured into your lap" (see Luke 6:27-38). Our Lord in Luke and St. Paul in Colossians urge us to confident and generous service of God and others; if this is what God wants, we need not worry about ourselves. "Sing[ ] . . . with gratitude in your hearts to God. And whatever you do, in word or in deed, do everything in the name of the Lord Jesus."

Friday of the Twenty-Third Week in Ordinary Time—
Turning a critical eye on ourselves

Readings: 1 Tim 1:1-2, 12-14; Luke 6:39-42
Resp. Psalm: Ps 16:1b-2a and 5, 7-8, 11 (L 441)

"I was once a blasphemer and a persecutor and an arrogant man" (1 Tim 1:13). The author of the First Letter to Timothy shows some of the self-knowledge which Jesus urges on us. The ill-willed exposure of other's faults is the target of his words. There's no law against exposing our own faults for any good purpose. But before making judgments, or simply to foreclose any judging of others, Jesus urges on us genuine self-knowledge. We're so close to ourselves that we often find it hard to be clear-sighted about "dear old me." Some people get profound self-knowledge through psychotherapy or counseling, but for most of us it's probably a lifetime project not involving professionals. Events and people who are close to us and honest to us may trigger flashes of insight about ourselves. It seems a paradoxical axiom that what we so willingly criticize in others is often a good indication of what is wrong with us. Acting on that principle seems very fruitful. It also fulfills Jesus' demands by making us more sympathetic to others and less willing to judge them. When we take Jesus' demands to heart, we inevitably end up needing to put our trust in God for the inadequacies which remain. Self-analysis should not prevent us from doing the works of service. Spending all our time getting to know ourselves would be too much self-concentration. Experience teaches that we learn about ourselves in the course of trying to serve others. The prayers of this Eucharist presume that we are always going to be in need of the forgiveness and help of God. "Lord, have mercy."

Saturday of the Twenty-Third Week in Ordinary Time—
Christ our rock

Readings: 1 Tim 1:15-17; Luke 6:43-49
Resp. Psalm: Ps 113:1b-2, 3-4, 5 and 6-7 (L 442)

For several decades it has been trendy for media personalities to have a guru (psychological, inspirational, or religious) in whom they trust. At the same time, in the same milieu, putting one's trust in Jesus Christ as the Word of God is often regarded as some sort of childish dependence. Christians believe that the Word of God is more trustworthy than any self-proclaimed wizard, guru, or preacher. This doesn't mean for thoughtful and informed Christians that they believe they can take the words of Scripture and shoot them at various targets like magic bullets. Trusting the biblical word of God supposes some reflection, thinking, prayer, and often assistance of scholars or authorities. Given all that, we find in the Scriptures an overall message assuring us of God's unfailing love for us and suggestions or exhortations for help through life and its trials, leading to ultimate victory over sin and death. Nothing or no one less than Christ can provide or be this same rock-like foundation. The Scriptures put it well in calling God and Christ over and over "my rock," "my refuge," "my stronghold" (see 2 Sam 22:2-3; Ps 18:3). Depending on God, on Christ, is simply a realistic recognition of our situation in this world. It is no more a sick dependence than is our dependence on the suppliers of our electricity and water. We, the church, its ministers, and the sacraments can point others and our world to Christ, the foundation of hope.

Monday of the Twenty-Fourth Week in Ordinary Time—
Praise and appreciation

Readings: 1 Tim 2:1-8; Luke 7:1-10
Resp. Psalm: Ps 28:2, 7, 8-9 (L 443)

The local Jewish elders tell Jesus that the centurion who is asking him for the cure of his servant deserves this favor. A little later as Jesus approaches the man's house, the centurion says to Jesus through friends, "Lord, do not trouble yourself, for I am not worthy to have you enter under my roof" (Luke 7:6). In effect, the elders tell Jesus that the centurion is worthy but the centurion himself says he is not. In many ways, isn't this the ideal arrangement? Others commend and promote us so we do not have to engage in self-promotion. This may not be the central point of this story, but it is one worth our pondering. Our desire for recognition and appreciation seems deeply rooted. Even when we know so much better than friends and associates what our defects are, we still find it hard to avoid hankering for commendation and praise. So, isn't it best if someone else does the recognizing, the appreciating? All this suggests that we should be more liberal, more generous in commending and appreciating others and what they do. Incidentally, this may also help us avoid some of our own self-pity and self-centeredness. Generous and genuine commendation of others puts the emphasis in our lives on praise and appreciation for God's creation, especially as shown in those we associate with and meet. Finally, we may learn to wait for and earn the appreciation of others. As we praise God through our Lord Jesus Christ at this Eucharist, may we learn too to praise the good surrounding us in family, friends, and co-workers.

Tuesday of the Twenty-Fourth Week in Ordinary Time—
Solidarity in our humanity

Readings: 1 Tim 3:1-13; Luke 7:11-17
Resp. Psalm: Ps 101:1b-2ab, 2cd-3ab, 5, 6 (L 444)

An occasional commentator complains that the author of the First Letter to Timothy does not uphold the high standards of the Gospel, but is rather too accommodating, simply going along with what is respectable in society. The author wants bishops, deacons, and women to be well thought of, moderate in drink, gentle, good parents, serious, trustworthy, etc. (The inclusion of women seems rather odd unless, as commentators suggest, this means deacons' wives or women deacons.) And it's true that the virtues listed here are often found in similar lists used by many outside the Christian community. This fact illustrates that whether Jews, non-believers, or Christians, we all have some common assumptions about how a good person acts. Further, it may be a good reminder to us that the more specifically Christian virtues presuppose or are built on natural virtues common to good people everywhere. For example, devotion to contemplation or a willingness to sacrifice for others does not dispense us from simple honesty and self-control. Over and over again the miracles of Our Lord (such as raising to life the young man in today's Gospel) attest to the Lord's compassion for and solidarity with the ordinary misery and sorrow of every human life. Our solidarity with suffering humanity comes before every distinction we make between "them" and "us."

Wednesday of the Twenty-Fourth Week in Ordinary Time—
Only experience will tell

Readings: 1 Tim 3:14-16; Luke 7:31-35
Resp. Psalm: Ps 111:1-2, 3-4, 5-6 (L 445)

"[W]isdom is vindicated by all her children" (Luke 7:35). This comes from Jesus as he expresses his frustration with his opponents who are so ill-willed that they blame John the Baptist for fasting and Jesus for feasting. Jesus seems to be saying that since these people dispute the value of everything he teaches or does, the final approval of his teaching has to come from practicing it. In effect, Jesus says the wisdom of God which he offers us reveals its worth in the life of anyone who tries to live by it. The difficulties our minds and hearts see in his teaching cannot be satisfied by some snappy answer or eloquent discourse. There is a risk; there is a surrender required before we can really know the value of the teaching of Jesus. It's like the man or woman who draws us into friendship or love. Giving ourselves to another always asks more than reason and words can justify. Couples who eventually marry do so, we hope, after learning over an adequate period of time that they can trust one other, that the relationship is worth every effort. To know the full value and impact of the following of Christ, we must be willing to try it day in and day out, over the long haul, through thick and thin, in excitement and boredom. Everything that is best and most worthwhile in life requires patience and time to prove itself. We realize what great wisdom there is in the way of Jesus only by living it and sharing it over a long period of time. People who are faithful to Christ through all the ups and downs of daily life reap a deep reassurance.

Thursday of the Twenty-Fourth Week in Ordinary Time—
The chain of love

Readings: 1 Tim 4:12-16; Luke 7:36-50
Resp. Psalm: Ps 111:7-8, 9, 10 (L 446)

Despite some confusion in the way the Gospel account has come down to us, the point seems to be that the woman loves so much because she has first been loved much by God and in the process forgiven much. That's the basic, incontrovertible essence of the New Testament teaching about God's love for us. It might be helpful to recall or remind ourselves of how much it means to us here and now to know that someone loves us. Hearing the words from someone loving or simply having that assurance from his or her behavior can keep us several feet off the ground for days, maybe even all our lives. A phone call, a card, or a bit of electronic mail giving evidence of someone's warm thoughts about us does the same to us. As we hear elsewhere in Scripture, "if God so loved us, we also must love one another" (1 John 4:11). A movie of recent years gained much attention for proposing that we should pass on the love we have received to others—to anyone—even if the person who gave love to us is not present nor even known. For those unfamiliar with the Christian message, this was an exciting and new idea; we hope it's old hat for Christians. We can never have too many reminders of the power of every bit of love and concern we show. In fact, to be exact, none of us can really know the power of our love and kindness. This is all the more reason not to be afraid of overdoing it. If we love being loved, we can be sure others love being loved as well.

Friday of the Twenty-Fourth Week in Ordinary Time—
An uncluttered life

Readings: 1 Tim 6:2c-12; Luke 8:1-3
Resp. Psalm: Ps 49:6-7, 8-10, 17-18, 19-20 (L 447)

"[W]e brought nothing into the world, just as we shall not be able to take anything out of it. If we have food and clothing, we shall be content with that" (1 Tim 6:7-8). These verses in the middle of today's first reading remind us of the contemporary movement toward a more simple life. The author goes on to talk about how wanting riches can destroy us: "[T]he love of money is the root of all evils" (6:10). Many people today, even without the benefit of this teaching, see the dangers in letting our lives be dominated by consumerism and by an inordinate desiring for and having things. An uncluttered life and environment leaves us more time for and helps point us toward more important elements of human life: the company of other people, family, friendships, conversations, contemplation, prayer, and reading. Human life is truly human when centered more on other human beings than on things. We become more fully human through our interaction with other people. When we fall for the lure of things, new gadgets, and all kinds of "stuff" we may never even have time to use, we easily become the prisoner of these possessions. Any movement toward a more simple life is often labeled counter-cultural, and it is. It takes some conviction and strong beliefs to resist the pull of our world of things and their accumulation. The real treasures are within our personalities and human nature, in life close to God and other human beings.

Saturday of the Twenty-Fourth Week in Ordinary Time—
Welcoming the word

Readings: 1 Tim 6:13-16; Luke 8:4-15
Resp. Psalm: Ps 100:1b-2, 3, 4, 5 (*L* 448)

Modern Catholics (many of them unfamiliar with the Scriptures) are often surprised to find so little in the New Testament about Mary, the mother of Jesus. But what we do have is extraordinarily helpful and it is found primarily in the opening two chapters of Luke's Gospel from which we are currently reading on these weekdays. Here she is depicted as the ideal or first disciple of the Lord, the one who is most open to God's coming into her life. In response to the angel's words about God's plan, she says: "May it be done to me according to your word" (Luke 1:38). The point of today's easily remembered parable is that God's word is fruitful only in those who open themselves to it: "But as for the seed that fell on rich soil, they are the ones who, when they have heard the word, embrace it with a generous and good heart, and bear fruit through perseverance" (Luke 8:15). That line, fulfilled so well in Mary, outlines the whole of Christian life from beginning to end: to be open to God's transforming word and through perseverance to allow it to bear fruit in one's life.

Monday of the Twenty-Fifth Week in Ordinary Time—
Let it shine

Readings: Ezra 1:1-6; Luke 8:16-18
Resp. Psalm: Ps 126:1b-2ab, 2cd-3, 4-5, 6 (*L* 449)

The Temple which the returning exiles are going to rebuild in Jerusalem is described at times as a light for the world, set on a mountain top, to illumine the whole world. We hear a similar idea in the Gospel: a light is not put under a bushel basket but put on a stand so as to be light for more people and shine a greater distance. All who have some gift bringing hope, joy, faith, and love owe it to the world—to their fellow human beings—to share it, to let it shine. Perhaps thinking of what our material world would be like without the benefits of electricity might help us realize the importance of light in any sense. It's probably impossible for most of us really to imagine what life would be like without electric light. True, there would be some benefits in being able to experience a starry night unimpeded by light from our cities. Human-made light, like everything we produce or do, has two sides to it. But leaving that aside for now, light makes possible so many joyous moments in our social life, in the world of music, theater, and sports. And on a deeper level, the light we can bring each other or be for each other is also a real treasure, one that shouldn't be hidden but raised high for everyone. How are we lights for each other, for our world? We are light through the good use of our talents and skills, and by the use of the unique gifts each of us has, of course. But, even more, we are light by bringing to the darkness of a world without Christ the hope, joy, and love flowing from our life in Christ and our belief in Christ.

Tuesday of the Twenty-Fifth Week in Ordinary Time—
Grace is everywhere

Readings: Ezra 6:7-8, 12b, 14–20; Luke 8:19-21
Resp. Psalm: Ps 122:1-2, 3-4ab, 4cd-5 (*L* 450)

The book of Ezra, which we hear this week, expresses Ezra's conviction that the Jews in exile were able to return to their own land because of the support of a well-disposed, non-Jewish ruler. Although the Jews did not even favor contact with such people, in this case Ezra and his fellow Jews owed King Darius gratitude. Christians have at times acted as if non-believers could not possibly do us any good. But experience tells us that we all depend upon each other in many ways and that the dependence crosses religious and family boundaries. Jesus points to something similar in today's Gospel. When told his mother and brothers are trying to get in, he says that there is a deeper relation to him than that of blood: "those who hear the word of God and act on it" (Luke 8:21) are his mother and brothers. Happily for many, family members do provide support and encouragement to faith. Others, unfortunately, have the experience of finding more sympathy and understanding outside the family. Everyone finds his or her spouse, of course, outside the family and often more understanding, deeper kinship. We discover in the course of growing up that compatibility and congeniality are not predictable in terms of family and background. We all need support and encouragement. We obstruct it by requiring that it come in a particular color or shape or from a particular source. Nothing in our created world is incapable of being the channel for God's grace, illumination, and support.

Wednesday of the Twenty-Fifth Week in Ordinary Time—
For body and soul

Readings: Ezra 9:5-9; Luke 9:1-6
Resp. Psalm: Tob 13:2, 3-4a, 4befghn, 7-8 (*L* 451)

Jesus sent the Twelve out "to proclaim the Kingdom of God and to heal the sick" (Luke 9:2). Later in today's Gospel the mission of the disciples is described similarly: "Then they set out and went from village to village proclaiming the Good News and curing diseases everywhere" (9:6). One part of their agenda is to proclaim the reign of God or spread the Good News—to teach what helps bring us to salvation. The other part is to heal the afflicted or cure disease, to take care of the body. Jesus is concerned for both the spirit and the body. The spirit needs to hear the Good News; the body needs to be healed of illness. All this warns us against the temptation to think that religion or faith is indifferent to the body and to our more earthly needs. Missionaries have been faulted at times by the comfortable in their armchairs for spending time on overcoming hunger and poverty. But it seems to be implicit in Jesus' teaching that there is no point in trying to speak to people about God and lofty religious matters when they are having a miserable time just surviving on the material level. It's especially insensitive for us who are comfortable to tell others who don't have basic needs that it doesn't matter. Christian faith is concerned about the welfare of the whole person; individually we, too, must share that concern. Collections, volunteering, and service for the poor, the hungry, the oppressed, and refugees are intrinsic to following Christ.

Thursday of the Twenty-Fifth Week in Ordinary Time—
Who is Jesus to me?

Readings: Hag 1:1-8; Luke 9:7-9
Resp. Psalm: Ps 149:1b-2, 3-4, 5-6a and 9b (L 452)

We are so used to the clear terms about Jesus with which we have grown up that we do not realize how hard it was for his contemporaries to figure him out. We call him Son of God, Savior, Redeemer, Lord, Messiah, or Christ. Yet it took Christians several centuries to hammer out agreement on these titles and descriptions. Luke's Gospel and the other Gospels show us the difficulty people around him had in figuring out who this Jesus was. In today's Gospel we hear of Herod's puzzlement; but he wasn't the only one. The Gospels also show us the difficulties his closest disciples had in, as we say, "figuring him out." Surely, we benefit from the struggles and work of our ancestors in the faith with respect to who Jesus is. But we need to continue the search or struggle in the sense that we try to comprehend what the meaning is for us in calling Jesus Lord, Savior, or Son of God. More particularly, what does Jesus especially mean to us in our lives today? How we think of him may vary

181

from time to time in our lives, depending on our circumstances. For what do we look to him? What do we expect from him? When do we especially seek his help? As we are united to God and each other in Communion with the Body and Blood of Christ, we might spend some time reflecting on how we think of him. Is he primarily our friend, our hope or strength, our judge, our joy and consolation, our Lord and Savior?

Friday of the Twenty-Fifth Week in Ordinary Time—
We are with the Lord in our sufferings
Readings: Hag 2:1-9; Luke 9:18-22
Resp. Psalm: Ps 43:1, 2, 3, 4 (L 453)

"Who do the crowds say that I am?" (Luke 9:18). This question of Jesus to his disciples continues Luke's focus on the identity of Jesus. Peter says that he regards Jesus as the Messiah, the Christ, the One long expected by his people. Jesus apparently pays little attention to this and forbids Peter to tell this to anyone. Then he calls himself simply "Son of Man," a very unpretentious title. Further, he emphasizes that he will suffer and be rejected before being raised up. At Mass we are assisting at the remembrance and representation of the suffering, death, and resurrection of Jesus. Many who come very faithfully to daily Mass are people of great faith and great hardships who confidently put before God their needs and those of suffering family members and friends. There is no better place to bring these concerns than to this daily recalling of the One who shared and still shares all that with us. Jesus' whole life showed his identification with the lowly, the suffering, and the rejected. He continues to be especially present to the same people: "a broken and contrite heart, O God, you will not despise" (Ps 51:17b; NRSV). Coming before him in our sorrows, worries, pains, and desperation is most appropriate. The Son of Man suffers and the members of the Body of Christ do, too.

Saturday of the Twenty-Fifth Week in Ordinary Time—
Here and now or hereafter?
Readings: Zech 2:5-9, 14-15a; Luke 9:43b-45
Resp. Psalm: Jer 31:10, 11-12ab, 13 (L 454)

One of the complaints made about Christianity or Christian preaching has been its emphasis on another world, on life after death. Critics charge that this kind of talk prevents people from being serious about the problems of life here and now, the problems of our earth and its inhabitants. Talk of the "other world" sometimes persuades believers simply to endure this world's problems with no concern about solving them. Hearing some of today's television preachers and others, we get a different slant on how successful true believers are in this life, here and now. One with faith in the Lord does not need to wait for another world to enjoy the rewards of faith, they seem to say. Both approaches fail to face directly the challenges of the world in which we live. Christians cannot be indifferent to the world's ills. Christians, in view of their Founder's life, have no reason to think that their faith will be rewarded with this-worldly success. The emphasis of Jesus on the inevitability of some form of the Cross, that even he will share this, is more realistic. And, obviously, this approach is much harder to take and accept: "they did not understand this saying" (Luke 9:45). What the Lord asks in the Gospels is, first, that we work hard to heal and help the suffering and the oppressed in our world; and, second, that we trust there will be a new and better life—but not necessarily tomorrow and certainly not without the Cross.

Monday of the Twenty-Sixth Week in Ordinary Time—
The way of the ordinary and daily

Readings: Zech 8:1-8; Luke 9:46-50
Resp. Psalm: Ps 102:16-18, 18-21, 29 and 22-23 (L 455)

Probably the most famous saint of the 19th century is the Carmelite nun Thérèse of the Child Jesus, Thérèse of Lisieux. Her famous "little way" illustrates practically the teaching of Jesus in today's Gospel: "For the one who is least among all of you is the one who is the greatest" (Luke 9:48). Her "little way" stressed self-giving in matters of ordinary, daily life. It is too easy, at least in our imaginations, to be drawn to renunciation in grandiose and large matters, in the heroic, the unusual, even in the outlandish. These are the matters attracting the media's attention and so often ours. The temptation is to underrate the value of little acts of self-forgetting, self-giving, patience, and forgiveness. But these are the ones closest at hand and, perhaps, the most difficult because they are so unsung, unappreciated, and unnoticed. Think of what some of these might be in our everyday life: keeping a smile and a friendly word for others who really have it so difficult; taking on the less elegant tasks around the house or work place; being patient with the habitually tardy or forgetful; restraining our tongue when we know so well that we have the only right answer on an issue; allowing those we regard as less informed or inarticulate to get a

183

word into a conversation; bearing patiently another's sense of humor which may either bore or irritate us. Most days we aren't required to join Christ on a cross, but there are always instances of smaller matters where we make life better for others by patience, forgiveness, and generosity. These become our "little way," a way of self-giving and a way of sharing in the sacrifice put before us at this Eucharist.

Tuesday of the Twenty-Sixth Week in Ordinary Time—
Let us go with you for God is with you

Readings: Zech 8:20-23; Luke 9:51-56
Resp. Psalm: Ps 87:1b-3, 4-5, 6-7 (L 456)

"Let us go with you, for we have heard that God is with you" (Zech 8:23) are the words concluding the first reading. In the Gospel we are at that place in Luke where Jesus and his disciples are making their way to Jerusalem for what will be the climax of his life. The disciples are going with him because they believe God is with him. The story from the prophet Zechariah makes the point that people are drawn to a place or to others where they see God working. Where God is or in whom God is present is not always so evident. In our own time people have been stung by their belief that God is with or is speaking through some person. Popular media preachers have attracted many with what appear to be miraculous signs, only to disappoint their followers with unseemly behavior. Evidence that God is with us or working in us must appear through love and generosity. Nothing in practice seems to draw people to God more effectively than the generous and effective love of a believer. In the reprimand Jesus gives his disciples for their desire to retaliate against the hostile Samaritans, we see this love in practice. In our own day and world it may not be the Samaritans but the poor, the immigrants, the Arabs, or foreigners who may be left out of the love of Christians. People are drawn to the Christian way of life by seeing God in the actions of Christians.

Wednesday of the Twenty-Sixth Week in Ordinary Time—
I will follow you

Readings: Neh 2:1-8; Luke 9:57-62
Resp. Psalm: Ps 137:1-2, 3, 4-5, 6 (L 457)

The would-be disciple tells Jesus that he will be his follower wherever Jesus goes. Jesus is going at the moment only to one place: to Jerusalem and the Cross. Wherever we go, wherever our life leads, we're going up to Jerusalem and the Cross in some form or other. It may be simply the pains of old age, disease, family disharmony, poverty, or heartbreak. One can say that the Cross is part of every human life and that would seem a very dark view of life if it were not for the assurance of the resurrection through belief in and following Jesus. The more scientifically inclined show us that this pattern of suffering, death, and rebirth is also in the details of nature around us; it's the pattern of the cosmos. This should tell us that we do not need to go looking for a cross; it's built into a life well lived, love generously given, work carried out faithfully, and fidelity to promises and responsibilities. Perhaps "Cross" sounds too dramatic as a description of the pains and difficulties accompanying a life of faithfulness and good work. And our cross may be marked not so much by drama as by nagging continuance or dulling annoyance. The psychoanalyst Carl Jung saw the physical nature of the cross as an apt picture of what happens in some form or other to all of us. Our plans, our desires, and our hopes are cancelled, thwarted, or at least made more difficult ("crossed," as we say) by various circumstances, bad people, our own uncontrolled passions or those of others, natural disasters, and the resistance of many elements in our environment. Following Jesus means, fortunately, both Cross and Resurrection. By our active participation at this altar, we face reality and gain the strength that life's crosses require of us. The follower of Christ knows that life will not be free of pain, but finds its meaning in the life, suffering, death, and resurrection of the Master present daily at this altar.

Thursday of the Twenty-Sixth Week in Ordinary Time—
To give what we have received

Readings: Neh 8:1-4a, 5-6, 7b-12; Luke 10:1-12
Resp. Psalm: Ps 19:8, 9, 10, 11 (L 458)

I've seen a note like this on church bulletins listing the personnel: "Ministers: all the members of the congregation." The mission to announce that the reign of God is at hand and our own ministry is to call our world to live in loving response to God's love; this is the right and duty of all who believe, not just clergy and apostles. We all minister in different, even unique ways. A look at history shows us that the ministers of Christ, whether clerical or lay, were all human beings like ourselves with limitations and faults. The love of God which the minister is to announce is for those who need healing. The lesson may be that we cannot wait until we are perfect before beginning to announce the Good News of the Lord; none of us ever becomes perfect in this life.

Even in our inadequacy we can do our part to tell others that there is forgiveness and help for all of us. All of us who receive the love of God once again in this Eucharist can minister the same love to all we meet.

Friday of the Twenty-Sixth Week in Ordinary Time—
Faithful above all

Readings: Bar 1:15-22; Luke 10:13-16
Resp. Psalm: Ps 79:1b-2, 3-5, 8, 9 (L 459)

Prophet and Gospel both speak of besetting sins of our race: unfaithfulness and unresponsiveness. Both seem the result of some sort of spiritual fatigue. We get tired trying to hold up our end; we get tired trying to be awake and forthcoming to demands on ourselves. We feel like protesting, "Why do I always have to be the one to bail out my errant brother? Why does everyone ask me for help? Why do I notice the suffering of another and feel obliged to help?" We feel that we've been singled out for harassment. We'd like the world and everyone to lay off a bit. But just this responsiveness and faithfulness are what God asks. Mother Teresa of Calcutta, when asked by a reporter if she thought she was successful, replied, "We're not called to be successful but faithful." Yes, we are to be faithful to God, to each other, to ourselves, to spouse, to family. Faithfulness and responsiveness get so little press and seem too boring and pedestrian. They are portrayed as the virtues of the stolid or of unimaginative nerds. The fact that people can think this way tells us they have never tried faithfulness and responsibility for any more than a few days. Success, especially of the kind we can put in numbers, is celebrated daily. But the real heroism open to all of us lies in simple and constant faithfulness. Coming here to Mass day after day witnesses this faithfulness. Going to our job day after day, picking up the kids, preparing meals day in and day out—all these show faithfulness. And at the altar the Lord in turn shows us the ultimate example of faithfulness and constancy. United with him, we too learn faithfulness.

Saturday of the Twenty-Sixth Week in Ordinary Time—
They returned rejoicing

Readings: Bar 4:5-12, 27-29; Luke 10:17-24
Resp. Psalm: Ps 69:33-35, 36-37 (L 460)

This Gospel has a downright jubilant, ecstatic, and exultant sound to it. All the vocabulary is words like "jubilation," "rejoice," and "blest" or "happy." After the woes and disappointment expressed by Jesus regarding the towns where he preached comes this exulting report. In most human lives, thank goodness, pains and joy alternate. Fortunately, we all have these exultant moments in our lives, these happy times we should remember and use to motivate ourselves. These are moments to which we can look back and be encouraged in less happy times. They tell us joy can be experienced again, things can be better. That present sorrow or ennui or drudgery does not last. In some desperate moments, we may need something like memories of good times to hang on to. The hard thing may be to welcome, as we should, joy and exultation without expecting that to be our daily fare. Every dinner is not a gourmet experience. Some dinners may be only cold cuts or peanut butter sandwiches. Most days have a certain predictability and quietness about them; other days are marked by pain, sickness, or real tragedy. But there will be happier, more exciting days. Further, it isn't simply a matter of waiting for the good times to happen. We can often do something to make the day brighter, to bring some cheer, hope, and joy to daily life. Most of us who come so close so often to the Lord here at Mass can do quite a bit to bring some joy into the lives of those around us. For here is where we most deeply experience it.

Monday of the Twenty-Seventh Week in Ordinary Time—
The unavoidable presence

Readings: Jonah 1:1–2:1-2, 11; Luke 10:25-37
Resp. Psalm: Jonah 2:3, 4, 5, 8 (L 461)

The wildly imaginative Book of Jonah seems to be poking fun at the kind of Hebrew prophet who would begrudge salvation to pagans. Humorously and with great exaggeration, the story tells of this Jonah who resists God's order to preach repentance to the pagans of Nineveh and thus save them. Jonah's own narrow view of salvation has him believing they should be allowed to go to damnation while he goes by boat to Tarshish, what we would call the end of the world: "Jonah made ready to flee to Tarshish away from the Lord" (Jonah 1:3). If somehow God were not in Tarshish as Jonah most improbably thinks, it would indeed be a God-forsaken place. But the point is that Jonah wants to escape God's demand. In the Gospel story the priest and Levite cross the street to avoid the robbed and beaten man, and thus really to escape the Lord who tells us that we meet and serve him in such suffering human beings (see Matt 25). An overly romantic view of our spiritual life sometimes makes people think they should encounter God in great ecstasy and excitement. But more regularly we meet the

Lord in the sick whom we comfort and help, in the poor whom we clothe and feed or give a job, in the worried and anxious, etc. While we may not book passage to "Tarshish" in order to avoid God, we do similarly try to avoid serving God's poor and desperate whom we may meet in daily life. It is better to face God's presence in every moment and every place—even with argument and protest—than to think we could somehow or somewhere avoid God.

Tuesday of the Twenty-Seventh Week in Ordinary Time— *In quiet and stillness*

Readings: Jonah 3:1-10; Luke 10:38-42
Resp. Psalm: Ps 130:1b-2, 3-4ab, 7-8 (L 462)

"Mary has chosen the better part" (Luke 10:42): sitting at the Lord's feet in quiet. In our world we take busyness as a sign of being alive; parents and children both take it for granted. Everyone has to be involved in doing something every minute of the day or, worse, being entertained by something (TV) every minute of the day. Sitting in quiet or reading is not just being "alone" —it is too often equated with being "lonely," a terrible thing! But we need time for silence and for doing nothing, especially since we have made Sunday pretty indistinguishable from Tuesday or Wednesday. Doing nothing, being quiet, is not evil, is not a bad thing. In fact, it's necessary if we are to give our life any direction and keep it focused on the right things. The great mathematician and thinker about religious matters, Pascal, wrote a lot about what he called "diversion." By this he meant the great efforts we make to be so busy that there is no chance to reflect on our lives or on what is really important. Pascal believed that it was in quiet and silence that we would come to realize our own emptiness apart from God, and so turn to God. Whether we accept that formula or not, it does seem pretty evident that God does not break in on our consciousness if our ears, our senses, are always full of immediate sensations. "Be still and confess that I am God!" we read in Psalm 46 (v. 11).

Wednesday of the Twenty-Seventh Week in Ordinary Time—*Tell it abroad*

Readings: Jonah 4:1-11; Luke 11:1-4
Resp. Psalm: Ps 86:3-4, 5-6, 9-10 (L 463)

We've been hearing from the Book of Jonah the last few days, which is a story full of humor and fancy but also one with a profound lesson. The story tells the Israelites of the time that, although they may be God's chosen people, God's intention is to spread the story of God's love for all peoples. God does not intend that message only for the Israelites. They, and more particularly the prophet Jonah, are to carry it to other peoples. Jonah earned his fame by his resistance to the idea that the God of his people, the Israelites, would want to save other people from sin and evil. But the Book teaches that Israel is to understand that her position as God's chosen people was not simply an ornament, but included a responsibility. Israel was to be the light that would show the love and mercy of God to the world. Christian belief is that this same love for those God has created is shown most brilliantly in Jesus Christ; it is focused especially in him. Christians are not to hug it to themselves but show it, make it visible to those around them. Belief in Christ and his saving power is never an excuse for feeling ourselves superior to those of other religions. Rather, it should spur us on to live out our belief in love and genuine compassion for human suffering anywhere in our world. Christian belief shows its value by a genuine love not limited by the color or beliefs of those we love.

Thursday of the Twenty-Seventh Week in Ordinary Time—
The sun will rise with its healing rays

Readings: Mal 3:13-20b; Luke 11:5-13
Resp. Psalm: Ps 1:1-2, 3, 4 and 6 (L 464)

The prophet Malachi expresses the temptation of many a thoughtful believer: "It is vain to serve God, and what do we profit by keeping his command, . . . Rather must we call the proud blessed; for indeed evildoers prosper" (Mal 3:14-15). We might say, "What good is it to be faithful to God, to Mass, to prayer? People who break every commandment in the book and flaunt it do very well, are blessed with wealth, and are free from illness, while poor, faithful people are abused within their families or lose their young children to accident or illness." And so on. It's understandable that people wonder about the wisdom of a Christian life. The fruit, the good of it is so often hard to see and so hard to feel. Faithful perseverance in prayer and trust in God which Jesus stresses today are indeed the real test of a Christian life. Momentary fervor or excitement about religion or God means little; staying with it day in and day out is what real faith is all about. The temptation to judge by the standards of our world is strong; we are pelted with advertisements for it every day. If, as we hear this today, we find this very hard to take, the best we can do is to pray that God

confirm in us the worth of following Christ. "[A]sk and you will receive" (Luke 11:9) means that God hears all the desires of our hearts
and the spoken and unspoken cries of those who are suffering (or, at
least, discouraged) human beings. In God's way and time faith and
hope are justified. Simply being here expresses our trust in this, no
matter how shaky that trust may be. God, Jesus tells us, is at least as
generous and trustworthy as a good parent.

Friday of the Twenty-Seventh Week in Ordinary Time—
Replacements needed

Readings: Joel 1:13-15; 2:1-2; Luke 11:15-26
Resp. Psalm: Ps 9:2-3, 6 and 16, 8-9 (*L* 465)

The end of the reading from Luke speaks of the possibility of falling
back into our bad habits, something we all experience at least with respect to eating, maybe drinking and smoking, or the good use of time.
One lesson probably is that it isn't enough to break a bad habit; we
need also to replace it with some good habit. Otherwise, the vacuum
invites some new evil or the return of the same old bad habits. An
effective change of life or repentance includes turning to something
better or making some good plans, decisions, or resolutions. Time
spent on sleazy reading or TV viewing needs to be replaced with time
spent on more positive interests and activities. A habit of badmouthing
others or being excessively critical needs to be replaced by a habit of
looking for the positive and good in others and speaking of it. Money
once spent on drink needs to be channeled to helping someone. Each
of us can think of what needs to replace the old and deficient in our
life and what new habit or practice needs to be taken up. None of
this, of course, is simply a matter of technique, but needs to be rooted
in prayer and reflection leading to self-knowledge. Our falling back
into old bad habits teaches us that change is never simply a matter of
stronger determination on our part, but change is primarily a matter
of more receptivity to God's action in us.

Saturday of the Twenty-Seventh Week in Ordinary Time—
Worship and work

Readings: Joel 4:12-21; Luke 11:27-28
Resp. Psalm: Ps 97:1-2, 5-6, 11-12 (*L* 466)

Like the woman in today's Gospel who exclaims how impressive Jesus
is and how honored his mother should feel, we can too easily stay at

the level of admiration of Jesus or knowledge about him. Christian history and secular history, too, are full of examples of great admiration for Jesus and even great devotion to him, as well as much knowledge about him, all without any corresponding action. We are conditioned so that the connection between adoration of the Lord and service of the homeless can whiz right by us. At times Christians have spent vast amounts of money on the decoration of our worship spaces, while ignoring the poverty of the very people hired to do the work. It's not a matter of either/or: worshiping God fittingly and praying, on the one hand, and serving others, on the other. They go together. We praise and worship God, but ideally this is accompanied by seeing the implications for our treatment of others. Grace, will, and energy help us do this. The woman in the Gospel says to Jesus, in effect, "Your mother should be proud to have given birth to such an impressive son." Jesus says, in effect, "It's better yet if your belief in me gives birth to concern for the poor, the abused, the victims of oppression and hatred." We are one Body with and in Christ, the Eucharist tells us. That is true at Mass and outside the church too.

Monday of the Twenty-Eighth Week in Ordinary Time—
Unchanging but ever new

Readings: Rom 1:1-7; Luke 11:29-32
Resp. Psalm: Ps 98:1bcde, 2-3ab, 3cd-5 (L 467)

Paul knows his mission is to announce the Gospel, promised long ago through the prophets and realized in Jesus Christ. What is revealed to the world in Jesus Christ is, in one sense, nothing new. What is new is the dramatic expression in a living human being who shared our life, suffered, died, and rose. It is nothing new insofar as God didn't first begin to love human beings when Jesus was born. God has always loved creation and everything in it. The refrain in the first chapter of the first book of the Bible, Genesis, is that God looked on everything in creation and saw that it was good. We can see the apparently tough approach God takes with Israel as similar to the regulations parents must use with growing children. God has never really changed the message; it has always been that God loves us and wills what is best for us. There is no time when we could say that God did not love the human race. The packaging has been different, depending on human receptivity or maturity. The prophets, Jesus himself (presented so continually in Luke as the great prophet), and the apostles all have proclaimed one Gospel, one great assurance for human beings. We are not abandoned;

191

evil, sin, disease, war, and death do not have the last word. God is with us and for us; most concretely, the Eucharist assures us of that.

Tuesday of the Twenty-Eighth Week in Ordinary Time—
Useful criticism

Readings: Rom 1:16-25; Luke 11:37-41
Resp. Psalm: Ps 19:2-3, 4-5 (L 468)

In terms of what we expect at a dinner party, Jesus is a rather abrasive guest at the table of the Pharisee. Moments after entering the room, he throws some very critical words at his Pharisee host. This confirms that Jesus is indeed a prophet for, as Abraham Heschel says, the true prophet is not someone we would invite to dinner a second time. Listening to Jesus or reading his words is not like reading our favorite romance or mystery writer. His words provoke, irritate, and sometimes simply confuse. While much of what he says gives comfort and encourage-ment, his words often are full of nettles, full of criticism and challenge. How hard we all find it to take criticism! Even our closest friends must criticize us gingerly and only after finding the right moment. A steady diet of criticism is not for most of us. The ceaseless activist or agitator easily tests our patience, no matter how relevant the message. But, given all that, it's good to be shaken up, good to have our behavior and thought questioned, and good to have our comfort and satisfaction disturbed. Growth depends on it. Jesus does not leave the Pharisee, no matter how offended, in that state, but tells him that there is a way out: "[G]ive alms, and behold, everything will be clean for you" (Luke 11:41). In other words, if we are provoked to more genuine concern for others, we are well on the way to growth and to true discipleship. Any discouragement resulting from criticism would only serve to turn us more fervently to the Lord for strength and change: "But say the word and [my soul shall be] healed" (Luke 7:7).

Wednesday of the Twenty-Eighth Week in Ordinary Time—
Saving the essentials

Readings: Rom 2:1-11; Luke 11:42-46
Resp. Psalm: Ps 62:2-3, 6-7, 9 (L 469)

Institutions (the church included) are in constant danger of spending more time and effort on their own preservation and convenience than on the service of their members. The results of this occupy Jesus as he utters the woes in today's Gospel. First, there is all the attention and time given to minutiae, to little matters which are so insignificant in the big picture. We can become so preoccupied with legal matters, for example, that we drive willing but very mobile young Christians away from celebrating a marriage in the church when we surround it with rules and regulations suited to a more stable age. Another example: ecclesiastics become so concerned about getting sufficient honor and respect—"seat of honor in synagogues" (Luke 11:43)—that Christianity seems to be more about them than about the Lord. Prelates talk more about serving the pope than Christ. Or, as in the tenor of Jesus' complaint against the lawyers, people in authority make demands on others that only serve unnecessarily to burden Christian life. At the same time, little is done to highlight the essentials of service to the Lord. While all these seem to be lessons primarily for those in authority, they concern all of us insofar as we exercise authority at home or on the job. And, too, these lessons concern us since we Christians have a right to remind our leaders, when necessary, of where their priorities should be. *Help us all, Lord, not to lose sight of you and the service of God and neighbor amid the rules and rubrics of our faith.*

Thursday of the Twenty-Eighth Week in Ordinary Time—
All is gift

Readings: Rom 3:21-30; Luke 11:47-54
Resp. Psalm: Ps 130:1b-2, 3-4, 5-6ab (L 470)

The message of St. Paul in his Letter to the Romans (and elsewhere) often strikes us as so contrary. We feel the importance of what we do in our relation to God, yet he seems to knock it down and call it useless. He says, for example, "What occasion is there then for boasting? It is ruled out. . . . For we consider that a person is justified by faith apart from works of the law" (Rom 3:27-28). Faithful followers of Christ have nothing of which to boast, no claims to make on their own behalf; if we please God it is not due to anything we do. What counts before God is accepting what Jesus has done for us and trusting in it. Possibly this is a little easier to accept if we recall that our very existence and that of the universe itself is something God did not have to bring about. Everything is a gift from God: life, our good qualities, our families, friends, and abilities and what they achieve. Paul is extending this further by pointing out that any good we do is also the result of a gift; that the eternal life for which we hope and the presence of God for which we hope is, again, God's gift. There are moments in life when all this is clearer and we should hold on to them and remember them.

For example, the birth of a child, despite all we know of the biology of it, strikes us often as an extraordinary gift. Discovering that we are truly loved by someone comes to us as a wonderful gift. Some reflection can make clearer to us that the greatest things in life are gifts and not achievements of ours.

Friday of the Twenty-Eighth Week in Ordinary Time—
Non-essential fears

Readings: Rom 4:1-8; Luke 12:1-7
Resp. Psalm: Ps 32:1b-2, 5, 11 (*L* 471)

One commentary entitles this section of Luke's Gospel "Courage in time of danger." "Fear" in today's context is the anxiety we feel in the face of some threat or crushing possibility. Most of us are concerned to erase such fear from our lives and to live in confidence and hope. There may be justifiable fear, but many other fears do not merit the hold they have on us and which we'd do well to forget. The words of Jesus today urge us to cut down on what we might call "non-essential fears," fear of factors having no power to do ultimate harm. With time and deeper faith we can hope to diminish all the secondary fears that so often obsess us and disturb our sleep. Absorbing more of Saint Paul's teaching on faith and trust in God, and less focus on our own accomplishments, can lessen the hold of fear on us and replace it with courage rooted in trust in the God who cares for us. The final word must be the last in today's Gospel: "Do not be afraid" (Luke 12:7).

Saturday of the Twenty-Eighth Week in Ordinary Time—
Hope has more options

Readings: Rom 4:13, 16-18; Luke 12:8-12
Resp. Psalm: Ps 105:6-7, 8-9, 42-43 (*L* 472)

Abraham's faith, a recurring theme in Paul's Letter to the Romans which we hear for a couple of weeks, is a good springboard for thinking about facets of faith and particularly about our own faith. Today's first reading suggests pondering the relation of faith and hope. Our translation uses a well-known but odd English expression; we hear that "He [Abraham] believed, hoping against hope, that he would become the father of many nations" (Rom 4:18). Abraham believed, that is, trusted in God although all the evidence was against this. Or, although Abraham's hope seemed impossible, he persisted and did become the father of many nations. Abraham had been told that he and

Sarah in their advanced age would become parents and ultimately the father and mother of many nations, of offspring as plentiful as the stars of the heavens. Our trust in the Lord means, similarly, that we must in any number of moments during our life expect that God finds an out and brings about a solution for the terrible anxieties and fears besetting us. Humanly speaking and from our limited perspective, things look hopeless. But God has more options and, of course, more power than we can imagine. Like God's Son going to the Cross, we need to trust that there is more to life than what we perceive.

Monday of the Twenty-Ninth Week in Ordinary Time—
Our only true security

Readings: Rom 4:20-25; Luke 12:13-21
Resp. Psalm: Luke 1:69-70, 71-72, 73-75 (L 473)

Clearly, to "believe in the one who raised Jesus our Lord from the dead" (Rom 4:24) is much more than accepting someone's report that Jefferson High beat Yorkville in last Saturday's game. To believe in him is to have total trust in God's loving care for us: willingness to save us from sin and death and to raise us too from the dead. To be a Christian means that our security is in God and the risen Son of God. Today's Gospel is a mixture of an admonition against greed and an admonition to put one's trust in God and not accumulate wealth. This recurring refrain in Luke's presentation of the Lord's teaching may just be the most difficult demand of discipleship. Like the rich man in the Gospel, we readily collect "things"—everything from jewels and frozen food to property—in order to make ourselves feel secure, in order, as we say so revealingly, "to have something to fall back on." The desire for security seems to be one of the most deep-seated traits of our nature. It may explain many things in our behavior from teenage dating to the way people accept sightings of Christ on a warehouse wall. We want something or someone to hold on to. To trust ourselves completely to the God we do not see and not to have something more concrete to fall back on is very tough, indeed. The people who do it almost completely are the ones we call saints! We stand with mouths open at the sight of them. Most of us compromise quite a bit. Often, it seems, only misfortune can teach us to trust totally in God. *Help us, Lord, to learn some of that now.*

Tuesday of the Twenty-Ninth Week in Ordinary Time—
Present in the here and now

Readings: Rom 5:12, 15b, 17-19, 20b-21; Luke 12:35-38
Resp. Psalm: Ps 40:7-8a, 8b-9, 10, 17 (*L* 474)

When we look back at our life, no matter how much time that covers, we must be amazed at how unconscious, how unaware, we seem to have been so much of the time. What were we thinking? Were we thinking at all? Where have the years gone? Where were we? Absent, it seems, so often. Today the Lord tells us that it will be well for those of us whom the master finds wide-awake on his return. "Wide-awake" can be a summary term for our whole response to God, to God's love, to our own creation, and to our own existence. To be attentive is a matter of being fully present where we are and fully present in whatever we are doing—attentive to those we live and work with, to family members and friends, to opportunities to do good, and to the needs of suffering and hurt people around us. It means, too, of course, that we aim to be wide-awake to God in our prayer; that we don't let ourselves use our prayer time or Mass for planning the brunch menu or our next trip or calculating expenses. We try this split-focus in everything. We go to the gym and then keep a cellular phone nearby, the better to distract our attention from exercise. And why not "hang up and drive," as a bumper sticker puts it? It shouldn't be on the basketball court only that we focus our energies and thoughts on one thing; it's a program for every facet of life: "Blessed are those servants whom the master finds vigilant on his arrival" (Luke 12:37).

Wednesday of the Twenty-Ninth Week in Ordinary Time—
Gifted and giving

Readings: Rom 6:12-18; Luke 12:39-48
Resp. Psalm: Ps 124:1b-3, 4-6, 7-8 (*L* 475)

"Noblesse Oblige" is an old axiom. We might translate it as position, wealth, and privilege carry with them obligations to others. The last two lines of today's Gospel echo this axiom: "Much will be required of the person entrusted with much, and still more will be demanded of the person entrusted with more" (Luke 12:48). St. Paul says in the first reading that we have been given new life; we are under the power of grace. We should be slaves or servants of justice. The position of privilege obliging Christians to do more is our position in grace as sons and daughters of God raised to new life in Christ. As believers we trust

that God loves us, that we are destined for life with God, and that love and the good of our fellow humans is more important than wealth, position, or power. We might be propelled to more generosity and concern if we started each day by recalling what great gifts have been given to us. On a purely human level, too, we have reason to think the same way; we live in relative comfort and security, maybe even having wealth. What did we ever do to deserve this? Our best response to all this is to look for opportunities daily to pass on hope and help to the less fortunate. It shouldn't be a matter of fearing what happens if we don't use our gifts well, but more a matter of being happy that we are able to give to others. At this table we share with others the life of God through the Body and Blood of Christ. We can go from this celebration armed with enthusiasm and courage.

Thursday of the Twenty-Ninth Week in Ordinary Time—
Set ablaze by the Lord

Readings: Rom 6:19-23; Luke 12:49-53
Resp. Psalm: Ps 1:1-2, 3, 4 and 6 (L 476)

"I have come to set the earth on fire," Jesus says (Luke 12:49). He comes to light a fire under us. In many ways it's similar to the theme of being wide-awake which we heard this past Tuesday. Both themes mean to stir up some energy, vitality, and enthusiasm in us. The hope is that we should leave this Mass afire to make a difference in our environment; to live up to our high dignity as sons and daughters of God and as members of the Body of Christ; to be afire with the desire to meet enmity with love, indifference with care, backbiting with kindness, and gloom with hope and joy. If being afire doesn't happen today because we have a bad cold or are in the grip of a recurring ailment, maybe it will happen another day. But to be afire with God's life in us, with the power God gives us—we'd all like that, wouldn't we? All of us have our bad days, our low-energy days, our days when we feel heavy and even sad. But there's nothing wrong with praying for a little fervor and fire. If we can generate that for a football game or a shopping trip, as Christians we are certainly capable of generating some fire and enthusiasm for the way we face life with others.

Friday of the Twenty-Ninth Week in Ordinary Time—
Two sides of the self

Readings: Rom 7:18-25a; Luke 12:54-59
Resp. Psalm: Ps 119:66, 68, 76, 77, 93, 94 (L 477)

The opening line from St. Paul strikes us twentieth-century people as pretty harsh: "I know that good does not dwell in me, that is, in my flesh" (Rom 7:18). We live in what might be called "the age of affirmation." Teachers aim to encourage and affirm their students; education uses various ways of getting around "failing" students. We find it pretty hard to accept saying that no good dwells in us. We'd tend rather to say that much good dwells in all of us and it just has to be encouraged or brought forth. St. Paul's use of the word "flesh," too, causes problems. Other translations make a point that flesh here means one's non-spiritual self or worldly self. This gets the meaning across and avoids the suggestion that somehow the flesh, the bodily part of us, is the big problem. The other side of the coin is that what good dwells in us dwells in our spiritual selves, the selves who recognize God's right to guide our lives and actions. The unspiritual self is that part of us or those forces within us which are guided by selfish considerations and worldly standards. Most of us can recognize ourselves in the description of the spiritually interior contest about what will prevail—selfishness or God's will. The struggle may be between lust and genuine love for another. It may be between the desire to make a lot of money dishonestly and the desire to serve the good of our fellow human beings. As Paul says, the answer to our struggle is not in laws or knowledge, but in the power of the risen Christ in us through baptism and the Eucharist.

Saturday of the Twenty-Ninth Week in Ordinary Time—
Some urgency

Readings: Rom 8:1-11; Luke 13:1-9
Resp. Psalm: Ps 24:1b-2, 3-4ab, 5-6 (L 478)

In Luke's Gospel Jesus is on his way to Jerusalem. His hearers, he tells them, still have time to repent before the Day of Judgment, that is, the death of Jesus. We say God's mercy is infinitely patient, but the words of Jesus today say that we should not take that for granted. Somehow, despite God's limitless patience and love, we still need to recognize that there is some urgency to how we respond. Procrastination almost defines the way we so often live our lives. So much is put off until another day. For example, we put off repentance and change in our lives; we put off a visit to a parent or sick friend; we put off quitting smoking or cutting down on the alcohol; we put off taking the initiative in some bad situation; or we put off a decision to give time daily to prayer or holy reading. God's mercy is no excuse for inaction or procrastination or for self-satisfaction. Just as it is not right to take for granted our patient and forgiving friends, so also the patience of God must awaken in us some energetic determination to make some changes in our lives. The fact that we may not be able to change everything in our lives for the better doesn't mean we cannot begin somewhere and at some time, here and now. God still looks for some fruit on the tree which is our life.

Monday of the Thirtieth Week in Ordinary Time—
The inseparable duo

Readings: Rom 8:12-17; Luke 13:10-17
Resp. Psalm: Ps 68:2 and 4, 6-7ab, 20-21 (L 479)

The expression, "to live according to the flesh" (Rom 8:12), means for many a life of sensuality—primarily of sexual indulgence. We can't help but wonder if St. Paul's use of the term in Romans has been at least partly responsible for the long tradition in the West of blaming so much sin on the body, on the flesh. Our Lord himself says that the worst sins are those that come from within a person: sins of hatred, envy, aggression, etc. Yet in much of Christian spirituality over the centuries, the body has taken it on the chin as the leading cause of our sins. A more careful look at St. Paul reveals that in condemning a life lived according to the flesh he was not talking primarily about indulgence in cheesecake and Chivas Regal or even sex. Paul speaks of two sorts of people: those who live according to the spirit and those who live according to the flesh. The terms refer to what dominates our thinking and acting. According to the spirit means a life lived under the influence of the Holy Spirit. "According to the flesh" means a life governed by our human weakness or under the domination of human and worldly values. Pride, arrogance, self-righteousness, avarice, and aggressive abuse of others are the most obvious qualities of such a "fleshly" life. No more than any other authentically biblical writer does Paul imply that the body, the flesh, is evil. The human being as created by God is good, very good, Genesis tells us (see Gen 1:31). The concern of Jesus to cure so many bodily ills itself illustrates God's respect for the body. The body deserves as much or more respect from

199

Christians than it gets in a fitness center. For us it works hand in hand with our spirit to honor God and serve others.

Tuesday of the Thirtieth Week in Ordinary Time—
Offering hope

Readings: Rom 8:18-25; Luke 13:18-21
Resp. Psalm: Ps 126:1b-2ab, 2cd-3, 4-5, 6 (*L* 480)

There are so many translations of the Bible because there is room for differences about the meaning of certain ancient expressions. Our first reading today ends with the sentence, "But if we hope for what we do not see, we wait with endurance" (Rom 8:25). Others take the Greek original to mean waiting with eager expectation. It is more like a person looking for the first signs of the dawn. "Endurance" seems more passive. "Eager expectation" puts a bit more zest into the enterprise. Today's parables about the mustard seed and the leaven also point to hope—hope that the kingdom of God grows and that more of us accept the reign of God in our lives. While "what the world needs now" may still be love, it also very much needs hope. We need to offer the young and those around us reasons for hope. Vatican Council II reminded Christians of their responsibility to be strong enough themselves to leave the next generation a reason for hope. Aren't we, by reason of our faith, those who are this strong? Our own experience in most cases offers reasons for hope, reasons we can pass on to others. Instead of griping about all that is new or complaining that the world is getting worse in every way, we can look for signs of improvement and for the good people do: amnesty for political prisoners, forgiveness of debts, easing the pain of the terminally ill, etc. Possibly we can even hope for the day when the influence of money is removed from politics. There are signs of hope around us and in our own lives. We witness to hope by our speech and our activity.

Wednesday of the Thirtieth Week in Ordinary Time—
More study or more practice?

Readings: Rom 8:26-30; Luke 13:22-30
Resp. Psalm: Ps 13:4-5, 6 (*L* 481)

"[W]e do not know how to pray as we ought" (Rom 8:26). This expression of St. Paul's could have come out of the mouth of many a Christian. Many Christians, indeed, complain that they do not know how to pray. One suspects at times that this is our old ploy for excusing

ourselves from doing something by saying that we need more instruction and more knowledge. In that way we put off doing something we
are really unwilling to undertake. It's like the "we'll have to study that"
approach so popular in institutions. An ability to pray certainly comes
partly from just doing it. But there is more, and this is what Paul ad-
dresses. We don't know how to pray? He tells us that even our groan-
ings, our inarticulate desires, our sighs, our tears, and discouragement
can all be prayers. Paul says the Spirit is ready to pray for and within
us if we allow it. Such situations probably do just that. Another reason
why the Spirit must pray within and why we must allow the Spirit to
pray is that we do not actually know ourselves well enough to get too
specific in our prayer. We do not know for sure what is for our best or
for the best of others around us. While nothing forbids our praying for
parent, husband, child, or our own self, our prayer needs to be rooted
in our great confidence that God loves each one of us and hears us. If we
know God loves us, we can leave our prayer more open ended. We can
leave the results up to God. For the Spirit "intercedes for the holy ones
according to God's will" (Rom 8:27).

Thursday of the Thirtieth Week in Ordinary Time—
Christ to each other

Readings: Rom 8:31b-39; Luke 13:31-35
Resp. Psalm: Ps 109:21-22, 26-27, 30-31 (L 482)

Paul's beautiful statement of confidence in God's love for us and its
power to conquer everything contrasts starkly with the talk of Jesus
about his rejection by his people, a rejection of the One who brings the
message of God's love. It makes us wonder sometimes why God chose
this apparently difficult and messy way of making clear divine love
for the world. Why not paint it in bright and bold colors across the
skies for everyone to see? In one part of the sky it could have been in
English, in another in Arabic, in another in Swahili, etc. No, God seems
to make it purposely difficult by tying the revelation of divine love to
acceptance of a fellow human being. This really is another way of un-
derlining a fundamental truth about God's relation to human beings:
we cannot be related in love to God without a willingness to accept
and love our fellow human beings. We only truly accept God's love
if we are willing to see God's love around us by accepting assurances
of God's love for us in the good actions and care of others. The other
side of this, equally important, is that others know God loves them if
someone cares for them in their loneliness, their need, their pain, their

discouragement, their hunger, and their homelessness. In this sacrament we become Christ's Body in order to be Christ to and for others.

Friday of the Thirtieth Week in Ordinary Time—
Beyond our disappointment

Readings: Rom 9:1-5; Luke 14:1-6
Resp. Psalm: Ps 147:12-13, 14-15, 19-20 (*L* 483)

"I have great sorrow and constant anguish in my heart" (Rom 9:2), is Paul's confession about his disappointment that his fellow Israelites have not embraced belief in Christ. Something similar occurs in our time in the hearts of parents and friends who are saddened by the apparent indifference of sons and daughters or friends to Christ, the sacraments, and life in the Christian community. Often they have been brought up in the practice of the following of Christ, taught about and educated in it, and given some very good example; yet some seem to reject it all. Neither Paul nor we can force the wills and choices of others. We need such confidence in the intrinsic value of our own commitment that such disappointments do not lessen generosity or good spirit. Like Paul's Israelites, we have been blessed with closeness to God and Christ, life in the Body of Christ and, it is to be hoped, the assurance and strength this brings. Rather than wailing over what isn't and dreaming of some other time, we do better to give the present (and those who have disappointed us) our best, our gifts, our hope. Whining, nagging, complaining, self-pity, grumpiness, and bitterness—even if supposedly for religious reasons—are not, as Paul would say, the fruits of the spirit but of the flesh (see Rom 5:19-23), the fruits of an attitude too short-sighted. Rather, our true following of Christ shows itself in joy, kindness, forgiveness, trust in the future, and perseverance in prayer and worship.

Saturday of the Thirtieth Week in Ordinary Time—
Jesus and Paul in other words

Readings: Rom 11:1-2a, 11-12, 25-29; Luke 14:1, 7-11
Resp. Psalm: Ps 94:12-13a, 14-15, 17-18 (*L* 484)

It's too easy and a shame that we often leave our understanding of this parable of Jesus on such a merely self-serving level. We end up having Jesus make the point that rather than taking the first place at a banquet, take the last place. Then the host, if he so wishes, can bring us up to a more prominent place and we get a double reward: our humility is praised and our special value to the host is made apparent. Why should Jesus spend time making such a banal point revolving around self-interest? This story, like so many others of Jesus, says much more, and teasing more meaning out of the parable is partly the point of teaching in parables. They are meant to challenge us. The point of this story is not that some human being recognizes self-effacement and rewards us with a better position, but that if we recognize our own inability to save ourselves, if we, therefore, put our trust in God, then God saves us. Jesus is saying in his own language what Paul says in Romans in much different terminology. We are not saved by trying to impress God with all the great things we have done or can do, but by putting our trust in grace. Too simple? Too easy? That's part of the scandal of the Gospel: it doesn't tell us that we are saved by the exercise of our great minds or talents.

Monday of the Thirty-First Week in Ordinary Time—
How unsearchable are his ways

Readings: Rom 11:29-36; Luke 14:12-14
Resp. Psalm: Ps 69:30-31, 33-34, 36 (L 485)

God's gifts are forever. God's love is persistent. God, it seems, is always, in a sense, "after" us. We are usually not that patient with others. After a certain number of disappointments in others, we wash our hands of them. God doesn't act that way toward us. God is the "Hound of Heaven" (of Francis Thompson's famous poem). Although St. Paul at times sounds very hostile to his fellow, not-converted Jews, these remarks here show his belief that God's agreement (covenant) with the Jews has not been disowned and that God remains faithful: "The gifts and the call of God are irrevocable" (Rom 11:29). This is all the more reason for us not to presume that anyone is lost or beyond God's love. In the second part of today's first reading, Paul underlines how unsearchable are the ways of God, suggesting that we need to be more tentative in attempting to tell others the will of God. Throwing around that term "God's will" too easily is dangerous. It can actually be frightening when one thinks of how it has been used historically. The crusaders used the conviction that they were doing God's will to do a lot of harm even to fellow Christians. Any presumption we have that we know God's will must always be tempered by some consultation with others and by the standard of love. Love is the fulfillment of the law, Paul tells us, and anything less can hardly be God's will.

Tuesday of the Thirty-First Week in Ordinary Time—
Given in order to give

Readings: Rom 12:5-16ab; Luke 14:15-24
Resp. Psalm: Ps 131:1bcde, 2, 3 (L 486)

Sometimes we think that individualism such as we are all familiar with had its beginnings only in the modern era or the American West, but Paul faced it as a problem in the churches to which he wrote, especially to the Corinthians and here to the Romans. Putting our own fulfillment and desires ahead of the welfare of all others may, in fact, be one of the consequences of our share in the world's sin. "I, me, and mine" have always been pretty popular with us. Paul's response to this is the image of Christians as one Body in Christ: "We, though many, are one Body in Christ and individually parts of one another. . . . [W]e have gifts that differ according to the grace given to us" (Rom 12:5-6). Ideally, like the members of our own human body—the various senses and limbs and faculties—the members of the Body of Christ work together for the good of the whole without envying others, maligning them, or degrading them in any way. Further, each of us has indispensable gifts which we bring to this Body and without which the Body cannot function properly. Our talents or specialties are gifts and Paul tells us they are to be used so that they become gifts for others, for example, doing "acts of mercy, with cheerfulness." (12:8). The gospel tells us that if a major purpose of life is to find our particular gift, it is also of utmost importance to not hug it to ourselves but to give it away with the example and strength of our Lord.

Wednesday of the Thirty-First Week in Ordinary Time—
Let go and enjoy

Readings: Rom 13:8-10; Luke 14:25-33
Resp. Psalm: Ps 112:1b-2, 4-5, 9 (L 487)

What can the people one meets at weekday Mass make of the strong language of Jesus today? Are we going to put our home up for sale or, better yet, give it away, putting the family out in the streets? If we take into account the many references in Luke's Gospel to the dangers of wealth, it may help us make some sense of this strong statement: "Everyone of you who does not renounce all his possessions cannot be my disciple" (Luke 14:33). Mahatma Gandhi once summarized the Hindu religion in some words taken from one of its sacred books: "All is filled with God. Renounce it and enjoy it." This may offer a clue to the teaching of Jesus about renunciation. To simplify: all we have comes from God; we are caretakers of what is God's. Our response is to use it in love (see the first reading); above all, we are to take lightly property and possessions, not grasping them as if they were our true security. God knows we and all people need possessions, but there should be some looseness in our grasp of them, coupled with a readiness to let go of them, to share them, and to use them well.

Thursday of the Thirty-First Week in Ordinary Time—
Lost and found

Readings: Rom 14:7-12; Luke 15:1-10
Resp. Psalm: 27:1bcde, 4, 13-14 (L 488)

The context of today's Gospel is important for our understanding: Jesus is sitting with sinners, tax collectors, "the wrong people," and the nearby Pharisees are scandalized. They think he should be spending his time with those who observe the Law, not with this scum. The Lord's parables rebuke the attitude of the Pharisees; to paraphrase, "if you, you, and you lost a sheep, wouldn't you go in search of it?" The preceding chapter had ended with the words of Jesus: "Whoever has ears to hear ought to hear" (Luke 14:35). The Pharisees and scribes, too full of their own judgments, are not going to listen. What would they have to learn from some wandering preacher who hangs around with these bums? But it's the tax collectors and bad people who are willing to hear, to listen. So Jesus goes to them. So-called sinners, aware of their deficiencies and sins, are much more capable of receiving a call to change and reform than are those who think they've already arrived. In the first reading from Romans, Paul says, "Why then do you judge your brother or sister?" (Rom 14:10). Those who know themselves realize they have no time and certainly no expertise for judging others. Rather, they look to themselves. As Paul says in conclusion, "So then each of us shall give an account of himself to God" (14:12). Judging others is essentially a self-satisfying exercise by those who are unjustifiably contented with themselves. Rather, we are called to take seriously the Gospel invitation to rejoice with those who have found and been found.

Friday of the Thirty-First Week in Ordinary Time—
Initiative, ingenuity and inventiveness

Readings: Rom 15:14-21; Luke 16:1-8
Resp. Psalm: Ps 98:1, 2-3ab, 3cd-4 (L 489)

Think of all the gadgets and conveniences that have been devised to meet our needs, no matter how trivial: machines which buff our shoes before we leave the house; ways of turning on the lights with a sound; devices acting at a distance to save us steps and movement. The initiative and ingenuity of human beings with respect to matters that are not life and death, testify to the truth of Christ's words. We show a great deal of ingenuity when it comes to our comfort and security. But our world lacks inventiveness in delivering food to the hungry, health care to the poor, and protection to children. Christians, convinced that we are God's stewards, would be expected, Jesus says, to be as creative in facing basic human needs as others are creative in producing a profit-making gadget. The followers of Jesus develop sensitivity to the needs of those around them and an ability to respond practically to the problems in our own environment, family, home, and neighborhood.

Saturday of the Thirty-First Week in Ordinary Time—
What demands our time and energy

Readings: Rom 16:3-9, 16, 22-27; Luke 16:9-15
Resp. Psalm: Ps 145:2-3, 4-5, 10-11 (L 490)

It could be useful for any one of us to take the last line of today's Gospel and apply it in the most personal way possible to ourselves, leaving aside for the moment the original context: "[W]hat is of human esteem is an abomination in the sight of God" (Luke 16:15). Depending on our age, situation, and location, we think so many things are desperately important. It can be a football team, a kind of music, clothes, an economic theory, a certain kind of car, maybe a particular address, a specific diet, the tenets of a political party, a movie star, a certain bunch of friends, money or financial security, or even a particular person. Often we're not willing to face up to the fact that we consider one of these items so terribly important, but the amount of time, expense, and energy we're willing to spend on the item speaks volumes. A Christian with maturing faith begins to look on the icons of our culture and the things our world holds important with a critical eye. A famous theologian, Paul Tillich, defined religion or even God as that which ultimately concerns us, that which in the long run we consider non-negotiable. To what do we give our time and attention? About what do we worry? For what do we plan? What occupies our waking thoughts and motivates what we do? "What is of human esteem is an abomination in the sight of God."

Monday of the Thirty-Second Week in Ordinary Time—
Hurting and forgiving

Readings: Wis 1:1-7; Luke 17:1-6
Resp. Psalm: Ps 139:1b-3, 4-6, 7-8, 9-10 (L 491)

"You always hurt the one you love." That's a line from a very old popular song. Even among people deeply in love or among very close friends, having differences, arguments, actions, or words which one party takes as offensive is inevitable. "You always hurt the one you love." While we encourage those thinking of marriage to grow in mutual love, we might also help them by realistically indicating the serious differences. If all this is true among those who are very devoted to each other, all the more is it likely to be true in a diverse collection of people such as our local congregation or our neighborhood. Very good, conscientious people with high ideals can differ seriously and offend each other deeply; we are capable of looking at many matters in such different ways that division and argument, sometimes fairly bitter, are inevitable. We should not be too surprised at all this. If the lives of the saints and good Christians were presented with more realism, we'd hear about the serious disagreements and personality clashes taking place even among the most unselfish and Christ-like people. We see them in the New Testament. Further, there is the fact that a claim to be a follower of Christ does not prevent people from committing some of the crimes others in our world commit. Christians have been known to abuse their wives; Christians have been unjust to their employees; Christians have been unfaithful husbands and wives; they have sold and used drugs. All this is the context for the injunction of the Lord to forgive again and again, as often as the offending brother or sister asks.

Tuesday of the Thirty-Second Week in Ordinary Time—
Hope full of immortality

Readings: Wis 2:23–3:9; Luke 17:7-10
Resp. Psalm: Ps 34:2-3, 16-17, 18-19 (L 492)

The Book of Wisdom which we read this week dates most likely from the century immediately before the birth of Jesus. It is printed in almost all Bibles today, although it is among those books whose place in the Bible has been disputed. Today's reading is fairly familiar to Catholics from its frequent use in funeral Masses. Very few places in the Hebrew Scriptures express so strongly a belief in an afterlife. And that is one of the great consolations our faith offers to those grieving over the loss of a parent, spouse, child, or friend. Wisdom embraces the idea that we human beings have an immortal part—"imperishable" (Wis 2:23), the author says. This is not the Christian belief in resurrection but another view of afterlife. In our immortal part, the writer says, we are made in the image of God. Cynical and this-worldly people, Wisdom says, think that the goodness of believers is a waste of time but, the Book says, they are in peace: "yet is their hope full of immortality" (3:4). Believers counter the idea that the material world alone is real by trust and confidence that God's love for us extends beyond this short life. The prayer and worship of Christians and the time we take out of our human lives for God and what concerns God are a witness (signs) to those around us of our belief that there is more to life than these eighty or ninety years. Prayer and worship make no sense apart from belief in an invisible being. Hope and trust only make sense if we believe that God formed us for eternal life. Beyond this the joy and confidence which ideally mark us Christians depend on a belief that the whole person, body and spirit, will rise as Jesus has risen. Those who share his life here and now will share his resurrection.

Wednesday of the Thirty-Second Week in Ordinary Time—
Why me?

Readings: Wis 6:1-11; Luke 17:11-19
Resp. Psalm: Ps 82:3-4, 6-7 (L 493)

We hardly ever question the good that happens to us. We don't wonder why we feel so good or why the day is so sunny or the eggs just right. But when we're victims of a mugging, a tornado, an earthquake, a disease, or the envy or schemes of someone's bad intentions—when these happen, we have a lot of questions. Why me? Why did this happen? Why does God allow this or, worse, why did God do this to me? True, not to exaggerate, there are times when we hear people wonder about all the good happening to them. A young man fallen in love and preparing for marriage wonders, "How did I ever deserve to have the love of Nancy?" Parents may be awed at the goodness of their children. But so often we're like the nine lepers cured in the Gospel today. We implicitly say to ourselves, "Sure, we're cured; it's only appropriate.

Why not?" We're not surprised or overwhelmed, at least not so often as we should be, by a beautifully mild and sunny day. If it's cloudy and damp for five days, we may hear about it. It's one out of ten times that we praise and thank God for the good surrounding us; more often we take it for granted and complain about the bad. If we could only learn to take nothing for granted, our life would be so full of thanksgiving that we'd have no time for griping and complaining. In Psalm 90:12 we pray, "Teach us to count our days aright, that we may gain wisdom of heart." This is truly wisdom of heart: to be like the one leper who returned to give thanks; to be struck day after day with what a gift life is and how many other gifts enhance life daily. It is right to give God thanks and praise!

Thursday of the Thirty-Second Week in Ordinary Time— *Among you*

Readings: Wis 7:22b–8:1; Luke 17:20-25
Resp. Psalm: Ps 119:89, 90, 91, 130, 135, 175 (L 494)

"[T]he Kingdom of God is among you" (Luke 17:21). At certain seasons like the end of the church year, we hear more and more talk about the end of things and the return of the Lord. But Jesus does not give much encouragement to speculation about when and how: "The Kingdom of God is among you." It's here now. Why look in the clouds or in odd happenings for God's breaking into our world? God has come in Jesus and that simply reaffirms that God is in the ordinary here and now, right before us. God is present by the Holy Spirit to reign in our hearts, words, and lives if only we allow it. Too much looking for God and God's presence in the exotic and marvelous keeps us from finding God in today's work, in that ill and maybe slightly crotchety neighbor, in the boredom of faithfulness to duty, and in sorrowing friends at a funeral. Would anyone ever have expected to find God hanging in agony on a cross? We really have no right to think that God is only present in power, majesty, and awesome spectacle. If we limit our expectation of how and where God may appear, we risk missing that presence completely. The daily presence of Jesus Christ comes about through ordinary bread and wine, which serves as a constant reminder to us of God's presence. In Christ and our own ordinary-appearing world, the reign of God is already with us. The poet Francis Thompson expresses it in four exclamations: "O world invisible, we view thee; O world intangible, we touch thee; O world unknowable, we know thee; inapprehensible, we clutch thee!"

Friday of the Thirty-Second Week in Ordinary Time—
Getting and spending, buying and selling

Readings: Wis 13:1-9; Luke 17:26-37
Resp. Psalm: Ps 19:2-3, 4-5ab (*L* 495)

Yesterday in the Gospel we were reminded that the reign of God is already with us, in our midst. Today's Gospel suggests that we can be so preoccupied with daily concerns and this-worldly tasks that we miss the divine presence because we do not see the signs of God's presence: "The world is too much with us; late and soon, / Getting and spending, we lay waste our powers; / Little we see in nature that is ours" (Wordsworth). The Gospel focus is on the end of things, the return of the Lord; it urges us not to live solely in this one dimension of "getting and spending." Giving ourselves wholeheartedly to what is before us, to what the moment and these people require surely is appropriate. This is the way we serve each other and, through each other, the Lord. But when self-centered acquiring and power-grabbing take over, then we're in trouble. Our perspective has to be broader and deeper than the here and now, than what gives us more of the world's power and possessions. The examples in the first part of today's Gospel point out how heedless we can become: "they were eating, drinking, buying, selling, planting, building" (Luke 17:28). And they were unprepared for anything more! Again, it is not our daily activities and concerns that are wrong; it's only our unthinking and total submersion in them that puts them in opposition to our eternal destiny. Our first reading today from the Book of Wisdom rebukes those who are unable to go beyond the beauty and power of this world to their Maker. *Lord, help us to handle rightly this life and its goods; help us live rightly among its prizes and perils.*

Saturday of the Thirty-Second Week in Ordinary Time—
The power of perseverance

Readings: Wis 18:14-16; 19:6-9; Luke 18:1-8
Resp. Psalm: Ps 105:2-3, 36-37, 42-43 (*L* 496)

Heroic, generous, outstanding acts are always newsworthy, and rightly so. They show us human beings at their best or pushed to their limits. We've all heard of people who, under the stress of trying to save a child, have done something they probably could not have done under ordinary circumstances. All of us have done something extraordinary on at least one occasion in our lives, something we would have a very hard time duplicating. In many ways the tougher and less newsworthy thing would be if we could continue in some of these generous and skillful actions over a long time. To save a little child about to drown in a backyard pool is courageous and generous. To do that sort of thing every day and over a long period of time would be a wonderful habit, a virtue. It may be the same with prayer. Under the stress of concern for a friend ill with cancer, we may be able to pray long and continually for months. To persist in prayer when the crisis has passed and to live a life of persistent prayer is another matter requiring another kind of strength. Hardly anything we do is really a virtue unless we're able to sustain it over a long period and through varying circumstances. To persist in prayer when there is no great emergency occupying our thoughts or when we feel no reward from it or no sense of accomplishing anything (when the Person we pray to seems remote or absent), that is true perseverance. And that is the only way that prayer becomes a factor for change and renewal in our life. The final question of Jesus in this Gospel today is, when the Son of Man comes, will he find any persistent widows praying, any husbands and wives in constant and trusting prayer? Will he find us trusting and hoping despite dryness and silence?

Monday of the Thirty-Third Week in Ordinary Time—
Not answers but strength

Readings: 1 Macc 1:10-15, 41-43, 54-57, 62-63; Luke 18:35-43
Resp. Psalm: Ps 119:53, 61, 134, 150, 155, 158 (L 497)

Immediately before today's Gospel reading from Luke, the author tells us that the disciples could not comprehend at all the sort of prediction of his passion and death that Jesus had just made. Today's story about the restoration of sight to a blind man may refer back to the blindness of the disciples. The gift of seeing, of understanding to any degree, is a gift that only the Lord can give. The disciples, too, need to ask for it. We ask so often in the tragic and sad moments of daily life, why? how could this happen? The death of a young person or child in an accident, a death from a drug overdose, the unfaithfulness of a spouse to the promises so joyously given, the senseless beating of a poor elderly woman, and many other such situations raise questions for us. All these situations unavoidably bring to our lips, why? It cannot be stressed often enough that faith—belief in the Lord—does not give us a set of answers satisfying our minds. God does not come up with the over-simple answers we hear or occasionally use ourselves in such situations: "God wanted her"; "His time was up"; "God will bring good out of it." No, faith does not give answers for the mind. Faith gives strength for the spirit, the heart; faith gives trust and confidence in the enfolding hand of God. Faith is much more an attitude toward life and the world that trusts that God is in charge and will some day and in some way wipe away the tears, ease the grief, restore the lost. Continuous reflection on life and the Lord's words ultimately seems to give us two basic pointers: God genuinely loves us; and, second, our part is to persist in our trust in that love. Our sharing at this table strengthens this trust within us.

Tuesday of the Thirty-Third Week in Ordinary Time—
Whose house is it?

Readings: 2 Macc 6:18-31; Luke 19:1-10
Resp. Psalm: Ps 3:2-3, 4-5, 6-7 (L 498)

Jesus says to Zacchaeus, "today I must stay at your house" (Luke 19:5). Those observing the incident say, "He has gone to stay at the house of a sinner" (19:7). Perhaps this incident suggests some ideas about the place of church buildings in Christian life. Churches are buildings we human beings erect to honor God; they serve as a very real reminder of God's presence with us. But they are also primarily our own creation, something we need, and they are definitely the houses of sinners, in that sense. We might say that churches are built to be the place where God's glory and love meet human need and sinfulness. While the church is God's house, it is built by humans and, Scripture tells us, built up of human beings as the stones of its foundation and walls. God's love and mercy meet human emptiness and sin here. Those who judge everything in monetary or quantitative terms find church buildings a waste of space. But even more than we need such things as music and art, we need a place for worship, for prayer, and a visible reminder of the invisible God. The church building says of itself that God is with and among us, that like his Son, God is profoundly interested in us. Like Zacchaeus we are hosts to the Lord in this place and outside of it, too, insofar as we serve our fellow human beings. And in offering us forgiveness and love here, the Lord is also the host.

Wednesday of the Thirty-Third Week in Ordinary Time—
Accountable

Readings: 2 Macc 7:1, 20-31; Luke 19:11-28
Resp. Psalm: Ps 17:1bcd, 5-6, 8b and 15 (L 499)

Today's new word of the month (we've had community, codependency, diversity) may well be "accountability." At least in business and academic circles, this seems to be a tendency. So often the more we use a particular term, the more it means that we have little real grasp of it. Christian belief in God's initiative never means that our accountability is wiped out or taken away. The stories we hear this week of the vigorous opposition of the Maccabees to their persecutors show us that what God does for us does not take away what we can and must do for God. The Gospel story about what the new king expects from his managers illustrates the same point; they must be accountable, responsible for what they do with what they've been given. Japanese custom takes accountability to the extreme where a manager who presides over a failure commits suicide. In the Western world we're near the other extreme: when a government official says he takes responsibility for, say, the deaths of large numbers, that is usually purely verbal. He or she doesn't resign, leave office, or make reparation. As our society reacts against the belief that parental upbringing and society are solely responsible for our faults and failures, we may find room again for the acceptance of some responsibility and for being accountable for what is done under our supervision. We may understand that each of us is accountable.

Thursday of the Thirty-Third Week in Ordinary Time—
Irreplaceable for others

Readings: 1 Macc 2:15-29; Luke 19:41-44
Resp. Psalm: Ps 50:1b-2, 5-6, 14-15 (L 500)

"If this day you only knew what makes for peace" (Luke 19:41). These charged words of Jesus express very strongly his assumption that each of us can make a responsible decision about what he says. His teaching presupposes our basic freedom to say yes or no to him and the fact that each of us has a conscience. Hence, his strong emotional reaction to the unresponsiveness of his contemporaries is understandable. The decisive behavior of Mattathias, described in today's passage from Maccabees, points to the same conviction: we are responsible. Conviction about this is not an excuse for lording it over others or for taking upon ourselves all the sins of the world. But it could be an encouragement to each of us to see the value of our life, our words, and our example for our family, our friends, our neighborhood, and our world. What we do or do not voluntarily do in the way of worship, love, and honesty does strengthen or weaken the fabric of the community of which we are a part. For our little part of the world and for many people around us, we are irreplaceable; without the things we do or say others are diminished. No one of us is an island, as the poet wrote; we are all interrelated. Our lives, words, and actions build up or tear down. Our encouraging words or gestures may be just what help someone else get through the day. Our sympathy and listening express to others they are not alone. The respectfulness or dignity we bring to what we do helps others believe in the worth of living. What we do in response to our conscience is vital to the world around us and is our way of responding to the call of the Lord in a practical way.

Friday of the Thirty-Third Week in Ordinary Time—
Ridding the temple of thieves

Readings: 1 Macc 4:36-37, 52-59; Luke 19:45-48
Resp. Psalm: 1 Chron 29:10bcd, 11abc, 11d-12a, 12bcd (*L* 501)

Elsewhere in the New Testament we hear that our bodies are temples of the Holy Spirit (see, for example 1 Cor 1:16). It's a truism that our minds and hearts can be a house of prayer. Like the Temple in the Gospel, they can become dens of thieves, too, especially at Mass or at prayer when cares, idle thoughts, or plans steal our attention and energy. These thieves and hucksters may also be such things as our concern about what movie we'll see, what so-and-so meant by that remark last evening, how we'll ever get more attention from that gentle fellow in our fitness class, how tough that team will be on Saturday, worry about that homily for Sunday or that test Monday, or anxiety about our medical tests. We can, of course, gently ask the Lord to free us from these cares, but we can also help with this by more indirect means. We might, for example, repeat mantra-like some phrase from the texts of today's Mass. We can make these intruders themselves material for prayer—for petition, forgiveness, thanksgiving, praise. Our participation at Mass doesn't have to be a continual and literal attention to the texts we hear daily; we can in a more general way confirm in our own words our desire to join with Christ in praise, thanksgiving, and self-giving.

Saturday of the Thirty-Third Week in Ordinary Time—
Justice for the poor and oppressed

Readings: 1 Macc 6:1-13; Luke 20:27-40
Resp. Psalm: Ps 9:2-3, 4 and 6, 16 and 19 (*L* 502)

The First Book of Maccabees tells of the end of King Antiochus, the ruler who was behind the attempts to make the Hebrews more like the Greeks. Antiochus dies after hearing of the successful revolt in Judah and he dies in a foreign land—apt punishment, the writer feels, for his oppression. It fits well with our sense of justice when an oppressive tyrant comes to a bad end or loses everything. It fulfills a desire for justice for the poor and those who suffer under such tyrants. However, we know that such justice in this world is not guaranteed and some tyrants die comfortably and luxuriously amid their ill-gotten prizes and possessions. At the same time, the poor, oppressed, starving, and the most unfortunate of our world often live and die in misery and hardship. They are so often the thousands who are killed or at least bereaved by earthquakes and natural disasters. After noticing repeatedly in their history that God's justice was not by any means always served in this world, the Hebrew people came to believe by the time of Christ that there was an afterworld in which all was righted. Part of that belief, of course, was belief in resurrection. That the belief was not accepted by all is apparent in the way the Sadducees attempted to make fun of it with their question to Jesus in today's Gospel. In our world, too, belief in resurrection, heaven, and hell is often greeted with condescension as a bit childish and, at least, wishful thinking. "It's too good to be true," they think. But justice cries out for another life. A central belief for us Christians is that God does not abandon or forget the poor, the suffering, the oppressed, the have-nots, nor even the simply conscientious people we all know. And where does that happen?

Monday of the Thirty-Fourth Week in Ordinary Time—
Faithfulness

Readings: Dan 1:1-6, 8-20; Luke 21:1-4
Resp. Psalm: Dan 3:52, 53, 54, 55, 56 (L 503)

"Give us vegetables to eat and water to drink" (Dan 1:12). Daniel's words in the first reading to the king's official are not a plea for vegetarianism, but a request designed to avoid eating ritually unclean food. Jewish law had prohibitions against certain foods and the Book of the Prophet Daniel, like the Books of Maccabees, encourages the Jews to be faithful to the Law. In this book the setting is life in exile amid alien non-believers. Daniel and associates had been conscripted into the foreign king's service. Like the Maccabees, Daniel and his friends are presented as models of faithfulness. They figure out a way to avoid eating the unclean foods and are rewarded with glowing health and superior wisdom. In our day whole television series are built around unfaithfulness since, one can only guess, faithfulness seems so boring and unexciting. Yet perhaps nothing, outside of love, so defines the follower of Christ as faithfulness. And probably nothing is so basically heroic than day by day loyalty to our commitments, no matter what the weather or our moods or our other options. We are called to faithfulness to husband or wife, to obligations, to our work and promises, to children and friends, to religious practice and prayer, to daily routine and civility, to God and Christ. Faithfulness means consistency, fulfillment of what is expected of us, staying with what we've committed ourselves to despite hardships and discouragement. All of us rely on the faithfulness of many people for the smooth running of daily life, but so often we take it for granted and/or find it hard ourselves. At this altar we are united with the One who was faithful even to death, death on a cross.

Tuesday of the Thirty-Fourth Week in Ordinary Time—
The continual tension

Readings: Dan 2:31-45; Luke 21:5-11
Resp. Psalm: Dan 3:57, 58, 59, 60, 61 (L 504)

What we read about in the newspapers daily and see on the television news is, in many ways, old stuff. Kingdoms, empires, and powers have passed and crumbled before. Long before the Soviet collapse, the world has seen other empires disappear. Today's readings heighten the tension which must exist in our lives between concern about and work to change our world and the conviction that it is not eternal. Somehow it is worth our while to be involved in politics, to be responsible citizens, and to work to change the injustices around us. At the same time, all our hope cannot be in our political party or in free enterprise or the American way. Christian life is inevitably a tension between the here and now and the hereafter. Here and now we care about and for the disabled child, all the while knowing someone, somewhere continues to suffer. Each of us must reach some balance between involvement and detachment. Good material for meditation is how to be serious about our world and still keep our focus on the eternal. Only time, age, prayer, and hard-gained wisdom can settle that for any one of us.

Wednesday of the Thirty-Fourth Week in Ordinary Time—
He's got the whole world in his hands

Readings: Dan 5:1-6, 13-14, 16-17, 23-28; Luke 21:12-19
Resp. Psalm: Dan 3:62, 63, 64, 65, 66, 67 (L 505)

That first reading today is almost made for TV! The exaggerated and fantastic details and the color and sweep of the story all suggest great pictures: a banquet for hundreds of nobles, the precious vessels from the Temple, the dramatic writing on the wall, the offers made to Daniel, and the clear pronouncement from him to the king. Behind it all is the author's theme: that God has the whole world in his hands. God knows the king's pride and rebellion; God will sweep away his kingdom and power. Human beings cannot in any lasting way take over this world or universe. For us whose lives are played out on a smaller screen and with a smaller cast, these are still words of warning and encouragement in this great story. Our own life, with its tensions and stresses, is in the hands of God. And the often terrifying world around us of crime, war, poverty, and seemingly insoluble problems—this, too, is in God's hands. Our response is suggested in Jesus' words about how his followers should handle persecution: Be resolved not to worry, but to trust.

Thursday of the Thirty-Fourth Week in Ordinary Time—
Stand erect and raise your heads

Readings: Dan 6:12-28; Luke 21:20-28
Resp. Psalm: Dan 3:68, 69, 70, 71, 72, 73, 74 (L 506)

Another memorable story from the Book of the Prophet Daniel illustrates what we heard yesterday from the Lord in the Gospel. Although we are persecuted and put to death, we are still safe in the hands of God. Daniel's faithfulness in prayer to the one God leads to his imprisonment in the lions' den where God keeps him safe from harm. Luke's account of Jesus' words about the last things continues today its mix of warnings and encouragement: "And then they will see the Son of Man coming in a cloud with power and great glory. But when these things begin to happen, stand erect and raise your heads because your redemption is at hand" (Luke 21:27-28). Standing with heads raised up—that age-old position of attention and respect in Christian worship—expresses well the total and radical confidence of Christians in their Lord. It is still necessary this late in time for the followers of Christ to make it clear publicly that their faith brings joy, confidence, hope, and assurance; that their faith is not a way of crushing what is human, a way of cowing people, or of making us live in fear and distrust. Many today spend hours and much money on schemes and treatments designed to give hope, confidence, and joy in living. Do we Christians draw enough of this from our faith and our relation to God?

217

Many of the schemes referred to rely almost completely on a kind of self-hypnosis. We have reasons for hope, confidence, and joy rooted in what actually happened in the life, the death, and resurrection of the Son of God—and not simply in wishful thinking. In our baptism we were raised to the new life of Christ. That life means the ability to rise daily from sin, disappointment, suffering, and failure to the new life of Christ in us. "[S]tand erect and raise your heads."

Friday of the Thirty-Fourth Week in Ordinary Time—
What will last

Readings: Dan 7:2-14; Luke 21:29-33
Resp. Psalm: Dan 3:75, 76, 77, 78, 79, 80, 81 (*L* 507)

Like the last book of the New Testament, the Book of the Prophet Daniel has large sections of the kind of writing we call "apocalyptic." The strange beasts described today in the first reading and the vision of the Ancient One and of the son of man coming on the clouds of heaven are all part of an effort to make sense of world events during the life of the writer. With that, apocalyptic literature adds always a note of reassurance and encouragement for believers. God *does* triumph over evil. At the end of the church year and the beginning of Advent, our liturgy is full of such readings meant to press us to think about ultimate matters. A term occurs in Daniel's vision today which was to become very significant in the Gospels. The term "son of man" is in itself a neutral, descriptive term for a human being. But in the context of Daniel's vision this son of man comes on the clouds of heaven and is given authority and power. Jesus eventually uses the term of himself. By doing so he may have meant to leave room for his contemporaries to figure out his identity without imposing it on them himself. Was he just another human being, a son of man, or were the signs he did and what he said evidence that he comes from above and has authority? After his miracles people around him often asked: who is this man? Christians are those who believe they have a good idea of the answer. He is the Son of God and the Savior of the world. As a consequence, we owe his words a place of honor in our thoughts and lives. We make this real by devoting some time to study and reflection on his word. "Heaven and earth will pass away, but my words will not pass away" (Luke 21:33).

Saturday of the Thirty-Fourth Week in Ordinary Time—
Standing before the Son of Man with trust

Readings: Dan 7:15–27; Luke 21:34–36
Resp. Psalm: Dan 3:82, 83, 84, 85, 86, 87 (*L* 508)

Two days ago the discourse from Jesus presented in the selection from Luke's Gospel ended by telling us, "when these signs begin to happen, stand erect and raise your heads because your redemption is at hand" (Luke 21:28). Today's part of this discourse by Jesus on the last days ends similarly with the recognition that the Christian who has been vigilant in prayer and watchful has "the strength to escape the tribulations that are imminent and to stand before the Son of Man" (21:36). The apocalyptic language of Daniel and this discourse of our Lord have their share of what are called today "scary" scenarios. Just listen to that first reading today, for example, with its beasts with iron teeth and bronze claws, devouring the earth and laying low kings. And Jesus says that the great day can surprise like a trap. The fact that such literature is meant to encourage and console the faithful is almost lost in the use of these more bizarre phrases. But, again, the purpose of this kind of discourse is to bolster and console believers. With what better words can we end the church year and face the end of our world and time than with these words of the Lord? They tell us that we have reason to stand secure before the just Judge. Isn't God honored more by our total trust than by our cowering in fear? Our confidence, after all, is in the Lord and not in ourselves. That confidence, that faith and trust, are what, St. Paul tells us, really save us.